To Nicholas

READINGS IN ECONOMIC HISTORY AND THEORY

Capital Accumulation in the Industrial Revolution

Edited with an Introduction and Notes by

B. L. Anderson

Lecturer in Economic History
University of Liverpool

J. M. Dent & Sons Ltd   London
Rowman and Littlefield, Totowa N. J.

Dent edition
No. 194   Hardback ISBN 0 460 10194 3
Rowman and Littlefield edition
Library of Congress Cataloging in Publication Data

Anderson, Bruce Louis, comp.

   CONTENTS: Smith, A. Of the accumulation of
capital, or of productive and unproductive labour.—
Ellis, W. Effect of the employment of machinery, etc.,
upon the happiness of the working classes.—Rae, J.
On the nature of stock. (etc.)

   1. Capital—Addresses, essays, lectures.
2. Saving and investment—Addresses, essays,
lectures. 3. Great Britain—Economic conditions—
1760–1860—Addresses, essays, lectures, I. Title.
HB501.A595   1974   332'.041   73–17277
ISBN 0–87471–401–x

Contents

Introduction

In recent years few subjects have attracted so much attention in the literature of economics—history and theory—as the part played by capital formation in the process of economic growth. It is a question that has been widely pondered ever since the beginnings of that first phase of modern growth experienced by Britain just two centuries ago; and today capital is a major issue of controversy among theorists and historians. As a result of a massive increase in the volume of empirical work on data collection and hypothesis testing, much of it in connection with the need for policy determination in undeveloped countries, there is little left of whatever faith economists once held in a straightforward relationship linking capital formation and economic growth. A wide range of factors, many of them not lending themselves easily to precise measurement, have entered into the analysis of growth. Technical change, population increase, and a host of relative shifts in the allocation of resources within an industrializing economy that cannot be easily identified when the discussion is in terms of large aggregates, have all complicated the task of historical explanation. Social and institutional factors, hardly measurable yet clearly important, have also been instrumental in bringing about a general retreat from mono-causal explanations of the Industrial Revolution.

Yet, if modern evidence has made theorists and historians alike sceptical of the rate of growth of capital stock as the prime determinant in the transformation of the economy, there is no doubt that an important connection remains to be explained. For the classical economists, such a connection seemed self-evident; the growth of capital was a central feature of the revolutionary changes that had turned the

British economy from a basically agricultural society into an industrial and commercial power of the first rank. From the publication of Smith's *Wealth of Nations* in 1776 to the first edition of John Stuart Mill's *Principles of Political Economy* in 1848, the accumulation of capital was afforded an increasingly dominant role in the classical system as it developed. By the mid-nineteenth century, as the Industrial Revolution in Britain was coming of age, political economy seemed to have arrived at a broad consensus as to how a general analysis of the working of the economy should be composed. The fact that in this analysis considerable space was devoted to the definition of capital, and the factors influencing its accumulation, represented a significant advance on most eighteenth-century discussions of growth.

Mercantilist writers gave little consideration to capital and, even when they recognized it as a distinct factor, generally concentrated their attention on labour and land as the primary agents of production. Sir James Steuart, who paid most attention to the subject, was clearly thinking in traditional terms when he posed the questions, 'Why do people wish to augment population, but in order to compass these ends? Wherein does the effect of a machine differ from that of new inhabitants?'[1] Of course the concept of capital held by eighteenth- and early nineteenth-century writers included much more than simply machinery, and was in general broader and less exact than that of modern theory. It was not until much later, beginning principally with Böhm-Bawerk, that the term was used specifically to refer to the 'produced means of production' or 'intermediate goods'. Adam Smith and those who followed him in elaborating and extending classical economics normally understood capital to include not only production facilities but, in addition, all that was necessary to sustain labour during the actual process of production. Logically, at least, inventories, cash and credit would fall within this definition as well. Smith also introduced the important distinction between fixed and circulating capital. Although those who came after were not always agreed or

[1] Sir James Steuart. *An Inquiry into the Principles of Political Economy*, 1767, ed. A. Skinner (1966), Vol. 1, pp. 121–5.

consistent on the essential meaning of the terms, the former seems to have been taken as comprising the factories and machines in the more or less permanent possession of the capitalist, while the latter was to include raw materials and the means of subsistence for labour. Most subsequent writers, even Ricardo, who thought the distinction was not essential, recognized that a higher and more variable rate of turnover attached to circulating than to fixed capital.

Yet while Smith is rightly credited with giving capital a separate status for the first time, there can be no doubt that for him the really crucial factor in explaining growth in an exchange economy was the division of labour. Because this principle accorded so well with the facts of eighteenth-century economic life as he saw them, Smith's discussion of the division of labour, contained in the first three chapters of the first book, is the most developed part of the *Wealth of Nations*. Compared with the working of this principle, capital formation, much less technological change, was of secondary importance. Thinking in terms of a basically agricultural economy, partly a Physiocratic influence but also a reflection of reality, Smith conceived of output and accumulation as consisting of a single commodity—corn. Corn was what was regularly consumed for subsistence in the normal way; it was also that which was saved or accumulated in order that the production of future output could take place in due course and, by implication at least, that which was expended as wages for the production of current output. In this simple model of production the supply of capital is made to depend on the existence of prior saving which thus became a necessary, even sufficient, condition for investment to occur. At the same time, since saving could only come from what would otherwise have been consumed, it was important to distinguish those who saved and those who laboured productively from those whose labour was unproductive, 'whose services generally perish in the very instance of their performance'. In this way Smith laid lasting emphasis on the supply of capital as the main factor likely to limit growth. There was no problem that investment might not ultimately equate with savings, because the latter would be consumed as they were expended to meet the needs of labour during the production period.

The idea that accumulation was automatically beneficial to society, which arose from this analysis, was taken up by James Mill in *Commerce Defended* (1807). This was an affirmation of Smith in reply to William Spence's *Britain Independent of Commerce*, which argued that agriculture was the real origin of national wealth, being the only sector to produce a surplus. According to this view, it was the expenditure of the landed classes on manufactures that provided the engine of growth in the economy, and so luxury spending and increases in the national debt were to be applauded, not parsimony: writers of this stamp, like Malthus later, were concerned that the diversion of expenditure away from consumption towards investment would reduce the war-time prosperity. To Smith's followers this amounted to encouraging the unproductive consumption of unproductive labour, and James Mill, as well as Torrens in *The Economists Refuted* (1808), set about the task of denying that capital formation could be excessive and reasserting Smith's notion that, since saving is spending, it cannot harm consumption. For this purpose Say's law of markets was adopted, though not as Say himself had first used it in 1803 when he applied it to the working of a barter economy only. Mill fixed it to the conditions of a monetary economy as well and concluded '. . . that a nation can never be naturally overstocked either with capital or with commodities; as the very operation of capital makes a vent for its produce.'[1]

In this way the classical school came to hold a 'real' capital theory which, given the assumption that production creates its own market, for most of the time referred to circulating capital only and saw it as a commodity that was constantly being recycled during the process of production. This view was clearly over-simplified, even misleading. It left out of account any influence from the capital market, as well as the action of the rate of interest on the supply of funds available for investment. More important, this theory of capital formation

---

[1] James Mill. *Selected Economic Writings*, ed. D. Winch (1966), p. 135.

gave rise to the possibility, as argued by Ricardo in particular, that the stock of fixed capital could increase only at the expense of circulating capital, and that the wages fund, out of which labour was sustained throughout the production cycle, might therefore be reduced. For the Ricardians, acceptance of Say's law meant that there could be no limits on the side of demand to the accumulation of capital, so that the phenomena of overproduction and unemployment could be regarded as being aberrations from the norm.

In the first edition of his *Principles* (1817) Ricardo maintained the basic classical position on capital accumulation. It was the essential element in the process of economic growth; but growth itself was cast in terms of increments to the stock of capital rather than in terms of technological change. It continued to be seen as the result of capital fructifying the range of techniques then available to society; 'improvements' were thought to arise much more from the application of capital than from technical innovation itself. The publication of John Barton's *Observations on the Conditions of the Labouring Classes* just after the first edition of Ricardo's *Principles* was an important landmark in the development of classical thinking on capital accumulation. Barton raised the whole question of the relationship of fixed to circulating capital by pointing out that investment in technical improvements, involving the conversion of some part of circulating capital into machinery, etc., could no longer continue to exert the same influence, in fixed form, on the demand for labour. One argument used in reply to this assertion that the growth of fixed capital might actually have adverse effects on employment and be harmful to the interests of the working classes, was that given by J. R. McCulloch; while accepting some effect in employment and wages, he believed this would only be temporary because any labour made redundant by fixed capital would soon redirect itself to the expanding capital goods industries. It is interesting that the classical economists consistently assumed that all technical change was labour-saving in effect. This was certainly at variance with actual experience at the time, yet the view can be traced at least as far back as Sir James Steuart, as we saw above. He had also thought that any dislocation could only be temporary: 'The introduction of machines can, I think, in no other way prove hurtful by making people idle, than by the suddenness of it.'[1]

In the third edition of his *Principles* (1821), Ricardo did not take up the idea that the growth of fixed capital could be accommodated within the basic framework of classical theory by accepting that an 'automatic compensation' would occur with respect to employment. Instead he declared himself to have been mistaken on the issue and followed a more pessimistic line on the machinery question.[2] We have seen how much importance was given to saving in the classical theory of accumulation; the acts of saving and investment seemed, as a matter of common observation, to be undertaken by much the same sort of person in society so that, even to critics like Lord Lauderdale and T. R. Malthus, who believed that oversaving and under-consumption could occur, it was natural to assume that savings were automatically invested.[3] At the same time it was generally accepted that as the stock of capital increased, the rate of profit would show a tendency to decline. Adam Smith had considered this to be a natural consequence of competition between many small capitalists, few of whom were capable of exerting an undue influence in the market for very long. Following him, Ricardo attributed the phenomenon much more to the increasing costs of labour which, he believed, would result not in any reduction of the surplus coming available for new production but in a smaller share of it going to profits. Both Ricardo and Malthus, unlike Smith, believed that savings were an increasing function of the rate of profits. Ricardo was a man of the City, who knew more of the

[1] Op. cit., p. 122.

[2] Ricardo's pessimism also extended to the export of capital: 'It can never be allowed that the emigration of capital can be beneficial to a state'. *The Works and Correspondence of David Ricardo* (ed. P. Sraffa), III, p. 269 and IV, p. 16, note. It is interesting to compare this with J. S. Mill's view that 'Up to a certain point, the more capital we send away, the more we shall possess and be able to retain at home'. *Principles of Political Economy* (ed. Ashley), pp. 736–9.

[3] According to Schumpeter, Lauderdale was the first important theorist to set up capital as a distinct factor of production. J. H. Schumpeter. *History of Economic Analysis* (1954), p. 560.

working of the London money market than he did of manufacturing industry; possibly his prospect of declining incomes
accruing to capital as growth proceeded fitted the facts of his
own experience, such as the downward secular trend in
interest rates.

In the prosperous optimism of the 1830s more attention
was to be paid to the possibilities for economic growth inherent in an inventive society. Popular writers like Andrew
Ure (*The Philosophy of Manufactures*, 1835) and Charles Bab-
bage (*The Economy of Machinery and Manufactures*, 1832) had
an important impact on the way in which nineteenth-century
society interpreted the far-reaching economic changes taking
place in its midst. Nevertheless they cannot be counted with
those who contributed at the highest level to the analysis of
the economic system, and even here, in the theory of economic
growth and the role of capital accumulation within it,
Ricardo's long-run pessimism was exceptional and not so
extreme as is popularly believed. Perhaps a more accurate
reflection of classical thought on the subject of capital accumulation is that represented here by William Ellis.[1] The discussion shifts away from the possibility that unemployment
might result from technological change and returns to the
position of Smith, James Mill and the early Ricardo by
looking upon capital as consisting of very little else but the
wages fund and making profits depend on the level of wages.
Taking the beneficial effects of accumulation for granted,
much of the discussion becomes concerned again with
analysing the motivation towards saving and investment.

The 'Machinery Question', while it produced no major
adjustment in the basic classical view of capital formation,
did serve to draw attention to the importance of the time
taken for the production process to work itself through. This
had been first noticed by Adam Smith, though he never
actually stated that profits were the reward for the entre-
preneur's parsimony, thus enabling the accumulation necessary for sustaining labour to take place. Smith and Ricardo
were rather more concerned with revealing how the division

[1] On Ellis see B. A. Corry, *Money, Saving and Investment in Classical Economics*
(1962), pp. 45–8.

of labour raised productivity, a process involving applications of fixed and circulating capital: the productivity effects
of capital as a distinct factor of production were not really considered until it was seen, for example by Torrens and Malthus,
that there was a cost of production as well as a labour approach to the theory of value. Ricardo had seen that a time
period as well as the notion of accumulated labour was im-
plicit in the concept of capital, but it was left to Senior to
elaborate the point and extend the discussion.[1] Both Samuel
Bailey and G. Poulett Scrope, among others, had already
noticed that the time concept necessitated regarding accumulation as a cost, but it was Nassau Senior's 'abstinence'
theory which showed how the division of labour, and the
roundabout production process connected with it, were
ultimately dependent upon the fact of capital being forth-
coming. The supply of capital, in turn, depended on the
willingness to forgo present consumption; and this abstinence
found its reward in profits. The price of capital now joined
wages in any assessment of the cost of production, although
the conditions necessary to produce abstinence remained
unclear; thus, as the importance of capital in the economy,
especially fixed capital, increased, so it became increasingly
difficult to retain the labour theory of value in simple form.

One of the earliest writers to treat the whole theory of
capital as an entity was John Rae; and his extensive discussion of the influences surrounding the willingness to post-
pone present for future enjoyment was, perhaps, his most
important contribution in the task of explaining the supply
of capital. Although, as we saw, this had become the chief
problem in classical capital theory, the treatment given by
Rae, who had a wider experience of different economic and
social conditions than many classical writers, showed much
more appreciation of the role of technological change in
capital formation. With him we find that the dependence of
economic growth on increases of capital rests on two principles—the 'inventive' and the 'accumulative'. The first
allowed the natural tendency of diminishing returns to capital

---

[1]M. Bowley, *Nassau Senior and Classical Economics* (1937), pp. 140–1.

as its stock increased to be overcome; the second stimulated savings and the desire to possess durable goods. Rae's first-hand observations of an undeveloped economy (Upper Canada) appear to have exerted a considerable influence on his theory of capital. His approach, unlike that of say Adam Smith, did not stem from the observation of an increasing division of labour as part of the response to population growth. Instead of the Malthusian spectre of population pressure lurking in the background, we find Rae starting from the fact of accumulation itself, and seeing at once how invention was capable of arresting the natural tendency for returns on capital to decline.

The perennial problem of the capital theorist has been how to devise a method of quantifying capital, inherently heterogeneous as it is, in such a way as to facilitate analysis of the functional relationships that exist between it and quantities of labour and land. The obvious solution, if one wants to add, say, textile machinery and railway lines, is to convert to money values; but this not only treats capital differently from the other factors of production, it also raises the question of which values should be used, its costs in the past or its earnings in the future. Another difficulty is to discover what is the return on capital, in the same way as one can know the return on labour. Rae's attempt to deal with these problems was highly original. The objects of accumulation he defined as 'instruments' formed, directly or indirectly, by labour for the purpose of yielding a return over a time period, at the end of which they became 'exhausted'. Since instruments were the product of human labour, their cost could be measured in units of labour and so could their return, which Rae called their 'capacity'. To take account of the fact that instruments became exhausted at different times, he grouped them into 'orders' according to how long they took to return double their cost; in effect he classified instruments according to their rates of return and those in the higher orders we would now call capital goods. The capacity of an instrument could be raised by either extending its life, making it more durable or by improving its efficiency, usually through inventions. For Rae, invention, rather than parsimony, was the cause of

capital accumulation and the primary source of economic
growth; indeed in his analysis it occupied a similar place to
that held by the division of labour in the *Wealth of Nations*.
Saving—'the effective desire of accumulation'—was to be
fostered as an essential requirement for growth, but without a
propensity to invent, technical change would cease and further
capital accumulation would only serve to drag new instruments down into the lower orders of productivity.

It was Senior who drew the attention of John Stuart Mill
to Rae's *New Principles*; of its significance Mill wrote that 'in
no other book known to me is so much light thrown, both
from principle and history, on the causes which determine
the accumulation of capital'.[1] It is clear, however, that it was
not Rae's forward-looking analysis of technological change
which Mill saw as important, but rather his penetrating discussion of savings. In correspondence he admits that 'I have
made more use of your treatise than you appear to have been
informed of, having quoted largely from it, especially from
your discussion of the circumstances which influence the
"effective desire of accumulation", a point which you appear
to me to have treated better than it had ever been treated
before.'[2] In Book One, Chapter Five of his *Principles*, Mill
maintains, and frequently re-emphasizes, that long-standing
direct relationship between total net savings and total additions to capital in the long run; the simple essentials of
classical capital theory, given in his *Fundamental Propositions*,
differ little from those of Smith and Ricardo earlier. At any
given time industry was limited by the available stock, but in
the long term capital could grow indefinitely. If growth was
to be explained in terms of accretions to the productive
capacity of the economy, if capital was 'wealth appropriated to reproductive employment', then the increase of
total capital (fixed capital and the wages fund) must ultimately rely on saving and the motives surrounding it. Given
the long-run assumptions, which characterized so much of
classical thinking on capital accumulation, Mill found little

[1] J. S. Mill, *Principles of Political Economy* (1848), p. 165.
[2] J. S. Mill to John Rae, 19th Sept. 1854. Quoted in R. W. James, *John
Rae, Political Economist*, Vol. 1, pp. 426–7.

difficulty in setting aside the earlier objections of Lauderdale, Chalmers and Malthus that a shortfall in the propensity to consume might be an obstacle to further growth. The accumulation of capital depends on savings, which are the result of abstinence on the part of capitalists, not landlords who 'grow richer, as it were, in their sleep, without working, risking or economising'.[1]

The conversion of saving into investment, either by the capitalist himself or by borrowers, prevents the appearance of any discrepancy between production and consumption because what is saved will, in due course, be spent by productive labour.

Thus for Mill the rate of capital formation was dependent upon the net produce, or income, of industry and the proportion of this going to savings. Abstinence from current consumption was a function of the rate of profit and ultimately depended on the willingness of individuals to save. Indeed anything that increased 'the net produce of industry', the return to capital or savings, the 'strength of the disposition to save', or any of them, would increase the rate of accumulation.

In theorizing about how the economy functioned and the factors responsible for its growth, the classical economists generally paid less attention than some earlier writers to providing a quantitative basis for their analyses. The momentum of interest in statistical inquiry that had been set on foot by the earlier work of Graunt, Petty, Davenant and King in the seventeenth century proved difficult to sustain. In the first half of the eighteenth century Political Arithmetik, 'the art of reasoning by figures upon things relating to government', attracted few writers of detachment and originality. Instead the estimates of national income and wealth compiled by the pioneers were simply quoted verbatim, or used indiscriminately, in pamphlets and broadsides with little attempt to re-work or improve upon them.[2] Even after mid century, when the growth of the economy and the changes occurring

[1] Quoted in Edwin Cannan, *A Review of Economic Theory* (1929), p. 403.
[2] For example, see the use made of such estimates by Matthew Decker in 'An Essay on the Causes of the Decline of the Foreign Trade' (1740).

in its trade, finance and manufactures were becoming evident, genuine attempts at empirical work were made much more difficult by the paucity of official statistics. In the case of capital it was much less important for an eighteenth-century administrator to know how rapidly it was increasing, and how it was composed, than it was to know something of those factors, primarily relating to trade, agriculture and population, which had a bearing on the national revenue and taxation.

With a few notable exceptions, of which the most important was the work of Joseph Massie, more systematic contributions were made in the field of providing useful commercial information than in the hastily prepared arguments of pamphleteers on the economic problems of the moment.[1] The compilation of dictionaries was a popular means of disseminating such information, the best-known example being Malachy Postlethwaite's *Universal Dictionary of Trade and Commerce* (1751–5). And in the case of the *Description of Trades* (1747) we find a useful breakdown of the occupational structure of the English economy on the eve of the Industrial Revolution, together with broad estimates of the basic capital requirements and average remuneration for the various trades (see passage 5). The most striking impression created by the author's findings is of the extent to which a consumer society of considerable depth and sophistication had already developed by the middle of the eighteenth century. The picture provided shows how far the Industrial Revolution was founded upon earlier progress in, for example, the growth of foreign trade and agricultural productivity, and upon the existence of developed urban centres of consumption depending upon outside supplies of food, raw materials, etc. At this stage London was much the largest of these urban centres and few other towns exhibited the same wide range of economic activities. A large segment of the nation's income was earned and spent there; and the capital was a constant attraction for migrants from elsewhere in the country and abroad.

[1] For Massie's contributions, see P. Mathias, 'The Social Structure in the Eighteenth Century; A Calculation by Joseph Massie', *Economic History Review*, X (1957).

Accordingly, average wages, and probably capitals also, were somewhat higher there than in other centres, reflecting a greater prosperity and a larger number of skilled workers.

Although the data are clearly very approximate, and refer almost entirely to the traditional trades of London, they do show how low was the threshold of entry into so many eighteenth-century occupations. Of course differences in the size of concerns within a single trade or industry could still be considerable. The numerous cases where wide margins were given for initial capital needs are often a reflection of the significant disparities in masters' requirements, depending on whether they operated at the wholesale or retail level of the same trade. In many cases, too, the capital of a large country dealer would need to be very much greater than that of his smaller counterpart in town. Again, retailers who kept a shop would invariably require more capital for stock, credit, etc., than those who did not; in fact the expense involved in opening up a full retail business was perhaps the most important stumbling block in the way of a petty retailer *en route* to becoming a merchant. Most of the additional capital was needed for the extension of credit facilities rather than for the purchase of equipment and fixtures; indeed the ability to grant ample credit was an important ingredient of success in almost any business activity, not just in shopkeeping trades. In the case of a plasterer in the building trade, for instance, a mere '£50 will furnish a Master with Tools and Stuff sufficient to begin work with; and what he wants more must be in Proportion to the Credit he thinks proper to give'. Or again, the calico printer, where 'The Materials only to set up one a Master will take £300 after which they had need to have £1,000 more to pay Work-Folks, and give Credit to the Merchants, Linen Drapers etc. many of whom do not make up Accounts with them above once a year.'

This picture of the growth of individual capitals from relatively small beginnings, with large provisions for credit given and received, was not a new phenomenon. It was characteristic, and increasingly so, of the role of capital in the organization of trade, including most manufacturing industry; even in the early years of the eighteenth century it was claimed that

five-sixths of the country's trade was in the hands of men of
£500–£1,000 capital, whose credit might amount to five
times their own worth.[1] Even more important, by the middle
of the century, was the degree of specialization of function
achieved, particularly in the metal-working trades where the
term 'blacksmith', for example, had become a generic description to include a wide variety of different specialities of
the smith's work. It was this development which Adam Smith
was so concerned to illustrate; for him the organization of the
pin factory was an example of the potentiality of division of
labour, rather than an instance of the application of fixed
capital in machinery.[2] Purely industrial activities, however,
take up a small part of the *Description of Trades*, the remainder
being devoted to employment in trade and distribution. Here
the dominant figure is the merchant. 'The term merchant,'
the author explains, 'is very general, tho' commonly understood; but, to make it a little more particular, it signifies one
who merchandizes or traffics Abroad, by Sea as well as by
Land, Goods for Goods as well as Money; deals at home
only Wholesale, keeps no Shop, but Warehouses, Store-
houses, Vaults, Cellars, etc. To distinguish one from another,
they either have the Title from the principal Commodity in
which they traffic, or from the Chief Place they trade to and
from.' In an age of increasing specialization, it was becoming
difficult to incorporate all the activities of the merchants
within one definition. The same was true of another important group in the consumer society of the eighteenth
century, the grocers—'for the most part a set of wealthy Shop-
keepers and Traders, and their Name originally denoted such
who bought up Goods in large Quantities, and sold them out
in Small Parcels, which in Fact is their real Business . . . and
many of them are entirely in the Wholesale Way, dealing
much like Merchants.'

If the capacity to finance substantial investments already
existed in the English economy before the Industrial Revo-

[1] Anon. *The Reasons of the Decay of Trade and Private Credit*, by a Merchant of
London (1707).

[2] For a discussion of this point see T. S. Ashton, *An Economic History of
England: The Eighteenth Century* (1955), p. 103.

lution was under way, and most of the evidence available to date suggests that this was the case, then much of the explanation can be found in the already considerable capital accumulations of the merchant communities. This is not to say that investment funds moved easily from one region of the country, or one sector of the economy, to another. There were certainly, also, times when particularly heavy, and often competing, requirements for funds produced conditions of tightness in the money markets. But overall, and beyond the very short-term, most new capital needs appear to have been met from somewhere along the chain of financial connection that led from the land to trade, to industry and back again; it was the merchant more often than not who forged these links.

While mercantile capital was relatively mobile, it was frequently at risk and so less permanent than landed wealth. From Gregory King on, every social observer seeking to assess the national capital had, inevitably, to begin with the land. Modern convention leaves land and resources outside the concept of reproducible capital in order to assess the rate of growth of capital more accurately. But in the eighteenth century, when agriculture was by far the largest sector of the economy and so greatly influenced its development, the land requires to be considered. Not only did contemporary estimates include it throughout the period of industrialization, but they continued to testify to its dominant position in the economy. In King's day around 64 per cent of the national capital could be attributed to it: and by the time Giffen wrote it was still thought to represent one-third of the total. During the period between, the stock of utilized land had been enlarged and improved to sustain a considerable increase in agricultural output; the scattered figures relating to the costs of enclosure that are available are a quite inadequate guide to the applications of capital which this lengthy process of agricultural change involved.[1] If eighteenth-century writers were justified to some extent in thinking of the land as a major item in the national capital, they faced formidable problems when they attempted to place a value on it. Until

[1] See, for example, B. A. Holderness, 'Landlord's Capital Formation in East Anglia, 1750–1870', *Economic History Review*, XXV (1972).

late in the nineteenth century the standard method was to value land by the rental it received, and then multiply by the number of years' purchase to obtain a capital figure. An obvious weakness of this technique was that the movement of rents may have little to do with changes in the amount of capital invested in the land, so that capitalized values were usually arbitrary and unrealistic.

Next to the land itself, building and construction were responsible for the largest segment of the national capital during the eighteenth century. The available estimates for housing, which included not only domestic dwellings but also a variety of structures used in trade, manufactures and on the land, show a small decline from $17\frac{1}{2}$ per cent to 14 per cent, approximately, over the century as a whole. Much of the capital expenditure undertaken during the course of the Industrial Revolution did not take a directly productive form in the strict sense. Dwelling houses are only one of a number of items coming somewhere between expenditure on consumers' goods and investment in producers' capital. In eighteenth-century terms, 'personal stock' was frequently meant to include movable possessions that contributed nothing to the productive process and yielded no income. Similarly with circulating or liquid capital, which was often understood to include the monetary circulation, and which it was only too easy to confuse with the concept of revenue. Gregory King had estimated this item at £86 million, and when Andrew Hooke set out to show how small was the burden of the national debt on the national capital it was his exaggerated estimate of this item that was chiefly responsible for the inflated, and altogether spurious, figures for the stock of capital in existence by the mid-eighteenth century.

It was natural for eighteenth-century writers to be concerned with the stock of capital, inasmuch as it seemed to offer some guide to the nation's capacity to carry a public debt whose origin was within living memory and the size of which was a matter of widespread concern. But modern research has been equally, if not more, interested in discovering the rates at which capital investment was undertaken; and such evidence as there is suggests that until the very end of the eighteenth century new investment as a proportion of national income was relatively low. Moreover there appears to be no reason to think that this proportion underwent a dramatic change at any stage during the industrialization period, and certainly not before the coming of the railway. King's figures had implied an investment proportion of around 5 per cent towards the close of the seventeenth century; it is doubtful whether this figure shifted by more than 2 per cent either way over the next hundred years. The most likely periods for any shift to have occurred were during the middle years and again at the end of the century, though the expenses of war probably limited any tendency for the level of investment to rise too much before 1815.

As already mentioned, most of this earlier phase of capital formation centred on agriculture—before and after the onset of population growth—and building—where the physical asset normally had a long life and was often put to productive use in an economy based on domestic industry. But increasingly trade, and the need for better communications, were setting up significant new demands for capital. Some portion of these funds went to fixed capital creation in roads, canals and shipping, but much more went to meet the requirements for circulating capital from trade and industry, where in both sectors fixed capital was barely significant before the 1830s in aggregate. For the merchant and industrialist, the Industrial Revolution brought many more problems in the way of financing stocks and credit than it did in the equipment and maintenance of production units. This was the case even in the cotton and iron industries where technological change and fixed capital growth were most rapid. On the other hand, if the physical capital of industry was not a large item in the national capital even by Giffen's time, its qualitative importance in terms of the growth of reproducible capital was much greater. Perhaps the classic example of this is the development of steam power. The contemporary estimate (see passage 7) of the growing number of steam engines, and the uses found for them, is only one of many that tell how rapidly this single item of capital equipment searched out and solved a whole range of industrial problems, often changing its were not also given on a per-mile-of-road basis; if they had been they would have shown more clearly the concentration of road investment in the growth areas, where the costs of wear and tear would obviously be greater. This 'failure of capital accounting', as it has been described, was even more limiting in the case of investment in the infrastructure of the growing economy than it was in industry; but more generally it meant that much of the empirical work on capital accumulation in the nineteenth century had little relevance to the needs of theorists. On the other hand, the theoretical analysis of accumulation in terms of the savings propensity of the community did influence the nature of empirical work, as in Porter's case. Although the latter played a major part in the rapid improvement of statistical science and investigation during the 1840s, and was plainly aware of how much of gross investment was taken up with making good depreciation, his comments show that he was more concerned with the growth of savings and the objects to which they were put than with isolating the net additions to the stock of capital and measuring their rates of growth. He wrote,

> It might occupy much space, and would afford but little profit, to attempt making a minute enumeration of the various forms in which the savings of individuals in this country have been invested. Any such enumeration must almost necessarily be incomplete, and even inaccurate, for this, among other reasons, that it would be impossible to determine, with reference to many of such investments, in what degree they can truly be considered in the light of accumulated capital, and in what degree they should be accounted as a part of current expenditure, serving to repair the ravages of time and accident ... and as no advantage could follow from such an undertaking that would be adequate to the labour it would occasion, we may conclude that the task will never be accomplished.[1]

Increasing legislative intervention during the course of the nineteenth century provided civil servants with the need

---

[1] G. R. Porter, *The Progress of the Nation* ... (1857 ed), pp. 624–5.

of a gap appears to have developed in classical political economy between theorist and statistician. Even as moves towards administrative reform began to hold out the promise of new and more varied sources of economic information in the first half of the nineteenth century, with few exceptions, the leading economists seemed to be less disposed than before to subjecting theoretical conclusions to the test of empirical proof. Their known preference for the deductive method of reasoning has been suggested as one explanation. Certainly John Rae was almost alone in the conscious use he made of Baconian inductive philosophy, an approach that was quite foreign to most of the Classics, except perhaps McCulloch. That British economic statistics continued to be inadequate for the tasks of theory is indisputable; but the importance of this deficiency seems doubtful in the face of the wide acceptance of doctrines whose basic propositions were at variance with the known facts, e.g. the theories of population and diminishing returns in agriculture.

On this question the truth probably was that Ricardo and J. S. Mill had set themselves an altogether different goal, nothing less than comprehending the causes of the growth of income and wealth and of their distribution in society. As to the role of capital accumulation in this system, the theorists, struggling to uncover the correct conceptual basis of the new variable, received small assistance from the statisticians and accountants of the time. Modern research has encountered great difficulty in its attempt to apply the concept of net investment to the Industrial Revolution period; because of its modest size, never much more than 10 per cent of the national income before the 1860s, in most cases it is almost impossible to extract from the much larger item representing repairs and maintenance to existing capital. The problem is illustrated in the example of the accounts relating to turnpike roads for 1836 (see passage 9). A confusion of capital and current items was typical of prevailing accountancy practice and stems from the fact that capital expenditure was, in general, only rarely a major item and so was not normally distinguished from current outlays. In the particular instance shown, it is unfortunate that income and expenditure figures occupation several times during the course of its life. In this respect, as Crouzet remarks, 'Capital formation does not matter as much as capital utilization'.[1]

The early attempts to quantify changes in the stock of capital clearly had little chance of success when sources of even remotely reliable data simply did not exist; even the well-established returns available for foreign trade and shipping had grown to be of limited value. In consequence, the so-called 'political chemistry' of the type contained in Hooke's essay, particularly when its conclusions were so agreeable, had to meet with little resistance from anything better informed. But after 1750 there were signs of improving standards in the work of Webster, Whitworth, Chalmers and Macpherson. Much of this renewed interest arose out of the contemporary debate on the growth in population: poverty and agricultural improvement were also topical issues and stimulated the researches of Eden, Price, Sinclair and Young. But the growth of capital was neither so well understood, nor indeed so much in evidence as yet, as to impress upon investigators the need to measure its progress. Hume and Smith among the theorists had begun to recognize the increasing specialization of factors of production, and to consider the profits of stock as another distinct source of revenue in addition to the wages of labour and the rent of land. We have already seen how, in the nineteenth century, capital was never far from the centre of theoretical discussion, but in the field of empirical work it was hardly ever a major preoccupation, unlike national income accounting. Before 1815 writers such as Joseph Massie and Patrick Colquhoun, who were aware of the changes in the social structure and in the nature of the economy which the growth of capital was bringing about, felt it necessary to provide their discussions of social phenomena with quantitative support, and showed considerable ingenuity in the process. This willingness and ability to ground the display of opinions on a marshalling of facts represents the tradition of political arithmetic at its best; it also contrasts with the situation after 1815 when something

[1] F. Crouzet (ed), *Capital Formation in the Industrial Revolution* (1972), p. 18.

and opportunity for gathering a growing body of information and improving methods of compilation; but the chief beneficiary was national income estimation which was taken much further as a result of the work of McCulloch and Smee before 1850, and Baxter, Mulhall and Giffen later. But, after the earlier efforts, only Giffen and Mulhall showed real interest in the growth of capital, and Giffen, at least, was forced to rely on the income approach for obtaining his results, with all the weaknesses that this implies for them. It was still relatively easy for private interests to baulk any official attempts to improve the quality and scope of statistical information and, as Mulhall later complained, government indifferences continued to be a major obstacle. In the absence, then, of any direct estimates, those resulting from Giffen's researches could only reflect the broad changes in the magnitude and character of the growth of capital over the preceding century of industrialization. What they show is that by 1875 the items making up most of the capital employed in industry and commerce (excluding railways) amounted to not much more than 15 per cent of the total; technical innovation and organizational change had clearly been at least as important as capital formation to industrial development. The structure of the national capital appears to have changed little before 1830, since Giffen shows that the major impacts here came first from the rise of railway capital and next from the growth of investment overseas. Gains in these sectors were made largely at the expense of the land, which now at last was showing appreciable relative decline. Finally, as recent research confirms, the process of capital accumulation was long drawn out and much more complex than is suggested by the simple model of classical economics; for much of the eighteenth and early nineteenth centuries it is doubtful if the rate of growth of capital was as fast as that of incomes and it was only after the immediate strains of the Industrial Revolution were over that it grew apace.

EDITOR'S NOTE

My thanks are due to Miss L. Wood and Mrs E. V. Greer for secretarial assistance, and to my colleague Richard Rodger for commenting on the typescript.

It should also be pointed out that all footnotes in this book keyed in by numerical indicators are my own, and those keyed in by asterisks are those of the author concerned.

Part One

CAPITAL AND ECONOMIC GROWTH

1 Adam Smith

OF THE ACCUMULATION OF CAPITAL, OR OF PRODUCTIVE AND UNPRODUCTIVE LABOUR[1]

In this chapter of the *Wealth of Nations* Smith lays down all the important ingredients for a theory of Capital Accumulation that was to have an overriding influence far beyond the classical period. In the first chapter of the Second Book he has already distinguished Capital as a separate factor of production and introduced the concepts of fixed and circulating capital. The Physiocratic influence is marked in this part of the work and the notion of a distinction between productive and unproductive labour certainly owes something to Quesnay. Although his meaning was much debated later, Smith appears to have regarded labour as productive if it replaced the value of the capital used in its employment to show a profit, and unproductive labour as that which went to the provision of services.[2] This proposition leads him on to the uncompromising emphasis on the savings propensity of a nation as the reason for the growth of capital. To the extent that savings are used to maintain productive labour, then the nation's capital is increased. Smith's emphasis has been well attested by modern research, whose findings have shown how crucial were the private accumulations of the early entrepreneurs for capital growth, particularly in industry.

[1] From *An Inquiry into the Nature and Causes of the Wealth of Nations* (1776), Ch. 3, Book 2.

[2] This clearly opened the way for the development of a theory of surplus value by Marx later. The latter's contribution stands apart from the mainstream of classical thought on accumulation and, since it is best considered in the context of the rest of his political economy, no attempt has been made to include it here.

There is one sort of labour which adds to the value of the subject upon which it is bestowed: there is another which has no such effect. The former, as it produces a value, may be called productive; the latter, unproductive* labour. Thus the labour of a manufacturer adds, generally, to the value of the materials which he works upon, that of his own maintenance, and of his master's profit. The labour of a menial servant, on the contrary, adds to the value of nothing. Though the manufacturer has his wages advanced to him by his master he, in reality, costs him no expense, the value of those wages being generally restored, together with a profit, in the improved value of the subject upon which his labour is bestowed. But the maintenance of a menial servant never is restored. A man grows rich by employing a multitude of manufacturers: he grows poor by maintaining a multitude of menial servants. The labour of the latter, however, has its value, and deserves its reward as well as that of the former. But the labour of the manufacturer fixes and realizes itself in some particular subject or vendible commodity, which lasts for some time at least after that labour is past. It is, as it were, a certain quantity of labour stocked and stored up to be employed, if necessary, upon some other occasion. That subject, or what is the same thing, the price of that subject, can afterwards, if necessary, put into motion a quantity of labour equal to that which had originally produced it. The labour of the menial servant, on the contrary, does not fix or realize itself in any particular subject or vendible commodity. His services generally perish in the very instant of their performance, and seldom leave any trace or value behind them for which an equal quantity of service could afterwards be procured.

The labour of some of the most respectable orders in the society is, like that of menial servants, unproductive of any value, and does not fix or realize itself in any permanent subject, or vendible commodity, which endures after that labour is past, and for which an equal quantity of labour could afterwards be procured. The sovereign, for example,

* Some French authors of great learning and ingenuity have used those words in a different sense. In the last chapter of the fourth book I shall endeavour to show that their sense is an improper one.

with all the officers both of justice and war who serve under
him, the whole army and navy, are unproductive labourers.
They are the servants of the public, and are maintained by a
part of the annual produce of the industry of other people.
Their service, how honourable, how useful, or how necessary
soever, produces nothing for which an equal quantity of
service can afterwards be procured. The protection, security,
and defence of the commonwealth, the effect of their labour
this year, will not purchase its protection, security, and defence for the year to come. In the same class must be ranked,
some of the gravest and most important, and some of the most
frivolous professions: churchmen, lawyers, physicians, men
of letters of all kinds; players, buffoons, musicians, opera-
singers, opera-dancers, etc. The labour of the meanest of
these has a certain value, regulated by the very same principles which regulate that of every other sort of labour; and
that of the noblest and most useful, produces nothing which
could afterwards purchase or procure an equal quantity of
labour. Like the declamation of the actor, the harangue of the
orator, or the tune of the musician, the work of all of them
perishes in the very instant of its production.

Both productive and unproductive labourers, and those
who do not labour at all, are all equally maintained by the
annual produce of the land and labour of the country. This
produce, how great soever, can never be infinite, but must
have certain limits. According, therefore, as a smaller or
greater proportion of it is any one year employed in maintaining unproductive hands, the more in the one case and the
less in the other will remain for the productive, and the next
year's produce will be greater or smaller accordingly; the
whole annual produce, if we except the spontaneous productions of the earth, being the effect of productive labour.

Though the whole annual produce of the land and labour
of every country is, no doubt, ultimately destined for supplying the consumption of its inhabitants, and for procuring a
revenue to them, yet when it first comes either from the
ground, or from the hands of the productive labourers, it
naturally divides itself into two parts. One of them, and frequently the largest, is, in the first place, destined for replacing

a capital, or for renewing the provisions, materials, and finished work, which had been withdrawn from a capital; the other for constituting a revenue either to the owner of this capital, as the profit of his stock, or to some other person, as the rent of his land. Thus, of the produce of land, one part replaces the capital of the farmer; the other pays his profit and the rent of the landlord; and thus constitutes a revenue both to the owner of this capital, as the profits of his stock; and to some other person, as the rent of his land. Of the produce of a great manufactory, in the same manner, one part, and that always the largest, replaces the capital of the undertaker of the work; the other pays his profit, and thus constitutes a revenue to the owner of this capital.

That part of the annual produce of the land and labour of any country which replaces a capital, never is immediately employed to maintain any but productive hands. It pays the wages of productive labour only. That which is immediately destined for constituting a revenue, either as profit or as rent, may maintain indifferently either productive or unproductive hands.

Whatever part of this stock a man employs as a capital, he always expects it to be replaced to him with a profit. He employs it, therefore, in maintaining productive hands only; and after having served in the function of a capital to him, it constitutes a revenue to them. Whenever he employs any part of it in maintaining unproductive hands of any kind, that part is, from that moment, withdrawn from his capital, and placed in his stock reserved for immediate consumption.

Unproductive labourers, and those who do not labour at all, are all maintained by revenue; either, first, by that part of the annual produce which is originally destined for constituting a revenue to some particular persons, either as the rent of land or as the profits of stock; or, secondly, by that part which, though originally destined for replacing a capital and for maintaining productive labourers only, yet when it comes into their hands whatever part of it is over and above their necessary subsistence may be employed in maintaining indifferently either productive or unproductive hands. Thus, not only the great landlord or the rich merchant, but even the common workman, if his wages are considerable, may maintain a menial servant; or he may sometimes go to a play or a puppet-show, and so contribute his share towards maintaining one set of unproductive labourers; or he may pay some taxes, and thus help to maintain another set, more honourable and useful, indeed, but equally unproductive. No part of the annual produce, however, which had been originally destined to replace a capital, is ever directed towards maintaining unproductive hands till after it has put into motion its full complement of productive labour, or all that it could put into motion in the way in which it was employed. The workman must have earned his wages by work done before he can employ any part of them in this manner. That part, too, is generally but a small one. It is his spare revenue only, of which productive labourers have seldom a great deal. They generally have some, however; and in the payment of taxes the greatness of their number may compensate, in some measure, the smallness of their contribution. The rent of land and the profits of stock are everywhere, therefore, the principal sources from which unproductive hands derive their subsistence. These are the two sorts of revenue of which the owners have generally most to spare. They might both maintain indifferently either productive or unproductive hands. They seem, however, to have some predilection for the latter. The expense of a great lord feeds generally more idle than industrious people. The rich merchant, though with his capital he maintains industrious people only, yet by his expense, that is, by the employment of his revenue, he feeds commonly the very same sort as the great lord.

The proportion, therefore, between the productive and unproductive hands, depends very much in every country upon the proportion between that part of the annual produce, which, as soon as it comes either from the ground or from the hands of the productive labourers, is destined for replacing a capital, and that which is destined for constituting a revenue, either as rent or as profit. This proportion is very different in rich from what it is in poor countries.

Thus, at present, in the opulent countries of Europe, a very large, frequently the largest portion of the produce of the land is destined for replacing the capital of the rich and independent farmer; the other for paying his profits and the rent of the landlord. But anciently, during the prevalency of the feudal government, a very small portion of the produce was sufficient to replace the capital employed in cultivation. It consisted commonly in a few wretched cattle, maintained altogether by the spontaneous produce of uncultivated land, and which might, therefore, be considered as part of that spontaneous produce. It generally, too, belonged to the landlord, and was by him advanced to the occupiers of the land. All the rest of the produce properly belonged to him too, either as rent for his land, or as profit upon this paltry capital. The occupiers of land were generally bondmen, whose persons and effects were equally his property. Those who were not bondmen were tenants at will, and though the rent which they paid was often nominally little more than a quit rent, it really amounted to the whole produce of the land. Their lord could at all times command their labour in peace and their service in war. Though they lived at a distance from his house, they were equally dependent upon him as his retainers who lived in it. But the whole produce of the land undoubtedly belongs to him who can dispose of the labour and service of all those whom it maintains. In the present state of Europe, the share of the landlord seldom exceeds a third, sometimes not a fourth part of the whole produce of the land. The rent of land, however, in all the improved parts of the country, has been tripled and quadrupled since those ancient times; and this third or fourth part of the annual produce is, it seems, three or four times greater than the whole had been before. In the progress of improvement, rent, though it increases in proportion to the extent, diminishes in proportion to the produce of the land.

In the opulent countries of Europe, great capitals are at present employed in trade and manufactures. In the ancient state, the little trade that was stirring, and the few homely and coarse manufactures that were carried on, required but very small capitals. These, however, must have yielded very large profits. The rate of interest was nowhere less than 10 per cent, and their profits must have been sufficient to afford this great interest. At present the rate of interest, in the improved parts of Europe, is nowhere higher than 6 per cent, and in some of the most improved it is so low as 4, 3 and 2 per cent. Though that part of the revenue of the inhabitants which is derived from the profits of stock is always much greater in rich than in poor countries, it is because the stock is much greater: in proportion to the stock the profits are generally much less.

That part of the annual produce, therefore, which, as soon as it comes either from the ground or from the hands of the productive labourers, is destined for replacing a capital, is not only much greater in rich than in poor countries, but bears a much greater proportion to that which is immediately destined for constituting a revenue either as rent or as profit. The funds destined for the maintenance of productive labour are not only much greater in the former than in the latter, but bear a much greater proportion to those which, though they may be employed to maintain either productive or unproductive hands, have generally a predilection for the latter.

The proportion between those different funds necessarily determines in every country the general character of the inhabitants as to industry or idleness. We are more industrious than our forefathers; because in the present times the funds destined for the maintenance of industry, are much greater in proportion to those which are likely to be employed in the maintenance of idleness, than they were two or three centuries ago. Our ancestors were idle for want of a sufficient encouragement to industry. It is better, says the proverb, to play for nothing than to work for nothing. In mercantile and manufacturing towns, where the inferior ranks of people are chiefly maintained by the employment of capital, they are in general industrious, sober, and thriving; as in many English, and in most Dutch towns. In those towns which are principally supported by the constant or occasional residence of a court, and in which the inferior ranks of people are chiefly maintained by the spending of revenue, they are in general idle, dissolute, and poor; as at Rome, Versailles, Compiegne, and Fontainebleau. If you except Rouen and Bordeaux, there is little trade or industry in any of the parliament towns of France; and the inferior ranks of people, being chiefly main-

tained by the expense of the members of the courts of justice,
and of those who come to plead before them, are in general
idle and poor. The great trade of Rouen and Bordeaux
seems to be altogether the effect of their situation. Rouen is
necessarily the entrepôt of almost all the goods which are
brought either from foreign countries, or from the maritime
provinces of France, for the consumption of the great city of
Paris. Bordeaux is in the same manner the entrepôt of the
wines which grow upon the banks of the Garonne, and of the
rivers which run into it, one of the richest wine countries in
the world, and which seems to produce the wine fittest for
exportation, or best suited to the taste of foreign nations.
Such advantageous situations necessarily attract a great
capital by the great employment which they afford it; and the
employment of this capital is the cause of the industry of
those two cities. In the other parliament towns of France, very
little more capital seems to be employed than what is necessary for supplying their own consumption; that is, little
more than the smallest capital which can be employed in
them. The same thing may be said of Paris, Madrid and
Vienna. Of those three cities, Paris is by far the most industrious; but Paris itself is the principal market of all the
manufactures established at Paris, and its own consumption
is the principal object of all the trade which it carries on.
London, Lisbon and Copenhagen, are, perhaps, the only
three cities in Europe which are both the constant residence
of a court, and can at the same time be considered as trading
cities, or as cities which trade not only for their own consumption, but for that of other cities and countries. The situation of all the three is extremely advantageous, and naturally
fits them to be the entrepôts of a great part of the goods
destined for the consumption of distant places. In a city
where a great revenue is spent, to employ with advantage a
capital for any other purpose than for supplying the consumption of that city is probably more difficult than in one
in which the inferior ranks of people have no other maintenance but what they derive from the employment of such a
capital. The idleness of the greater part of the people who are
maintained by the expense of revenue corrupts, it is probable,

the industry of those who ought to be maintained by the employment of capital, and renders it less advantageous to employ a capital there than in other places. There was little trade or industry in Edinburgh before the union. When the Scotch parliament was no longer to be assembled in it, when it ceased to be the necessary residence of the principal nobility and gentry of Scotland, it became a city of some trade and industry. It still continues, however, to be the residence of the principal courts of justice in Scotland, of the boards of customs and excise, etc. A considerable revenue, therefore, still continues to be spent in it. In trade and industry it is much inferior to Glasgow, of which the inhabitants are chiefly maintained by the employment of capital. The inhabitants of a large village, it has sometimes been observed, after having made considerable progress in manufacture, have become idle and poor in consequence of a great lord having taken up his residence in their neighbourhood.

The proportion between capital and revenue, therefore, seems everywhere to regulate the proportion between industry and idleness. Wherever capital predominates, industry prevails: wherever revenue, idleness. Every increase or diminution of capital, therefore, naturally tends to increase or diminish the real quantity of industry, the number of productive hands, and consequently the exchangeable value of the annual produce of the land and labour of the country, the real wealth and revenue of all its inhabitants.

Capitals are increased by parsimony, and diminished by prodigality and misconduct.

Whatever a person saves from his revenue he adds to his capital, and either employs it himself in maintaining an additional number of productive hands, or enables some other person to do so, by lending it to him for an interest, that is, for a share of the profits. As the capital of an individual can be increased only by what he saves from his annual revenue or his annual gains, so the capital of a society, which is the same with that of all the individuals who compose it, can be increased only in the same manner.

Parsimony, and not industry, is the immediate cause of the increase of capital. Industry, indeed, provides the subject which parsimony accumulates. But whatever industry might acquire, if parsimony did not save and store up, the capital would never be the greater.

Parsimony, by increasing the fund which is destined for the maintenance of productive hands, tends to increase the number of those hands whose labour adds to the value of the subject upon which it is bestowed. It tends, therefore, to increase the exchangeable value of the annual produce of the land and labour of the country. It puts into motion an additional quantity of industry, which gives an additional value to the annual produce.

What is annually saved is as regularly consumed as what is annually spent, and nearly in the same time too; but it is consumed by a different set of people. That portion of his revenue which a rich man annually spends is in most cases consumed by idle guests and menial servants, who leave nothing behind them in return for their consumption. That portion which he annually saves, as for the sake of the profit it is immediately employed as a capital, is consumed in the same manner, and nearly in the same time too, but by a different set of people, by labourers, manufacturers, and artificers, who reproduce with a profit the value of their annual consumption. His revenue, we shall suppose, is paid him in money. Had he spent the whole, the food, clothing, and lodging, which the whole could have purchased, would have been distributed among the former set of people. By saving a part of it, as that part is for the sake of the profit immediately employed as a capital either by himself or by some other person, the food, clothing, and lodging, which may be purchased with it, are necessarily reserved for the latter. The consumption is the same, but the consumers are different.

By what a frugal man annually saves, he not only affords maintenance to an additional number of productive hands, for that or the ensuing year, but, like the founder of a public workhouse, he establishes as it were a perpetual fund for the maintenance of an equal number in all times to come. The perpetual allotment and destination of this fund, indeed, is not always guarded by any positive law, by any trust-right or deed of mortmain. It is always guarded, however, by a very powerful principle, the plain and evident interest of every individual to whom any share of it shall ever belong. No part of it can ever afterwards be employed to maintain any but productive hands without an evident loss to the person who thus perverts it from its proper destination.

The prodigal perverts it in this manner. By not confining his expense within his income, he encroaches upon his capital. Like him who perverts the revenues of some pious foundation to profane purposes, he pays the wages of idleness with those funds which the frugality of his forefathers had, as it were, consecrated to the maintenance of industry. By diminishing the funds destined for the employment of productive labour, he necessarily diminishes, so far as it depends upon him, the quantity of that labour which adds a value to the subject upon which it is bestowed, and, consequently, the value of the annual produce of the land and labour of the whole country, the real wealth and revenue of its inhabitants. If the prodigality of some was not compensated by the frugality of others, the conduct of every prodigal, by feeding the idle with the bread of the industrious, tends not only to beggar himself, but to impoverish his country.

Though the expense of the prodigal should be altogether in home-made, and no part of it in foreign commodities, its effect upon the productive funds of the society would still be the same. Every year there would still be a certain quantity of food and clothing, which ought to have maintained productive, employed in maintaining unproductive hands. Every year, therefore, there would still be some diminution in what would otherwise have been the value of the annual produce of the land and labour of the country.

This expense, it may be said indeed, not being in foreign goods, and not occasioning any exportation of gold and silver, the same quantity of money would remain in the country as before. But if the quantity of food and clothing, which were thus consumed by unproductive, had been distributed among productive hands, they would have reproduced, together with a profit, the full value of their consumption. The same quantity of money would in this case equally have remained in the country, and there would besides have been a reproduction of an equal value of consumable goods. There would have been two values instead of one.

The same quantity of money, besides, cannot long remain in any country in which the value of the annual produce diminishes. The sole use of money is to circulate consumable goods. By means of it, provisions, materials, and finished work, are bought and sold, and distributed to their proper consumers. The quantity of money, therefore, which can be annually employed in any country must be determined by the value of the consumable goods annually circulated within it. These must consist either in the immediate produce of the land and labour of the country itself, or in something which had been purchased with some part of that produce. Their value, therefore, must diminish, as the value of that produce diminishes, and along with it the quantity of money which can be employed in circulating them. But the money which by this annual diminution of produce is annually thrown out of domestic circulation will not be allowed to lie idle. The interest of whoever possesses it requires that it should be employed. But having no employment at home, it will, in spite of all laws and prohibitions, be sent abroad, and employed in purchasing consumable goods which may be of some use at home. Its annual exportation will in this manner continue for some time to add something to the annual consumption of the country beyond the value of its own annual produce. What in the days of its prosperity had been saved from that annual produce, and employed in purchasing gold and silver, will contribute for some little time to support its consumption in adversity. The exportation of gold and silver, is in this case, not the cause, but the effect of its declension, and may even, for some little time, alleviate the misery of that declension.

The quantity of money, on the contrary, must in every country naturally increase as the value of the annual produce increases. The value of the consumable goods annually circulated within the society being greater, will require a greater quantity of money to circulate them. A part of the increased produce, therefore, will naturally be employed in purchasing, wherever it is to be had, the additional quantity of gold and silver necessary for circulating the rest. The increase of those metals will in this case be the effect, not the cause, of the public prosperity. Gold and silver are purchased everywhere in the same manner. The food, clothing, and lodging, the revenue and maintenance of all those whose labour or stock is employed in bringing them from the mine to the market, is the price paid for them in Peru as well as in England. The country which has this price to pay will never be long without the quantity of those metals which it has occasion for; and no country will ever long retain a quantity which it has no occasion for.

Whatever, therefore, we may imagine the real wealth and revenue of a country to consist in, whether in the value of the annual produce of its land and labour, as plain reason seems to dictate; or in the quantity of the precious metals which circulate within it, as vulgar prejudices suppose; in either view of the matter, every prodigal appears to be a public enemy, and every frugal man a public benefactor.

The effects of misconduct are often the same as those of prodigality. Every injudicious and unsuccessful project in agriculture, mines, fisheries, trade, or manufactures, tends in the same manner to diminish the funds destined for the maintenance of productive labour. In every such project, though the capital is consumed by productive hands only, yet, as by the injudicious manner in which they are employed they do not reproduce the full value of their consumption, there must always be some diminution in what would otherwise have been the productive funds of the society.

It can seldom happen, indeed, that the circumstances of a great nation can be much affected either by the prodigality or misconduct of individuals; the profusion of imprudence of some being always more than compensated by the frugality and good conduct of others.

With regard to profusion, the principle which prompts to expense is the passion for present enjoyment; which, though sometimes violent and very difficult to be restrained, is in general only momentary and occasional. But the principle which prompts to save is the desire of bettering our condition, a desire which, though generally calm and dispassionate, comes with us from the womb, and never leaves us till we go into the grave. In the whole interval which separates those two moments, there is scarce perhaps a single instant in which any man is so perfectly and completely satisfied with his situation as to be without any wish of alteration or improvement of any kind. An augmentation of fortune is the means by which the greater part of men propose and wish to better their condition. It is the means the most vulgar and the most obvious; and the most likely way of augmenting their fortune is to save and accumulate some part of what they acquire, either regularly and annually, or upon some extraordinary occasions. Though the principle of expense, therefore, prevails in almost all men upon some occasions, and in some men upon almost all occasions, yet in the greater part of men, taking the whole course of their life at an average, the principle of frugality seems not only to predominate, but to predominate very greatly.

With regard to misconduct, the number of prudent and successful undertakings is everywhere much greater than that of injudicious and unsuccessful ones. After all our complaints of the frequency of bankruptcies, the unhappy men who fall into this misfortune make but a very small part of the whole number engaged in trade, and all other sorts of business; not much more perhaps than one in a thousand. Bankruptcy is perhaps the greatest and most humiliating calamity which can befall an innocent man. The greater part of men, therefore, are sufficiently careful to avoid it. Some, indeed, do not avoid it; as some do not avoid the gallows.

Great nations are never impoverished by private, though they sometimes are by public prodigality and misconduct. The whole, or almost the whole public revenue, is in most countries employed in maintaining unproductive hands. Such are the people who compose a numerous and splendid court, a great ecclesiastical establishment, great fleets and armies, who in time of peace produce nothing, and in time of war acquire nothing which can compensate the expense of maintaining them, even while the war lasts. Such people, as they themselves produce nothing, are all maintained by the produce of other men's labour. When multiplied, therefore, to an unnecessary number, they may in a particular year consume so great a share of this produce, as not to leave a sufficiency for maintaining the productive labourers, who should reproduce it next year. The next year's produce, therefore, will be less than that of the foregoing, and if the same disorder should continue, that of the third year will be still less than that of the second. Those unproductive hands, who should be maintained by a part only of the spare revenue of the people may consume so great a share of their whole revenue, and thereby oblige so great a number to encroach upon their capitals, upon the funds destined for the maintenance of productive labour, that all the frugality and good conduct of individuals may not be able to compensate the waste and degradation of produce occasioned by this violent and forced encroachment.

This frugality and good conduct, however, is upon most occasions, it appears from experience, sufficient to compensate, not only the private prodigality and misconduct of individuals, but the public extravagance of government. The uniform, constant, and uninterrupted effort of every man to better his condition, the principle from which public and national, as well as private opulence is originally derived, is frequently powerful enough to maintain the natural progress of things toward improvement, in spite both of the extravagance of government and of the greatest errors of administration. Like the unknown principle of animal life, it frequently restores health and vigour to the constitution, in spite, not only of the disease, but of the absurd prescriptions of the doctor.

The annual produce of the land and labour of any nation can be increased in its value by no other means but by increasing either the number of productive labourers, or the productive powers of those labourers who had before been employed. The number of its productive labourers, it is evident, can never be much increased, but in consequence of an increase of capital, or of the funds destined for maintaining them. The productive powers of the same number of labourers cannot be increased, but in consequence either of some addition and improvement to those machines and instruments which facilitate and abridge labour; or of a more proper division and distribution of employment. In either case an additional capital is almost always required. It is by means of an additional capital only that the undertaker of any work can either provide his workmen with better machinery or make a more proper distribution of employment among them. When the work to be done consists of a number of parts, to keep every man constantly employed in one way requires a much greater capital than where every man is occasionally employed in every different part of the work. When we compare, therefore, the state of a nation at two different periods, and find, that the annual produce of its land and labour is evidently greater at the latter than at the former, that its lands are better cultivated, its manufactures more numerous and more flourishing, and its trade more extensive, we may be assured that its capital must have increased during the interval between those two periods, and that more must have been added to it by the good conduct of some, than had been taken from it either by the private misconduct of others or by the public extravagance of government. But we shall find this to have been the case of almost all nations, in all tolerably quiet and peaceable times, even of those who have not enjoyed the most prudent and parsimonious governments. To form a right judgement of it, indeed, we must compare the state of the country at periods somewhat distant from one another. The progress is frequently so gradual that, at near periods, the improvement is not only not sensible, but from the declension either of certain branches of industry, or of certain districts of the country, things which sometimes happen though the country in general be in great prosperity, there frequently arises a suspicion that the riches and industry of the whole are decaying.

The annual produce of the land and labour of England, for example, is certainly much greater than it was, a little more than a century ago, at the restoration of Charles II. Though, at present, few people, I believe, doubt of this, yet during this period, five years have seldom passed away in which some book or pamphlet has not been published, written, too, with such abilities as to gain some authority with the public, and

pretending to demonstrate that the wealth of the nation was
fast declining, that the country was depopulated, agriculture
neglected, manufactures decaying, and trade undone. Nor
have these publications been all party pamphlets, the wretched
offspring of falsehood and venality. Many of them have been
written by very candid and very intelligent people, who wrote
nothing but what they believed, and for no other reason but
because they believed it.

The annual produce of the land and labour of England,
again, was certainly much greater at the restoration, than we
can suppose it to have been about an hundred years before,
at the accession of Elizabeth. At this period, too, we have all
reason to believe, the country was much more advanced in
improvement than it had been about a century before, towards the close of the dissensions between the houses of York
and Lancaster. Even though it was, probably, in a better
condition than it had been at the Norman conquest, and at
the Norman conquest than during the confusion of the Saxon
Heptarchy. Even at this early period, it was certainly a
much improved country than at the invasion of Julius Caesar,
when its inhabitants were nearly in the same state with the
savages in North America.

In each of those periods, however, there was not only much
private and public profusion, many expensive and unnecessary wars, great perversion of the annual produce from maintaining productive to maintaining unproductive hands; but
sometimes, in the confusion of civil discord, such absolute
waste and destruction of stock, as must be supposed, not only
to retard, as it certainly did the natural accumulation of
riches, but to have left the country, at the end of the period,
poorer than at the beginning. Thus, in the happiest and most
fortunate period of them all, that which has passed since the
restoration, how many disorders and misfortunes have occurred, which, could they have been foreseen, not only the im-
poverishment, but the total ruin of the country would have
been expected from them? The fire and the plague of London,
the two Dutch wars, the disorders of the revolution, the war in
Ireland, the four expensive French wars of 1688, 1702, 1742, and
1756, together with the two rebellions of 1715 and 1745. In

the course of the four French wars, the nation has contracted
more than a hundred and forty-five millions of debt, over and
above all the other extraordinary annual expense which they
occasioned, so that the whole cannot be computed at less
than two hundred millions. So great a share of the annual
produce of the land and labour of the country has, since
the revolution, been employed upon different occasions in
maintaining an extraordinary number of unproductive hands.
But had not those wars given this particular direction to so
large a capital, the greater part of it would naturally have
been employed in maintaining productive hands, whose
labour would have replaced, with a profit, the whole value of
their consumption. The value of the annual produce of the
land and labour of the country would have been considerably
increased by it every year, and every year's increase would
have augmented still more that of the following year. More
houses would have been built, more lands would have been
improved, and those which had been improved before would
have been better cultivated, more manufactures would have
been established, and those which had been established
before would have been more extended; and to what height
the real wealth and revenue of the country might, by this
time, have been raised, it is not perhaps very easy even to
imagine.

But though the profusion of government must, undoubtedly,
have retarded the natural progress of England towards wealth
and improvement, it has not been able to stop it. The annual
produce of its land and labour is, undoubtedly, much greater
at present than it was either at the restoration or at the revolution. The capital, therefore, annually employed in cultivating this land, and in maintaining this labour, must likewise be much greater. In the midst of all the exactions of
government, this capital has been silently and gradually
accumulated by the private frugality and good conduct of
individuals, by their universal, continual, and uninterrupted
effort to better their own condition. It is this effort, protected
by law and allowed by liberty to exert itself in the manner
that is most advantageous, which has maintained the progress of England towards opulence and improvement in

almost all former times, and which, it is to be hoped, will do so in all future times. England, however, as it has never been blessed with a very parsimonious government, so parsimony has at no time been the characteristical virtue of its inhabitants. It is the highest impertinence and presumption, therefore, in kings and ministers, to pretend to watch over the economy of private people, and to restrain their expense, either by sumptuary laws, or by prohibiting the importation of foreign luxuries. They are themselves always, and without any exception, the greatest spendthrifts in the society. Let them look well after their own expense, and they may safely trust private people with theirs. If their own extravagance does not ruin the state, that of their subjects never will.

As frugality increases and prodigality diminishes the public capital, so the conduct of those whose expense just equals their revenue, without either accumulating or encroaching, neither increases nor diminishes it. Some modes of expense, however, seem to contribute more to the growth of public opulence than others.

The revenue of an individual may be spent either in things which are consumed immediately, and in which one day's expense can neither alleviate nor support that of another, or it may be spent in things more durable, which can therefore be accumulated, and in which every day's expense may, as he chooses, either alleviate or support and heighten the effect of that of the following day. A man of fortune, for example, may either spend his revenue in a profuse and sumptuous table, and in maintaining a great number of menial servants, and a multitude of dogs and horses; or contenting himself with a frugal table and few attendants, he may lay out the greater part of it in adorning his house or his country villa, in useful or ornamental buildings, in useful or ornamental furniture, in collecting books, statues, pictures; or in things more frivolous, jewels, baubles, ingenious trinkets of different kinds; or, what is most trifling of all, in amassing a great wardrobe of fine clothes, like the favourite and minister of a great prince who died a few years ago. Were two men of equal fortune to spend their revenue, the one chiefly in the one way, the other in the other, the magnificence of the person whose expenses had been chiefly in durable commodities, would be continually increasing, every day's expenses contributing something to support and heighten the effect of that of the following day: that of the other, on the contrary, would be no greater at the end of the period than at the beginning. The former, too, would at the end of the period, be the richer man of the two. He would have a stock of goods of some kind or other, which, though it might not be worth all that it cost, would always be worth something. No trace or vestige of the expense of the latter would remain, and the effects of ten or twenty years profusion would be as completely annihilated as if they had never existed.

As the one mode of expense is more favourable than the other to the opulence of an individual, so is it likewise to that of a nation. The houses, the furniture, the clothing of the rich, in a little time, become useful to the inferior and middling ranks of people. They are able to purchase them when their superiors grow weary of them, and the general accommodation of the whole people is thus gradually improved, when this mode of expense becomes universal among men of fortune. In countries which have long been rich, you will frequently find the inferior ranks of people in possession both of houses and furniture perfectly good and entire, but of which neither the one could have been built, nor the other have been made for their use. What was formerly a seat of the family of Seymour is now an inn upon the Bath road. The marriage-bed of James the First of Great Britain, which his queen brought with her from Denmark, as a present fit for a sovereign to make to a sovereign, was, a few years ago, the ornament at an alehouse at Dunfermline. In some ancient cities, which either have been long stationary, or have gone somewhat to decay, you will sometimes scarce find a single house which could have been built for its present inhabitants. If you go into those houses too, you will frequently find many excellent, though antiquated pieces of furniture, which are still very fit for use, and which could as little have been made for them. Noble palaces, magnificent villas, great collections of books, statues, pictures, and other curiosities, are frequently both an ornament and an honour, not only to the neighbourhood, but to the whole country to which they belong. Versailles is an ornament and an honour to France, Stowe and Wilton to England. Italy still continues to command some sort of veneration by the number of monuments of this kind which it possesses, though the wealth which produced them has decayed, and though the genius which planned them seems to be extinguished, perhaps from not having the same employment.

The expense too, which is laid out in durable commodities, is favourable, not only to accumulation, but to frugality. If a person should at any time exceed in it, he can easily reform without exposing himself to the censure of the public. To reduce very much the number of his servants, to reform his table from great profusion to great frugality, to lay down his equipage after he has once set it up, are changes which cannot escape the observation of his neighbours, and which are supposed to imply some acknowledgement of preceding bad conduct. Few, therefore, of those who have once been so unfortunate as to launch out too far into this sort of expense, have afterwards the courage to reform, till ruin and bankruptcy oblige them. But if a person has, at any time, been at too great an expense in building, in furniture, in books or pictures, no imprudence can be inferred from his changing his conduct. These are things in which further expense is frequently rendered unnecessary by former expense; and when a person stops short, he appears to do so, not because he has exceeded his fortune, but because he has satisfied his fancy.

The expense, besides, that is laid out in durable commodities gives maintenance, commonly, to a greater number of people than that which is employed in the most profuse hospitality. Of two or three hundredweight of provisions, which may sometimes be served up at a great festival, one-half, perhaps, is thrown to the dunghill, and there is always a great deal wasted and abused. But if the expense of this entertainment had been employed in setting to work masons, carpenters, upholsterers, mechanics, etc. a quantity of provisions, of equal value, would have been distributed among a still greater number of people who would have bought them in pennyworths and pound weights, and not have lost or thrown away a single ounce of them. In the one way, besides, this expense maintains productive, in the other unproductive hands. In the one way, therefore, it increases, in the other, it does not increase, the exchangeable value of the annual produce of the land and labour of the country.

I would not, however, by all this be understood to mean that the one species of expense always betokens a more liberal or generous spirit than the other. When a man of fortune spends his revenue chiefly in hospitality, he shares the greater part of it with his friends and companions; but when he employs it in purchasing such durable commodities, he often spends the whole upon his own person, and gives nothing to anybody without an equivalent. The latter species of expense, therefore, especially when directed towards frivolous objects, the little ornaments of dress and furniture, jewels, gewgaws, frequently indicates, not only a trifling, but a base and selfish disposition. All that I mean is, that the one sort of expense, as it always occasions some accumulation of valuable commodities, as it is more favourable to private frugality, and, consequently, to the increase of the public capital, and as it maintains productive, rather than unproductive hands, conduces more than the other to the growth of public opulence.

2 William Ellis

EFFECT OF THE EMPLOYMENT OF MACHINERY UPON THE HAPPINESS OF THE WORKING CLASSES[1]

William Ellis (1800–81) was the son of a Lloyd's underwriter of Huguenot descent. At its foundation in 1824 he was made assistant-underwriter to the Indemnity Marine Insurance Company, and became chief manager three years later. A member of the Utilitarian Society, he was also a notable educationist and founded the Birkbeck Schools at his own expense from 1848–52. Although he wrote a number of text-books on political economy, he is perhaps best known as the author of the article on 'Marine Insurance' in J. R. McCulloch's *Commercial Dictionary*. In fact the following re-view article was his most serious contribution; it is a landmark in the development of Ricardian economics, as J. S. Mill recognized when he described it as 'the most scientific treat-ment of the subject which I have met with' in reference to the machinery question. Essentially its importance lies in the extension of the simple Ricardian model, in which agri-cultural profits govern the profits of the other sectors of the economy, and capital consists largely of the subsistence of workers, to take account of the consequences of the growth of fixed capital. Ricardo himself, and John Barton,[2] saw this development as having a possibly adverse effect on employ-ment by reducing the wages fund. But Ellis makes the growth of fixed capital depend on the supply of savings, not on the conversion of circulating capital. Although Ellis is clear about the distinction between savings and investment, his dis-

[1] *Westminster Review*, 5, January 1826, Article IV.

[2] *Observations on the circumstances which Influence the Condition of the Labouring Classes of Society* (1817).

cussion of the motive for saving suggests that he felt it was independent of the prevailing rate of profit and that the portion of savings used to make additions to capital would depend very much on the profitability of innovations. This was one direction in which subsequent thinking on capital formation was to develop. But another, more important, effect of this form of analysis was to focus attention even more closely on the factors governing saving, rather than on the problems associated with the growth of fixed capital, particularly in cases involving technical change.

There is perhaps no question within the whole range of the science of Political Economy which has been left in a more vague and unsatisfactory state than that of the consequences which flow from the employment of Machinery. It is maintained by some that the use of machinery cannot but be attended with the most deplorable consequences to the working classes. The arguments, say they, by which the highly-vaunted advantages resulting from the use of machinery are pretended to be proved, rest upon the fact, that a large quantity of labour is superseded by a smaller. Are we not then entitled to conclude from this very admission, that mechanical improvements and inventions, however beneficial they may be to capitalists, are the source of misery and degradation to the working classes? By others, again, it is maintained that the benefits resulting from the use of machinery are not confined to the capitalists but are extended to all classes of the community. They appeal, in support of their views, to the dense population of England and other civilized countries, and ask, whether it would be possible to draw sustenance from the earth for such vast numbers, without the assistance of the plough and other equally useful instruments of production. If it would not be possible, and no one they affirm can pretend that it would be, it is madness any longer to dispute the advantages which all classes of society derive from the use of machinery.

Such may be stated as the principal arguments of the two parties by whom opinions of so contradictory a nature upon the employment of machinery are entertained. If it were forced upon us to come to a decision without further inquiry, we certainly should not hesitate a moment in pronouncing in favour of machinery. The arguments on the other side admit of so easy a reductio ad absurdum, as to lead us involuntarily to infer that in them some fallacy cannot fail to be involved. If the use of machinery is calculated to diminish the fund out of which labourers are supported, then by giving up the use of the plough and the harrow and returning to the pastoral state, or by scratching the earth with our nails, the produce of the soil would be adequate to the maintenance of a much greater number of labourers. There are many labourers now in England, and the gradations of ingenuity and skill in machinery are numerous; but as the number of labourers and the funds for their support would be gradually increased in proportion as we fell back upon the less perfect machinery, so, at last, when we deprived ourselves entirely of its assistance, the produce and hence the population of England would be increased beyond what has ever been exhibited in any country upon the surface of the globe, nay would exceed, perhaps, what the most exalted imagination warmed with the contemplation of ancestorial and primitive simplicity, and revelling in dreams of a golden age, could dare to conceive.

This reductio ad absurdum has fortunately been sufficient for most practical purposes, and has generally withheld legislators, who on this question can have but little if any sinister interest, from attempting to impede the development of skill and ingenuity in the application of machinery to the various branches of industry. But there is a class of persons who take for their motto 'medio tutissimus ibis;' who steer a middle course, by which is meant the course of wisdom; who say, admitting the general inference as to the benefit resulting from the use of machinery, still it is possible that the use of machinery may in some cases be attended with baneful effects to the labouring population. It is perfectly clear that the reductio ad absurdum leaves this class untouched. Although, strictly speaking, the task of shewing wherein these certain cases vary from the general rule should devolve upon them, every thing connected with the welfare of the labouring population is of such vital importance to society, that rather than that these possible cases should not be met, we will undertake the investigation of them ourselves. To pursue this investigation with effect, it will be necessary to trace the operation of the use of machinery upon society through all its ramifications, and to consider why the employment of machinery is beneficial in its general effects, or for what reasons its employment under particular circumstances should, if it ever can, be the cause of mischief.*

In the early stages of society, when the instruments employed in the cultivation of the earth were few and rude, when the draining and manuring of the land, and the rotation of crops were as yet unthought of, the attention of the husbandman was directed exclusively to the better description of soils. With his limited knowledge it would have been vain to attempt the cultivation of inferior soils. From good land he was enabled, after the payment of his labourers and replacing the stock expended, to draw some little profit as a remuneration for his exertion and risk. The same expenditure on less fertile land would perhaps have yielded him no return, or at least the return would have been such as not to afford him an adequate remuneration. With the progress of society, as knowledge increases and the arts of husbandry become better understood, the cultivator of the soil is enabled to employ his capital with advantage on those soils from which he found it impossible before to extract such returns as would afford him an adequate remuneration. Hence it is clear that a soil which is regarded as barren in one state of civilization may be highly productive in another more advanced, and that with the progress of society lands of a less and less degree of fertility may be brought under cultivation. Such, in reality, has been the course of events in every country where the inhabitants have been continually adding to their stock

* Mr. Ricardo, in the third edition of his work *On the Principles of Political Economy and Taxation*, added a chapter upon machinery, wherein he attempted to shew that the use of machinery might in some cases be for a time detrimental to the labouring classes. It is needless to say that we distinguish this enlightened philosopher from the vulgar objectors to machinery, although we think that his arguments are inconclusive.

of useful knowledge and pushing on their inventions and improvements in the arts and sciences.

One of the first symptoms of a nation's emerging from a state of barbarism, one co-eval with the practice of bartering, is the division of labour. Two savages soon learn, that if one confine himself to hunting and the other to fishing, each will obtain a larger quantity of food than if they were each to fish and hunt on alternate days. When agriculture is introduced, and other wants and desires beyond those of food spring up, the capitalists and labourers soon divide themselves into two great classes, the agricultural and manufacturing. The employment of the first is, to supply the community with raw produce, that of the second, to work the raw produce into the shapes in which, as they conceive, the community will be willing to give the greatest equivalent for it. The arts of the manufacturer are at first in as rude a state as those of the agriculturist. Every thing is made by the hand; and consequently the quantity of commodities produced is small in proportion to the quantity of labour set in motion. In that early stage of society in which no rent is paid, if half the labourers and half the capital in a country were employed in manufactures and half in agriculture, the produce of one would exchange for the produce of the other—they would be of equal value. If by improvements in manufactures, by the invention of machinery, or by a more judicious distribution of labour, the same quantity of commodities could be produced by one quarter instead of one half of the labourers and capital, there would then be one quarter of the labourers and one quarter of the capital to dispose of. Should the demand of the community be for an increased quantity of manufactures, that branch of industry would be extended. An increased quantity of manufactured produce would be given in exchange for the same quantity of agricultural; and the raw produce required for this extension of manufactures would occasion the cultivation of an inferior description of soil. But should the demand of the community be, not for an increased quantity of manufactured, but of agricultural produce, the capital and labourers spared from the manufacturing department would be transferred to the soil. The total produce of the community would in this case consist of the same quantity of manufactures as before and an increased quantity of agricultural produce. Agricultural produce would rise in value as compared with manufactures; and the increased command which the capitalists engaged in agriculture would thus have over the manufactured produce would compensate them for the cultivation of an inferior description of soil. From this we may conclude that the effect of improvements in manufacturing industry, as in agriculture, is to enable capitalists to derive a profit from lands not antecedently brought under cultivation. This conclusion seems so little open to dispute that the mere statement of it might be thought sufficient to ensure its reception. There were formerly, however, many writers, and some there are of the present day, who imagine that they see important distinctions in respect of utility between agriculture and manufactures; and they might hesitate about yielding to it their assent. We may, perhaps, by a short illustration, succeed in presenting to them our opinions in a new point of view. If, by some improvement, the cost of producing a loaf of bread is reduced one-half, the effect is the same to the community whether the saving of labour be made in the agricultural or manufacturing department, whether in the business of the farmer, or by the carrier, miller, and baker. The same remark may be extended to broad cloth, hardware, or any other commodity. What difference can there be in the result to society, whether the saving of labour is with the farmer who grows the wool, and the miner who extracts the metal from the earth, or with the manufacturer who weaves the cloth and polishes the steel?

Having thus established that it is owing to increased knowledge and skill, as exemplified in improved manufacturing and agricultural implements, that soils of a less and less degree of fertility can be cultivated to advantage, our next step will be to ascertain what appearance society would assume, supposing no further improvements were to be made.

The capital of a country is that portion of the sum total of commodities which is employed in production. That which is annually produced over and above what is requisite to replace the capital consumed (leaving rent out of the question) is profits of stock. Let the capital of a country be represented by 1,000 quarters of corn, and 1,000 yards of cloth: if the annual production is 1,150 quarters and 1,150 yards, the profits of stock are said to be 15 per cent; if the annual produce is 1,100 quarters and 1,100 yards or 1,050 quarters and 1,050 yards, the profits of stock are said to be 10 or 5 per cent. Let us assume in addition that the state of the country is such that no extension of tillage can take place except by resorting to soils inferior in fertility to any already under cultivation. Whatever the rate of profit might be, allowing that no further improvement is to be made in the arts of production, every addition to capital must be attended with a corresponding reduction in that rate. There is a certain rate of profit without which no person could be induced to employ his savings productively. What that rate of profits may be we shall not pretend to estimate. If profits were reduced to that lowest point, nothing more could be added to the existing capital; and consequently as no additional employment could be furnished to labourers, their numbers must remain stationary, unless they should be content to submit to a reduction in the quantity of food and clothing allotted to them as wages. If they were willing to consent to such a deterioration in their condition, as the profits of the capitalists would be thereby increased, a still further accumulation might take place; and would continue until the rate of profits were again reduced to its former level. The means of accumulation furnished by a deterioration in the condition of the labourers are of a temporary nature, and therefore may be entirely left out of consideration in this investigation. It may be assumed that a certain quantity of the produce of industry, either by habit or by necessity, is requisite for their maintenance, and that below this quantity they cannot be reduced.

After a certain period, then, if a stop were put to all further improvements, the rate of profit would be reduced to its minimum, no further additions to capital would be made, and consequently all further increase in the labouring population would be checked. The cause of this impediment to an increase of capital, it must be remembered, is to be found in the limited fertility of the soil. In the actual state of things, where improvements are continually taking place in the various branches of agricultural, manufacturing, and commercial industry, the tendency of profits is always to fall to this lowest point, but the actual fall is checked by these improvements, the operation of which is to enable capitalists to draw from soils of a certain degree of fertility, a larger sum of the necessaries and conveniences of life than they could previous to their introduction.

The capital of a country, as we have already observed, is that portion of the savings of previous labour which is employed in production. For the creation of capital, therefore, it appears that two sets of motives are necessary: the motives to save, and the motives to employ that which is saved in production. When once a correct estimate of these two sets of motives is made, the solution of the machinery-question will soon be stripped of its difficulties.

Before any addition can be made to capital, some fund from which this addition is to be derived must exist. This fund is accumulated from the savings of individuals, or rather it is the savings themselves. By what motives, then, are individuals swayed when they refrain from expending that which they have earned? It is universally allowed that the enjoyment to be derived from consumption is the real stimulus to exertion, and few words will be wanted to explain that the expectation of greater enjoyment from deferred than from immediate consumption must be the inducement to save. The numerous ills with which we are surrounded must make every man desirous of laying up a store in the period of prosperity, in order to ward off, if possible, the hour of adversity. The poor man is an object of comparative disregard; the rich man, by the mere influence of his wealth, commands respect. The insecure tenure upon which health is held, the prospect of old age when wants increase while the energies are impaired, the desire of making a provision for children, and the immediate advantages with which the possession of wealth is attended, are so many inducements, inducements too which operate strongly upon a large majority of mankind, to abstain from immediate consumption, to lay up a

store by which the suffering from future pain may be prevented and the enjoyment of future pleasure secured. That
these motives are more than adequate to counterbalance
those which lead to immediate consumption, is sufficiently
proved by daily experience. The motives which operate to
save exist totally independent of any addition which might
be made to the savings themselves. The inducement to save
a sum of money for fourteen years is no doubt considerably
strengthened by the knowledge that the sum saved will be
doubled at the end of that period; but even where no profit is
superadded, where the sum of money at the expiration of the
fourteen years is no greater than the sum originally laid by,
savings would still be made in conformity with the inducements which we have mentioned. In barbarous ages, when the
want of security formed an insuperable barrier to the accumulation of capital, hoards were nevertheless accumulated.
But in barbarous ages, while the human intellect was comparatively in a state of infancy, the chance of future evils was
less likely to be anticipated, and provision for their relief less
likely to be made. Security even for hoards was less perfect
than it now is. The motives to save, independent of any
pecuniary profit, therefore, are stronger in a civilized than in
a barbarous age.

Every augmentation of capital is made from savings. Our
next step, accordingly, is to investigate by what motives
mankind are induced to convert their savings into capital, or,
in other words, to employ their savings in production. The
control which an individual has over his savings, when drawn
from the hoard and employed in production, is considerably
weakened. He must either employ labourers himself, or lend
his savings to others for a similar purpose. In the term
diminished control over property, is implied an increase of
risk. What the exact value of this increased risk may be,
depends upon a variety of circumstances. Foremost in the list
of circumstances may be counted the state of the laws by
which the performance of contracts is enforced. It is sufficient
for our present purpose to assume a certain degree of risk. A
willingness to incur this risk can only be produced by some
commensurate advantage. This advantage is the profit which

it is anticipated will be realized by the transmutation of savings into capital.

To obviate misconstruction, we will here make a few remarks in explanation of what we comprise under the word profits. Where an individual employs his own savings productively, in the profit which he obtains is included, after deducting an adequate allowance for the risk to which his capital may have been exposed in his particular business, the remuneration for his time and skill, which remuneration may be called agency for superintendence; and the remuneration for the productive employment of his savings, which is called interest. The whole of this remuneration we may call gross profit. Where an individual employs the savings of another, he obtains, after deducting the same allowance, the agency only. Where an individual lends his savings to another, what he obtains is interest. This interest may, without impropriety, for our present purpose, be designated as neat profits. As the requisite capital and the requisite talent for conducting business to the greatest advantage, are seldom combined; as there are but few farmers, few manufacturers, and few merchants, who operate on their own means without credit, that is to say, without drawing upon the savings of others who are not directly engaged in business; we may assume that so long as savings are employed productively, so long there will be neat profits: at least until there is an arrangement of circumstances different from that of which we have hitherto had any experience, an arrangement of circumstances by which capital and talent for business will be appropriately combined in the same individuals. It will be understood, therefore, henceforward, in this article, that whenever the term profit occurs, neat profit, as explained above, is referred to.

It is seen, that a certain risk is attached to the employment of savings in production. This risk will be variously estimated, and different individuals will accordingly feel different degrees of reluctance to convert their savings into capital. One thing, however, is certain, that this reluctance, in the great majority of mankind, is not insuperable. In some it will vanish, perhaps, before a profit of 1 per cent, in some of 2, in some of 3, in some of 4, and in almost all before a profit of 5 per cent, unless indeed the existence of property should rest upon a very insecure basis, a supposition which we shall not contemplate.

From the previous reasoning, some general propositions may now, we think, be safely established. The higher the rate of profit in any community, the greater will be the proportion of the annual savings which is added to capital; and the greater will be the inducement to save. The lower the rate of profit, the smaller will be that portion of the annual savings, which is added to capital. Every improvement in the arts and sciences, therefore, or in the distribution of labour, the tendency of which is to raise the rate of profit, must occasion an increase of capital.

The strength of the motives to save, and to employ savings in production, has been called the vis medicatrix in society. Wars and seasons of famine, and the profligate expenditure of government, frequently make deep inroads into the national capital. Let but a few years expire after the baneful influence of these causes of human misery has ceased to operate, and all traces of their having existed are obliterated. The destruction of capital which is occasioned by such tremendous visitations, is shortly repaired, except where the people themselves have been made to retrograde in knowledge. The employment of a diminished capital with the same skill which existed previous to its diminution, must necessarily be attended with an increased rate of profit; and increased profit is the charm which draws savings from their hoard, and adds to the fund whence accumulations are to be made.

We can mention a few facts which are peculiarly illustrative of the powerful effects which have been wrought by the additional stimulus imported to the motives to accumulate by an increased rate of profit. In drawing a comparison between the ten years antecedent to the late war, and the ten years which have elapsed since its close, the most convincing proofs may be adduced to shew, that this nation has made a very considerable advance in wealth and population. The population has increased 40 per cent, the consumption of exciseable commodities upwards of 50 per cent, of tea 80

per cent, the manufacture of cotton 500 per cent, of wool
600 per cent, and of silk and flax 200 per cent. The increase of
shipping has been 70 per cent. The slaughter of cattle and
sheep in London, has increased 40 per cent; and in the manufacturing districts in a much greater proportion.* An increase
of consumption proves an increase of commodities, and an
increase of commodities proves an increase of capital. To be
perfectly safe from any charge of exaggeration, we will suppose that the capital of the country at the present moment,
does not exceed the capital at the commencement of the
French revolutionary war, by more than 40 per cent. During
the war, the expenditure of government was so enormous, as
to be quite out of proportion to the expenditure of any former
period, and the seasons of dearth were unusually severe and
numerous;† and yet not only were these inroads into the
national capital constantly repaired, but large additions
have been made to it. The causes of this great influx of savings
into productive employment may be traced to one cause,
the rise in the rate of profit; which rise in the rate of profit,
again, may be attributed to the large deductions from the
savings of individuals made by the unprofitable expenditure
of government, ‡ and to the wonderful improvements introduced into the various arts of production. That the rate of
profits rose during the war, and has declined since the peace
is matter of perfect notoriety to all who know any thing of
the commercial history of this country for the last thirty
years. The best authenticated evidence which can be brought
in corroboration of this notorious fact is, the price of the

* See Tooke on High and Low Prices.

† *Idem.*

‡ It must not be thought that we are by any means blind to the evil of a
large government expenditure. Because a diminution of national capital,
other circumstances remaining the same, is attended with a rise in the rate
of profit, the wealth, and consequently the happiness, of the community
is not the less certainly diminished. If the capital of a country, after contributing to a large government expenditure, were 900 millions with a rate
of profit of 5¼ per cent; before that expenditure it might have been 1,000
millions, with a rate of profit of 5 per cent. After the expenditure the
revenue of the country (exclusive of rent) would only be £47,250,000;
before the expenditure it would have been £50,000,000.

funds. The average price of the 3 per cent consols, with the rate of interest to which it corresponds in each year, from 1784 to 1824, may be quoted as follows:

Year	Consols	Interest	Year	Consols	Interest
1784	56	5·36	1805	58	5·17
1785	59	5·08	1806	61	4·92
1786	73	4·11	1807	62	4·84
1787	75	4·00	1808	66	4·55
1788	75	4·00	1809	68	4·41
1789	77	3·90	1810	68	4·41
1790	76	3·95	1811	64	4·69
1791	83	3·61	1812	61	4·92
1792	87	3·45	1813	58	5·17
1793	76	3·95	1814	67	4·48
1794	66	4·55	1815	60	5·00
1795	66	4·55	1816	62	4·84
1796	60	5·00	1817	75	4·00
1797	51	5·88	1818	78	3·85
1798	50	6·00	1819	71	4·23
1799	57	5·26	1820	69	4·35
1800	63	4·76	1821	74	4·05
1801	60	5·00	1822	79	3·80
1802	69	4·35	1823	80	3·75
1803	56	5·36	1824	93	3·23
1804	59	5·08			

This species of evidence is, we know, open to cavil. It may be said, that the funds were depressed during the war, from a feeling of insecurity. But granting the operation of this feeling, upon what species of property, especially of property employed in production, did it not operate? As far as it operated, its operation must have been to raise the rate of profit generally, and hence, of course, to depress the price of the funds. The largeness of the profit must be proportioned to the risk incurred in drawing treasure from the hoard, and employing it in production. It is the increasing rate of profit,

by which the consumption of capital is checked and counteracted. The fact that the rise in the rate of profit was not much
larger than it appears to have been when connected with the
events which we have mentioned, is, in itself, a strong proof of
the intensity of the desire to save and accumulate, which is
inherent in the human breast. The additional rise in the rate
of profit, which would otherwise have taken place, was anticipated by the conversion of savings into capital. Supposing
the facts which we have brought forward should, contrary
to our expectation, be disputed, granting even that they
could be shewn to be incorrect, our theory would not be
invalidated. We have been enabled to form it on completely
independent evidence, but the commercial history of the last
thirty years affords, as we think, a striking illustration of the
speed with which large masses abstracted from the national
capital, are replaced by fresh accumulations.

The ease with which an inroad into the national capital is
repaired, when the evil by which that inroad was occasioned
is removed, is a sure sign of the powerful influence which is
exercised over the majority of mankind, by the motives to
save and accumulate. These motives are in constant operation, and may be termed the vis progrediendi, with full as
much justice as the vis medicatrix. The constant and urgent
desire to find employment for additional savings, occasions
every opening which is made by improvements and inventions, to be instantly filled. As soon as a profit is presented,
fresh savings are converted into capital, either in the in-
closure and cultivation of new lands, in the more expensive
tillage of old ones, in the prosecution of a new trade, or in the
establishment of a new manufacture. When a tax is imposed,
the national capital is seldom diminished, the amount is
made up from savings by the influence of the vis medicatrix;
so when a lucrative employment for additional capital is
presented, it does not follow that any of the savings already
engaged in production, should be transferred to the new
employment; fresh savings will rather be provided for that
purpose, by the influence of the vis progrediendi. But even
supposing that the new opening, from whatever source
derived, were not instantaneously filled by fresh savings, the

rise in the rate of profit occasioned by the more lucrative investment of the old capital, would soon draw them forth into
productive employment. One of two events, then, will occur,
either the new employment for capital will be instantaneously
filled by fresh savings, or the consequent rise of profits, will
cause it to be so at no very distant period. The analysis of the
motives by which mankind are governed in saving, and in
employing their savings in production, leads to the inference
that the former, under most circumstances, would be the
more probable event of the two. This inference is strengthened
by our knowledge, that nations are generally adding to their
capitals, not only without any increase in the rate of profit,
but when it is well known that the rate of profit is declining.

For the sake of clearness, and in order not to encumber the
arguments which we shall hereafter have occasion to employ,
by any repetition, it will be useful to restate those propositions
which we have already established. 1st. That every improvement in the arts of production is a means of deriving profit
from an inferior description of soil. 2nd. That the limited
fertility of the soil, is the only impediment to an indefinite
increase of capital. 3rd. That the savings of individuals,
from which all additions to capital must be made, are the
consequence of the strong desire felt by the great bulk of
mankind, to preserve and to improve their station in society.
4th. That the magnitude of the additions to capital from the
savings of individuals, must in a great measure depend upon
the rate of profit. 5th. That, consequently, every diminution
in the national capital, from whatever cause arising, while the
skill and industry of the people are unimpaired, and every
improvement in the arts of production, the tendency of each
of which events is to increase the rate of profits, are necessarily attended with an immediate conversion of fresh savings
into capital, to take advantage of the opening thereby presented.

If these propositions are correct, there can be no necessity
to offer any thing further, to shew, that improvements in the
arts of production are beneficial to the capitalists. This fact,
indeed, we believe, has never been controverted. The allegation of those who lament improvements in the arts of production, or in any particular species of those arts is, that they

are at the same time a source of profit to the capitalist, and a source of misery to the labourer. We think we shall be able to establish satisfactorily, that this allegation is unfounded, and that all improvements in the arts of production, are beneficial to the working classes.

We call any event beneficial to the working classes, which places within the reach of the same number a larger quantity of the necessaries and conveniences of life, or which enables an increased number to maintain themselves as comfortably as the smaller number did at an antecedent period. The beneficial tendency of such an event may be counteracted, or even outweighed by other events of a mischievous tendency, brought about by the ignorance and want of foresight of the labourers themselves. No arguments, accordingly, against improvements in the arts of production, can be drawn from a comparison between the condition of the labouring classes, subsequent and antecedent to those improvements.

Supposing the capital of a country were wholly employed in the payment of wages, every improvement in the mode of employing that capital by a more judicious distribution of the labourers, would cause the same capital to yield a larger return; that is, the rate of profit would be increased—hence the capital, and hence the wages of the labourer. To illustrate as we proceed, let us suppose that the capital of a country were 1,000 quarters of corn, and 1,000 yards of cloth, the number of labourers 1,000, 500 employed in the production of corn, and 500 in the production of cloth, and profits of stock 5 per cent; the annual produce would be 1,050 quarters of corn, and 1,050 yards of cloth. Let us further suppose, that by some better distribution of labour, the annual produce should be increased to 1,100 quarters, and 1,100 yards; profits would rise to 10 per cent, and by the law which we have already explained, the capital of the country would be almost simultaneously increased, and would continue to increase, until profits were again reduced to 5 per cent. Should population increase in proportion to the increase of capital, inferior soils will be taken into cultivation. If the better distribution of labour should be confined to one of the commodities, say to the cloth, if for instance half the capital, and half the labour, were able to produce 2,100 yards of cloth, the price of cloth would fall, that of corn would rise; in other words, one yard of cloth, would no longer exchange for one quarter of corn. If the demand of the community were not for a double supply of cloth, but for an increased supply of corn, a portion of the capital and of the labourers, would be transferred from the production of cloth to the production of corn. In either case the result is an increase in the rate of profits, and the consequences which flow from that result are the same. It may, therefore, be stated as a general proposition that, if the capital of a country were wholly devoted to the payment of wages, every improvement in the arts of production would be beneficial to the labouring population.

We have taken this case as the most simple, thinking that its elucidation would lead the way to a ready comprehension of the more difficult ones. It is perfectly obvious that the existence of a capital wholly employed in the payment of wages is a mere supposition made for the purpose of illustration. The functions of capital are many. But they may be divided with advantage under two heads, the distinction between which it is of the utmost importance to observe. Under the first, is comprised the payment of the wages of the labourers; and under the second, the furnishing the tools, machinery, and raw produce employed in production. If it should be found that the consequence of improvements in the arts of production is, to increase that proportion of the capital which consists of implements &c., at the expense of that portion which is employed in the payment of wages, no doubt could remain that such an improvement would be detrimental to the working classes. It is here that the least decided class of objectors to the unlimited use of machinery make their stand. Their language is hesitating; they say that improvements in machinery may have the effect of diminishing that portion of the capital which is employed in the payment of wages. Our endeavours will be directed to the formation, not of an hypothetical but of an affirmative conclusion upon the subject. It seems to be granted by this class that, if it can be shown that improvements in machinery, instead of diminishing, actually add to that portion of the national capital which is devoted to the payment of wages, their opposition would cease.

Having divided the capital of a country into two portions, one of which is employed in the payment of wages, the other in furnishing implements, &c.; we will suppose that these two portions are of equal value, that is, are the produce of equal quantities of labour. A certain proportion of the labourers will necessarily be employed in keeping the implements &c. in a state of repair. If the effect of an improvement in machinery should merely be to render the implements &c. more productive, without adding to the number of labourers previously employed in keeping them in repair, it is obvious that the working classes would be benefitted. Let us suppose, that the capital of a country consists of 1,000 quarters of corn and 1,000 yards of cloth, and implements &c. equal to 1,000 quarters and 1,000 yards; that the number of labourers is 1,000, 500 engaged in the production of corn and 500 in that of cloth, each deriving equal assistance from the implements &c. and that the profits of stock are 5 per cent; the annual produce will be 1,100 quarters of corn and 1,100 yards of cloth, the implements &c. kept in a state of repair maintaining their original value. Now, let us suppose, that by an improvement in the implements of production the annual produce should be increased to 1,200 quarters and 1,200 yards; profits would rise to 10 per cent, and the same consequences would follow which we have already traced in a former case. Our former observations will likewise serve to explain what would be the consequences if the species of improvement under consideration were confined to one of the commodities, the corn or the cloth. The conclusion is, that such an improvement would be the opposite of detrimental to the labouring population.

Preserving the same division of capital as before, one more case remains to be examined, that in which the improvement in machinery has the effect of withdrawing some of the labourers from their previous employment. Let us suppose for instance, the produce at the end of the first year, during which the improvement was hit upon, to be only 600 quarters and 600 yards, and the implements &c. owing to the increased labour bestowed upon them, to rise in value to 1,500 quarters and 1,500 yards, the profits of stock would be 5 per cent as before. But it would appear that the capitalists will, for the next year's production, have their implements &c. worth 1,500 quarters and 1,500 yards, and only 500 quarters and 500 yards to distribute as wages among the labourers; the condition of the labourers will, therefore, be deteriorated. This is precisely the appearance by which so many have been misled, an appearance, as we hope to prove, altogether fallacious. Allowing, for a moment, that the wages of the labourers would, in conformity with this supposition, be reduced one half, it is no less true that the same number of labourers would be employed, and that they would be aided by improved machinery; the produce of their labour would, accordingly, be larger than it was before. We may assume that instead of 1,100 quarters and 1,100 yards, it would be 1,200 quarters and 1,200 yards, making the profits of stock 35 instead of 5 per cent. There is now an increased fund out of which to save, and an increased profit as a reward for the productive employment of savings; wages, therefore, would rise above their former level. But how would the case stand if wages only rose to their former level? Capital as wages 1,000 quarters and 1,000 yards; as implements &c. 1,500 quarters and 1,500 yards; produce 1,200 quarters and 1,200 yards—profits of stock 8 per cent. The reader can easily work out for himself the operation of this increased profit, in adding to the wages of labour by the stimulus which it would give to fresh accumulation. These increased wages would continue until the labouring classes in their turn increased in numbers, and occasioned a resort to the cultivation of inferior soils. It must always be remembered, that an improvement in machinery connected with the production of one commodity in a country, is in principle precisely similar to one connected with all the commodities. The commodity with which the improvement is exclusively connected, falls in exchangeable value. If the demand of the nation for that commodity should, contrary to the usual course of events, happen not to increase in proportion to the reduced cost of production, a portion of capital would be transferred to some other business. Under such circumstances, a number of labourers must be, what is called, thrown out of employment, that is, notwithstanding the increase of employment, a variation must take place in the distribution of labourers.

The strongest case, then, which can, with any appearance of plausibility, be stated against any given improvement in machinery is, that, by a sudden absorption of that portion of capital devoted to the payment of wages, wages may be temporarily reduced. It is evident that they must be ultimately raised, unless the rise be counteracted by an increase of population. But we are prepared to dispute the probability even of a temporary depression. For what would be the effect upon profits of such a depression in wages? According to the illustration which we have given, profits would rise from 5 to 35 per cent and fall again to 8 per cent. The motives which lead to the anticipation and prevention of such fluctuations have already been analysed. A fresh opening is presented for the profitable employment of savings. The additional capital devoted to the construction of a new machine is not drawn from the fund to which the labourers have to look for support, but from that fund which is constantly supplied by what we have denominated the vis progrediendi of society. We have shown that when that additional capital is introduced, motives in abundance are presented for a still further accumulation, since profits will have risen in as much as the same number of labourers, aided by more powerful instruments, will be able to produce a larger quantity of commodities.

If the validity of the foregoing arguments should be undisputed; and we confess that they appear to us perfectly conclusive, while at the same time they are collaterally strengthened by the aspect of every society, of the progression of which we have any record; the following advantages may be traced to the invention and improvement of machinery: 1st. To the landlords, an increase of rent, by the cultivation of a lower gradation of soils. 2nd. To the capitalists, an increase of profit, by rendering the same capital more productive. 3rd. To the labourers, an increase of wages, by adding to the fund which furnishes the means of their employment and maintenance.

In making use of the term 'inventions' in machinery, we

have confined ourselves to the consideration of such inventions as are the means of increasing the productive power of labour, in other words, of enabling the same number of labourers to produce a larger quantity of commodities. We should not, perhaps, be open to much animadversion if we were to neglect the consideration of all inventions of a different description, since it is hardly possible to conceive any invention of machinery applicable to the purposes of production which is not the means of saving labour. An individual who applies his mind or devotes his time and capital to the invention and manufacture of machinery, only does so in the expectation of gain; and his machinery will produce no gain to him unless he can supersede other machinery, less powerful in proportion to its cost, or unless he can prove to the capitalist that his capital would be more productively employed in its purchase than in the payment of wages. If we turn from the machinist to the manufacturer or farmer, we shall find but little encouragement held out to the mere inventor. Manufacturers and farmers who have their capitals already engaged cannot be tempted to abandon that employment from which their profit is uniform and secure, unless for some new employment in which the realization of a large additional profit may be reasonably expected. It is unnecessary to enumerate the difficulties which are opposed to change in any established series of operations in almost every branch of business. The loss of superseded machinery, the want of skill and practice in workmen, and the uncertainty of the result, all unite in preventing the adoption and application of that which is untried. These difficulties, doubtless, are constantly overcome, so constantly that to many, perhaps, they may appear unworthy of notice. They are only conquered, however, by the prospect of the great additional profit, with which the adopted invention is expected to be accompanied. Take away the prospect of this additional profit, and the difficulties would be insuperable. Take away even a part of it—suppose for a moment that the law were repealed by which the rights of a patentee are established—and who can pretend to estimate the check which would be given to the exertion of mechanical ingenuity?

Although it is perfectly clear that new machinery which is
unattended with an increased rate of profit to the capitalist
will seldom if ever be adopted, we may assume, for the purpose of investigation, that machinery of such a description
may be invented and applied. What would be the effect of the
adoption of such machinery upon the working classes? Reverting to our former figures, where we supposed the capital
of a country to be represented by 1,000 quarters of corn and
1,000 yards of cloth, and implements &c. equal in value to
1,000 quarters and 1,000 yards, and the annual produce to be
1,100 quarters and 1,100 yards (the wear and tear of the
machinery being regularly replaced) or profits 5 per cent,
let us suppose that the capitalists adopt some new machinery
by the use of which they will obtain no more than their
previous rate of profit. During the manufacture of the
machinery the wages of the labourers would remain as before. At the expiration of that period, the produce would be
600 quarters and 600 yards, and implements &c. equal in
value to 1,500 quarters and 1,500 yards. If there should still be
room for the employment of 1,000 quarters and 1,000 yards
as wages, without any diminution in the rate of profit, the
condition of the labourers would not be deteriorated; in fact,
it would be improved, since there would be an increased fund
to contribute to the exigences of the state; the annual produce
being increased from 1,100 quarters and 1,100 yards to 1,125
quarters and 1,125 yards. But should there no longer be room
for the employment of 1,000 quarters and 1,000 yards as
wages, except by a diminished rate of profit, as there would
then be no motive for an increase of capital, unless the
labourers were willing to submit to a reduction of wages, the
condition of the working classes would be deteriorated. A
reduction of wages would enable the capitalists to employ
further savings upon inferior soils, with the same rate of
profit as before; this, to the labouring classes, however,
would merely be a palliative to the evil, their only effective
and certain remedy, one happily at their command, being the
limitation of their numbers. One case may be supposed, then,
in which the introduction of new machinery might be injurious to the working classes, that is, where the invention of

the machinery is altogether unprofitable; and that no new machinery will ever be employed under such circumstances is sufficiently manifest. Inventions in machinery, therefore, are, without exception, a source of benefit to the working classes.

Machinery is the general term under which is comprised one only of the classes of means by which the objects of desire are produced. We must not entirely omit to notice the employment of cattle as instruments of production. The consequences resulting from the employment of machinery and of cattle are perfectly analogous; and a repetition of those arguments which we have already produced may be dispensed with. Another illustration may, perhaps, assist in placing the effects of an addition to that portion of capital which is not employed in the payment of wages in a still clearer point of view. The capital of a country may be supposed to be 1,000 quarters of corn, 100 as seed, 900 employed in the payment of wages; the annual produce, after replacing the seed, 950 quarters, or profits of stock 5 per cent. We may suppose, if we please, that the capitalists, after a time, choose to employ 200 quarters as seed, leaving only 800 as wages, and that the annual produce, after replacing the seed, is 850 quarters, or profits of stock 5 per cent as before. The numbers of the labourers, under such circumstances, must be reduced, or their condition deteriorated. This is the extreme, we may say, the impossible case. The capitalists alter the disposition of their capital without any prospect of benefit. Should the increasing the quantity of seed from 100 to 200 quarters occasion an increased produce; this increased produce, it must be remembered, is equivalent to a rise in the rate of profit; and we have already shown how a rise in the rate of profit, or the anticipation of such a rise, operates upon the conversion of savings into capital, that is, into the means of employment for additional labourers. For 'seed' read 'horses' or 'machinery', and the illustration holds equally good. None of these means of saving labour can be proved to be injurious to the working classes; their tendency is in a completely opposite direction.

The grand source of all the false reasoning upon machinery is to be found in the supposition that every new application of capital to other purposes than that of paying wages is a deduction from the fund devoted to that purpose. To be convinced of the groundlessness of that assumption it is merely necessary to bear in mind, that every improvement in the arts of production is uniformly attended with an increase of profit, which acts as a stimulus to an increase of capital; or, more correctly, it is attended with an increase of capital by which the rise in the rate of profit is anticipated. The capital, therefore, attracted to a new and more profitable employment, is not drawn from that fund to which the labourers look for support, but from fresh savings. The increase in the capital of a country keeps pace with the improvements in the arts of production. 'Discoveries', to use the words of Mr. Ricardo, 'rather operate in determining the employment of the capital which is saved and accumulated, than in diverting capital from its actual employment.'*

But here an objection may be started, one too which is deserving of the most attentive consideration. It may be said, according to your theory, when, because it is profitable to the capitalists, horses are introduced to do the work of men, the labouring classes are benefited; does it not follow, then, if foreign labourers could be introduced into England with profit to the capitalists, that their introduction would likewise be beneficial to the English labourers? Either, it may be continued by an objector, you must admit this conclusion or your arguments in favour of machinery and cattle are fallacious; and if you admit it the Malthusian theory of population must be abandoned. This would certainly be a most awkward dilemma, since we are firmly convinced of the incontrovertibility of the Malthusian theory of population. It cannot, however, be affirmed with truth that we are reduced to such a dilemma. We admit that the tendency of every increase in the numbers of the labourers is opposed to their welfare, we admit likewise that the immediate tendency of such an event is to add to the profits of the capitalists. Had we, therefore, maintained that every event which is profitable to the capitalists must be beneficial to the labourers, we should

* *Principles of Political Economy and Taxation*, 3rd edition, p. 478.

certainly be involved in a contradiction. But we maintain no
such thing; we contend, not that all events, but merely that
certain events which are profitable to the capitalists, are
beneficial to the labourers; and we allow that certain other
events which may be profitable to the capitalists are injurious to the labourers.

That these two propositions are correct and perfectly
reconcilable will shortly appear. There is, we wil¹ suppose, a
certain number of labourers and a certain amount of capital
devoted to the payment of wages, with a certain rate of profit,
the lowest which will serve as a motive for the productive
employment of savings. An immigration of labourers takes
place. An immediate reduction of wages is the consequence;
and as more work is done with the same capital, profits are
raised. By the rise of profits the capitalists are enabled to add
fresh capital to the soil. The capital, therefore, or the fund out
of which wages are paid is increased; but, owing to the law
by which every addition of capital to the soil is attended with
a less and less return, is not increased in proportion to the
increase in the number of labourers. The condition of the
labourers, accordingly, is permanently deteriorated. The
larger the addition to their numbers, the greater will be their
deterioration. The power of the capitalists to add to the
national capital, except by means of inventions and improvements in the arts of production, is absolutely dependent upon
a reduction in the wages of the labouring classes.

Supposing the number of labourers in England to be represented by 600, and the capital exclusively employed in the
payment of wages to be 1,200 quarters of corn, and profits of
stock 5 per cent, wages would be at the rate of 2 quarters per
man. It is possible, if an immigration of 1,200 Irish labourers
were to take place, that the national capital might be doubled
while the rate of profit remained unaltered, the larger number of labourers set in motion in proportion to the capital,
compensating for the decreased fertility of the soil. If the Irish
labourers were of a totally different species, and incapable,
accordingly, of competing with the English, their wages
might be 1 quarter per man while those of the English remained 2 as before. Under such circumstances it might even

happen that the quantity of work for which the English
labourers alone were qualified would be increased, and that
their wages would rise to $2\frac{1}{2}$ quarters while those of the Irish
were $\frac{3}{4}$ of a quarter per man.

	Quarters
600 English labourers at $2\frac{1}{2}$ quarters	1,500
1,200 Irish ditto at $\frac{3}{4}$ quarter	900
Total capital	2,400

There is a rate of wages below which not even an Irish
labourer can be maintained. Laying aside all objections to the
introduction of a poorer class of labourers on the ground of
contamination, an influx of Irish labourers until that lowest
rate was reached, might be a means of increasing the quantity
of employment for the English provided that employment
were above the abilities of an Irish labourer. The introduction
of horses and of Irish labourers would, if that were the case,
be analogous, as to their effects upon the English labourers.
But there is no such marked distinction between English and
Irish labourers. The former may, from superior education, be
a more generally skilful class than the latter. The chances,
however, are, that many individuals in the latter, will be
superior to individuals in the former class. The general tendency of wages, therefore, would be to an equalization between English and Irish. Taking the same figures, after the
immigration of the Irish labourers, the average rate of wages
would be $1\frac{1}{3}$ quarters per man, and supposing that $\frac{3}{4}$ of a
quarter were, on an average, sufficient to meet the habitual
wants of an Irish labourer, a fresh immigration would take
place, or those who had already immigrated would go on
procreating until the average rate of wages, of English and
Irish together, were reduced to nearly $\frac{3}{4}$ of a quarter per man.
Reading 1,200 horses for 1,200 Irish labourers, the different
consequences which would result to the English labourers
must be obvious to everybody. The food and stabling of the
horse, and his direction and superintendence while at work,
all require the agency of the labourer. The capitalist, in fact,
finds that the labourers whom he is obliged to employ are
most productive to him when employed through the medium

of horses. Turn the horses into Irish labourers again, and we find that their own agency assisted by capital is all that is required for their superintendence and the production of their food. The English labourer is not exclusively required for any particular employment, he must reduce his terms or a competitor is ready to supersede him altogether.

If, instead of an immigration of Irish labourers, a new piece of machinery were introduced; the reason for its introduction, as we have already shown, would be, that a profit above the ordinary rate of profit might be thereby earned—an increase of profit quite unconnected with any deterioration to the labouring classes. Fresh capital would be accumulated and flow into this new opening for its profitable employment. An addition to the number of labourers, or an addition to that portion of the capital of a country which is employed in implements &c., although both are profitable to the capitalist, differ with regard to the labourers in this, that the support of the additional number of labourers is partly drawn from that capital which formerly supported the original number; while the capital employed in the new implements &c. is entirely drawn from an independent fund. The profit on the new capital employed in the first case is a deduction from the wages of labour; in the second case it is a consequence of the productive power newly created.

Having thus established that our deductions are not in the least inconsistent with the principle of population, we will make one or two further remarks upon the different consequences resulting from the extended application of horse-labour or machinery, and from an increase of population, to the working classes. On the supposition that no capitalist will consent to alter the disposition of his capital except for an increase of profit, we have assumed that the extended application of horse-labour or machinery is always attended with that result. But allowing even that no additional profit accrued to the capitalist from the change, and that a portion of the capital devoted to the payment of wages were turned away to the new employment, the labourers are not without the means of warding off the mischief to which they would be exposed. A proportional reduction in their numbers would be an effectual remedy. When additional labourers are introduced, no prudence on the part of the original labourers can stop the contagion of low wages. If the newcomers are content with less of the conveniences and necessaries of life, they will either push the original labourers out of the market, or reduce them to their own level. Besides the motive for manufacturing machinery and for rearing horses is the profit of stock. When that motive ceases to be supplied, the manufacture of machinery and the rearing of horses stop. Not so with the rearing of labourers. Nothing short of necessity is found to operate invariably as a check upon that; and necessity is another word for the lowest degradation. It would be absurd, therefore, to talk of the degradation of the labouring classes by the introduction of new machinery and horse-labour under the unfavourable circumstances supposed, and which circumstances obviously cannot exist, while a remedy of so easy an application presents itself. On the other hand, it is almost beyond the powers of reasoning to determine to what extent the degradation arising from a redundant population may proceed. By the employment of newly-invented machinery, or by substituting the labour of horses for the labour of men, the capitalist calculates that with the produce of his capital he will be able to purchase the produce of a greater quantity of labour than he could before. The same quantity of labour better directed is attended by a produce of greater exchangeable value. The capitalist with whom the improvement originates is comparatively raised. An addition to the number of labourers leaves the comparative situation of the capitalists unaltered. It brings with it no increased power of production relative to a given number of labourers. Any increased gain, therefore, to the capitalist from an addition to the labouring population must proceed from a reduction in the rate of wages.

What we have attempted to prove may be summed up as follows: That every improvement in the arts of production, which does not disturb the proportion between those portions of capital which are and are not dedicated to the payment of wages, is attended with an increase of produce and consequently an increase of capital; that, to whatever extent it may diminish the ratio which that part of the national capital forming the fund for the payment of wages bears to that which is otherwise employed, its tendency is, not to diminish but to increase the absolute amount of that fund, and hence to increase the quantity of employment; and, consequently, that all improvements in the arts of production are a source of benefit to the class of labourers, no less than to the classes of capitalists and landlords.

After the foregoing elementary inquiry into the consequences which flow from improvements in the arts of production, but little attention will be required in order to understand the signs by which such improvements are generally attended. If improvements and inventions were extended simultaneously and equally to every branch of industry, no other outward sign would be presented to the eyes of the world beyond that of an increase of population and production regulated by the magnitude and frequency of the discoveries. The means of happiness to be divided among all classes of the community, among labourers, capitalists and landlords, would continue to increase in quantity. Whether such increased means were made the most of, whether the enjoyment which they are capable of affording were secured or wasted away, improved or neutralized and counteracted, would depend upon the wisdom of the respective classes. But improvements and inventions are not simultaneously introduced into all the branches of industry. First an invention is applied to one branch of industry, then to another, and so on. The outward sign by which the improvement manifests itself to the public is a fall of price in the commodity to which the improvement is applied. Let us suppose that a manufacturer with a capital of £20,000, half employed in the payment of wages, half in implements and raw produce which are annually replaced, while the profits of stock are 5 per cent, makes 44,000 pairs of stockings. The stockings will be worth 5s. a pair, or £11,000. Next let us suppose that the capitalist makes some grand discovery by means of which he finds that an increase of £20,000 to his machinery &c. will enable him, with the same number of workmen, after replacing the machinery &c. to produce 96,000 pairs of

stockings. He can then afford to sell his stockings at 2*s*. 6*d*.
a pair, or together for £12,000. The advantage to the public
is this, that every purchaser with 5*s*. is able to procure two
pairs of stockings instead of one. It may be said that the
demand for stockings might not be doubled; that 48,000
pairs of stockings, for example, would be a sufficient supply for
the market. The reverse is the case in general; but allowing
that 48,000 would suffice, the manufacturer with his
machinery &c. say £15,000 and wages £5,000, would only
employ half the number of labourers who would produce the
48,000 pairs of stockings at 2*s*. 6*d*. per pair. But the purchasers
in this case will not have expended much more than one-
half of the money which they formerly employed in the
purchase of stockings. The remainder of their money is to be
expended upon something, either upon an additional quantity
of some old production, or upon some new one. And to what
better purpose can the labourers who are released from the
manufacturer of stockings be turned than to the production
of the commodities which are demanded? Whichever event
takes place, whether the demand for stockings be extended or
not, the quantity of commodities produced and brought to
market cannot fail to be increased.

If the commodity in which the reduction of price takes place
is an article of consumption among the labouring classes, and
their money wages remain the same, it is evident that their
real wages, that is, their command over the necessaries and
conveniences of life, will be increased, or if their money
wages are reduced so as to compensate for the reduced price
of the commodity upon which part of their wages are expended, their real wages will remain unaltered. A rise in their
real wages is a stimulus to population and hence to extend
cultivation and production. An absence of rise in their real
wages would be a sign of a rise in profits, since the benefit of
the increased produce could only be shared by the landlords
and capitalists; and a rise in profits cannot fail to be attended
with additional accumulations to capital, and hence with a
rise of wages. Should the commodity, on the other hand, be
an article of consumption among capitalists and landlords,
capitalists would obtain greater enjoyment from the produce

of their capitals, which in fact to them is equivalent to a rise in profits, since, compatibly with that enjoyment to which they had been accustomed, they might find employment for additional capital. In whatever direction it is attempted to follow any improvement in the arts of production, it is easy to see that its tendency is, to add to the national wealth and to the happiness of all classes. Either such an improvement is accompanied by an increasing population, or if the population remain stationary, or does not increase in proportion to the enlarged supply of necessaries and conveniences, an indubitable symptom is manifested of an improvement in the habits of the people.

It will be observed that the particular benefit which would otherwise accrue to the inventor of the machinery is counteracted by the fall in price. He shares with the remainder of the community in the general benefit, according to the extent of his consumption of the article of which the cost is reduced. Until the application of the improvement became general, he might it is true, gain something in addition. He might, for a short space of time, obtain the original price for a commodity in the production of which he had effected a considerable saving. No very large profit could reasonably be expected from this source, since all other manufacturers would be eager to avail themselves, with the least possible delay, of his inventions. When the chances of failure and the certainty of expense in attempting an improvement in machinery, or in striking out some new employment for capital are taken into consideration, it will appear desirable that some profit beyond what can be derived from so precarious a source should be secured to the individual who is the means of conferring such an extensive benefit upon society. Any additional profit, however, which can be guaranteed to him must be so much cut off from the remainder of the community. There can be no difficulty in determining upon what principles this arrangement between the individual and the community ought to be conducted. The object is, to cultivate in individuals a disposition to benefit the community by exerting their ingenuity in attempting useful inventions and improvements. To accomplish this object, it is wise in the community to sacrifice a portion of the immediate benefit which they gain, such a portion as is sufficient to encourage this useful disposition, and no more. This is the principle on which patents and copyrights are granted, and on which, when patents and copyrights would be of no avail, premiums are awarded, or rather, as good governments do not abound, ought to be awarded. The laws of patent and copyright differ in different countries. It would be out of place to enter into a discussion upon that subject here. We must content ourselves with observing that, such as they are in this country, the rights which they guarantee, like all other rights, owing to the bad administration of the laws, are very imperfectly secured: if disputed or violated, it is frequently not worth while for the aggrieved party to seek redress.

A few words will suffice to explain the manner in which the patent operates to the benefit of the inventor. Reverting to the stocking manufacturer, the general cost of production is 5*s*. per pair. The number of pairs brought to market we may suppose to be ten millions; and the number which the patentee is enabled to produce 96,000 at 2*s*. 6*d*. per pair. To force his additional quantity into the market, he will consent to a trifling reduction in price, say 6*d*. per pair. At 4*s*. 6*d*. per pair 96,000 will yield him £21,000 or a profit of 29 per cent upon his capital, while the ordinary rate of profit is 5 per cent. This difference between the two rates of profit is a premium upon the extension of his works, and an inducement to other capitalists to purchase of him the permission to make use of his invention. The price of the stockings will thus be gradually reduced, but will not fall to 2*s*. 6*d*. per pair until the expiration of the patent, when the public come in for the whole benefit to be derived from the invention in question.

When these arguments have been weighed with the attention which they deserve, it is to be hoped that those benevolent persons who take a pleasure in exerting themselves to promote the happiness and well-being of the working classes will no longer be blinded to the means by which the fulfilment of their views may be secured. It is to be hoped that they will cease to imagine that improvements in the arts of production, either by the introduction of horses or of more powerful machinery can be productive of any thing but of benefit to the working classes; and that they will strive to communicate as generally as possible correct opinions upon this important subject to those who are principally interested. Nothing can be more pernicious than any fallacy, any prejudice, by which the working classes are persuaded to attribute their low wages and their consequent suffering to a cause other than the real one. It is easy to rail against machinery, to rail against cotton-fuz, to rail against the principle of population, to rail against the practice of doing the work of men with horses, and of harnessing men in the place of horses.* It is no difficult matter, in short, to foam at the mouth on account of the degradation of our fellow-creatures. The difficulty lies in conquering our own weak and silly prejudices, in separating the real from the supposititious causes of this degradation, and when we have conquered our own prejudices, in helping others to do the same, in pointing out to the objects of our compassion what are the real, what are the supposititious causes of their misery; what are the best means by which their misery may be prevented, not what is the grossest language in which those who are totally unconnected with it may be vituperated.

The rapidity with which during the last twenty years invention has followed upon invention may be taken as one of the signs of the increased quantity of knowledge and ingenuity which, by means of improved education, has been introduced into the community. The number of associations and partnerships where, by such means, from the nature of the operations to be performed, a great saving of labour could be effected, or a large capital could be concentrated, is likewise a sign of our increased wealth and enterprise. Companies connected with docks, canals, and railroads, colonization and mining, life, fire, and marine assurance, reversions and annuities, water, gas, and other objects, have lately started into existence, and present a spectacle at once novel and gratifying.† A few noisy and ignorant people, as if jealous of

* See Cobbett's Register, passim.

† Of course it will be understood that we do not pretend to vouch for the merits of all the establishments alluded to in the text.

being left behind by the age in which they live, are still to be found who cry out against this spirit of speculation. They would wish even to see it checked by the arm of power. Fortunately the arm of power is not wielded by such narrow minds. The better portion of our administration seem anxious to keep pace with the age; and, when unclogged by the dull intellects and sinister interests of the 'select few' under whose control it is their sad destiny to be, they shew themselves willing to give the enterprise of the community its full play, and to trust individuals with the superintendence of their own interests.

The objections which have been urged against machinery and horse-labour have been extended to other means of employing capital—to those by which it is transferred to foreign countries. The ground for objecting to the employment of capital in machinery was, that the fund from whence wages were paid was thereby diminished. This lamentable consequence of the employment of machinery, it was vaguely surmised, might be counteracted, but no compensation to the labouring classes, it was affirmed, could be connected with the diminution of the national capital by exportation. When we have shown that the fear of any evil to the labouring classes from this source is utterly groundless, this article may be deemed complete; for we shall then have proved that no suffering, no degradation on the part of the labouring classes, can be traced to the manner in which capital is employed.

In any particular country it may be impossible for all individuals to find productive employment for the whole of what they are disposed and are able to save. In their own country, the rate of profit may be such that no productive employment can be found for additional savings, excepting as new inventions and improvements slowly and gradually develop themselves. In another, the resources for the employment of additional capital may appear inexhaustible. In their own country they may find it impossible to obtain above a certain rate of profit. In another, it may be easy to obtain a much larger profit. In such a case, the savings of one country would be converted into capital in another, to their mutual advantage. The discovery of a new channel for the profitable

employment of capital in another country is, in its consequences, so far analogous to a similar discovery in our own,
that the new employment provided for capital would be
quickly supplied by fresh savings, without drawing upon those
already elsewhere employed. When individuals, no longer
finding in their own country sufficient inducements to employ
their savings productively, transfer them to a foreign land,
where, as they think, greater advantages are held out, it is
the part of a superficial observer to exclaim that 'such
speculators are inflicting an injury upon their country'.
If the savings which they export were withdrawn from
productive employment at home, the space which they
deserted would be immediately occupied by others, eager to
avail themselves of an opportunity to convert their savings
into capital. If they were not productively employed at
home, there would not be even the appearance of any
diminution of the national capital. To apply Mr. Ricardo's
expression once more, advantages which induce capitalists to
export their capitals to foreign countries, 'rather operate in
determining the employment of the capital which is saved and
accumulated, than in diverting capital from its actual employment'. The employment of capital abroad, therefore,
cannot justly be said to be detrimental to a country. It is
advantageous to the capitalists themselves, or they would not
encounter the increased risk which necessarily attends the
foreign investment of capital; and nothing which is profitable
to individuals, while it is neutral or immaterial to the state,
ought to be held in disrepute.

But on inquiring a little further we may be led to conclude,
not merely that the employment of capital abroad is harmless,
but that it is highly advantageous to the labouring classes;
not merely that it is inoperative in diminishing the national
capital, but that it is operative in increasing it. If from a
country where the price of wheat is 8*s.* per bushel, and where
no additional quantity can be produced at that price, capital
is exported to another, such as North America, or New South
Wales, where wheat can be produced at much less expense,
may not such a transfer of capital be highly advantageous to
the country whence the capital is supplied? If the supply of

wheat by such means, were increased, even without any reduction of price, would not the production of the commodities demanded in payment for this wheat, furnish employment for additional capital and additional labourers?
Should the fertility of the soil, in the country, to which the
capital was exported, be such as to occasion, besides, a reduction in the price; the means of employing additional
capital would be still further increased. A cheaper mode of
producing corn would be discovered, through the medium of
cloth, hardware &c. Thus the act of exporting capital would
be the means of increasing the capital of the country from
which it was exported.

We have selected one commodity, wheat, by way of illustration, but whatever the commodity which the exported
capital might be the means of producing in greater abundance,
the benefit, although it might be less in degree, would not be
the less indisputable. The general happiness of our species is
connected by such a multiplicity of ties, many of which are
so minute as to be apt to escape our notice, and the industry
of one country is so intimately blended with that of every
other with which it is in commercial intercourse, that it is
impossible to estimate the extent of the particular benefit
which a country may derive, directly and indirectly, from
adding to the powers of its neighbours.

Our general conclusion is, that capitalists ought not to
suffer themselves to be diverted from any profitable employment of their capitals by a fear of injuring the working classes.
Wherever their capitals can be most profitably employed for
themselves, whether in machinery or horse-labour, or in
foreign countries, there it is most for the interest of the labouring
classes that they should be invested. Where interest leads,
there capitalists, like other men, will follow. Accordingly,
whatever might be the commonly received opinion with regard
to particular modes of employing capital, it has nevertheless
been invested in machinery and in horses, and transferred to
foreign countries. Had our conclusion been the reverse of
what it is, we should still have deprecated any legislative
interference for the purpose of confining it to particular
channels. The evil of interference would, on many other con-

siderations, more than compensate for any advantages which might arise from circumscribing the operations of capital. Discordant as may be the opinions upon other points, all intelligent men appear to coincide upon this. It is pleasant, however, while capital is allowed to circulate freely, to be convinced that we are not merely enduring an incurable evil, but that we are enjoying a positive good.

3 John Rae

ON THE NATURE OF STOCK[1]

John Rae (1796–1872) was the son of an Aberdeen merchant
and studied medicine at Edinburgh until he left Scotland for
Canada in 1822. He settled in Williamstown as a school
teacher and in 1834 moved to Hamilton. But Rae's was a
restless spirit: in 1849 he left Canada for California and two
years later journeyed to the Hawaiian Islands, where he engaged in farming and practised medicine. The background to
the publication of his *New Principles* is an important pre-
requisite to understanding his fresh insights into capital theory.
In the first instance it was a by-product of extensive, empirical
research into the conditions of the early Canadian economy,
an experience which taught Rae the value of the inductive
approach as a basis for economic theorizing. One consequence
of this was to convince him that the standard classical assumption of an identity of causes for the growth of the national
wealth and that of the individual was erroneous. Unlike
Lauderdale, who made the same point earlier and who believed that the conflict between public and private interest
could give rise to a situation of under-consumption, Rae's
observations of an undeveloped society taught him the importance of invention as a force making for new additions to
the capital stock of an economy. His entire analysis of the
factors influencing the 'productivity of instruments' and the
maintenance of the 'effective desire of accumulation' ultimately depends upon the action of innovations bringing about
increases in the rates of return to capital. Yet 'the progress of
the inventive faculty' was only one of four causes which Rae
identified as determining the amount of instruments formed

[1] From the *Statement of some New Principles on the Subject of Political Economy
Exposing the Fallacies of the System of Free Trade* . . . (Boston, Mass. 1834).

by a society, notwithstanding the great importance he attributed to it. It is significant for understanding the main preoccupation of classical capital theory that, when J. S. Mill
came to give his definitive statement, it was Rae's discussion
of the second cause, the strength of the saving motive, which
he felt it necessary to incorporate into the analysis.

... As by the capacity of instruments is to be understood
their power to produce, or bring to an issue, events equivalent
to a certain amount of labour, and as they are also formed by
labour, it is evident that the capacity given to any of them,
and the labour expended in its formation, have determinable
numerical relations to each other. The length of time likewise, elapsing between their formation and exhaustion, may
be expressed in numbers. If a series then were devised, of such
a nature, that any relation that can exist among these three
quantities, in consequence of their varying proportions to
each other, might be embraced in it, every possible instrument
would find a place there.

It is to be observed that in consequence of a principle soon
to be explained, no instruments will be designedly formed, but
such as have a greater capacity, or issue in events, equivalent
to more than the labour expended in their construction. This
circumstance renders the formation of such a series more easy
as it renders it unnecessary to take account of any other instruments than such as issue in events equivalent to more
than the labour expended in their formation or, what may be
termed, the cost of their formation. To simplify the consideration of the matter, we may, for a little, proceed on the supposition that every instrument is constructed at one precise
point of time, and exhausted at another. In that case, every
instrument would find a place in some part of a series, of
which the orders were determined by the period of time at
which instruments placed in them issue, or would issue, if not
before exhausted, in events equivalent to double the labour
expended in forming them. These orders may be represented
by the letters A, B, C, Z, a.b.c. etc. The relation to each
other of the cost of formation, the capacity and the time

elapsing between the period of formation and that of exhaustion, of instruments in the order A, is such as may be expressed by saying, they in one year issue in events equivalent to double the labour expended on their formation, or would so issue, if not before exhausted. The relation between these, in instruments of the order B is such that in two years they issue in events equivalent to double the labour expended on them and are then exhausted. Instruments in the order C in three years issue in events equivalent to double the cost of formation; of the order D in four years; of the order Z in twenty-six years; of the order a in twenty-seven years, etc. For the sake of facility of expression, instruments in the order A or in the orders near it, will be said to belong to the more quickly returning orders; instruments in the order Z or in the orders near it or beyond it will be said to belong to the more slowly returning orders.

To imagine, in the first place, as simple a case as possible. An individual, say an Indian trader, is obliged to reside on a particular spot in the interior of North America somewhat more than a year. He arrives in Autumn and immediately sets about inclosing and digging up a piece of ground for the purpose of having it planted with maize. He expends on this twenty days' labour. That labour he reckons equivalent to ten bushels of maize. He gets the maize planted, hoed and harvested next season by Indian women, agreeing to give them part of the crop. After deducting their portion he has twenty bushels for himself, with which he leaves the place. The field he formed was then an instrument of the order A. The same individual has to reside a little more than two years in another quarter of the interior. He clears, or has cleared on his arrival, another piece of ground, and also expends on this operation twenty days' labour. Owing, however, to the soil being overrun with small roots and it being necessary to wait till they partially rot before a crop can be put on it, he is aware that it cannot be planted until the second year. It is then planted as before and, as it happens, with the same event as in the former field, yielding him net twenty bushels maize. This field then was an instrument of the order B. In the same way it is possible to conceive the formation and exhaustion of other instruments of this sort, answering to the orders C, D, E, etc. the capacity of them all being double the cost of formation, and the times intervening between the periods of formation and exhaustion being respectively three, four, five, etc. years. Although, however, instruments exactly corresponding to the conditions assumed may occasionally exist, and although it is possible at least to conceive their existence throughout a lengthened series, yet in fact they seldom do exist so as exactly to answer the suppositions. In by far the greater number of instances, neither the times elapsing between the periods of formation and exhaustion are any exact number of years, nor are the capacities double the cost of formation. But in all variations of these three quantities, from an exact correspondence with any of the orders, the proportions existing between them will, nevertheless, always be such as to make it possible to reduce the instruments in which they occur to some order or another in our series, or to an order that may be interposed between two proximate orders.

Such variations may be reduced to three sorts. The first consists of instances where the capacity is double the cost of production but the time, no exact number of years. In this case the instrument does not exactly belong to any of the enumerated orders, but falls between two proximate orders; it may therefore be said to belong to an order that may be supposed to be interposed between these two. Thus, an instrument being exhausted in between seven and eight years, and having a capacity equal to double the cost of production, might be said to belong to an order lying between G and H. This designation would mark its character with sufficient accuracy for our purpose.

There are only two other cases. The capacity of the instrument may be exhausted before it arrives at an amount equal to double the cost of formation, or it may not be exhausted until it has come to an amount greater than double the cost of formation. In the former case it is necessary to suppose the period of exhaustion prolonged, the excess of the capacity of the instrument over the cost of formation increasing at the same ratio, until the capacity doubles the cost. It will then be shown to belong to some particular order, or to lie between two proximate orders. Thus, let an individual have it in his power to make use of a small plot of ground for six months, and let him expend an equivalent to two days labour in preparing it for receiving the seeds of some plant, sowing them and cultivating the crop, and let it return him at the end of six months an amount, which, reduced to the value of days labour, would be 2,828. If then we suppose the period of exhaustion prolonged, the excess of the capacity over the cost increasing at the same ratio, in twelve months time the capacity will be 4; for, 2,828 is a mean proportional between 2 and 4. The instrument formed by the plants so cultivated would therefore belong to the order A, that order doubling in one year.

In the case where the capacity comes to more than double the cost of formation, the order in which the instrument should be placed, is to be found by retracing the progress of its capacity, under the supposition that it advanced at the same rate, until we arrive at a period when it was only double the cost. The interval between that and the period of formation will then indicate the order to which it really belongs.

The bread fruit tree is perhaps twenty years before it bear; but ten of these trees, when in bearing, will, it is said, nearly supply a family of South Sea Islanders with a sufficiency of this sort of food for eight months in the year. This sort of fruit tree requires too no other labour or attention than that bestowed in planting it. Suppose then that an inhabitant of one of those islands were to spend an hour in planting a few of these trees, and that, according to the hypothesis of sudden exhaustion on which we are proceeding, at the termination of the twenty-two years they are exhausted, yielding at that period an equivalent to two thousand and forty-eight hours labour. If then we retrace the progress at which the capacity of this instrument has advanced, we will find that it belongs to the order B. For, instruments in that order doubling in two years, one hour's labour, if employed in forming an instrument of that order, ought to yield an equivalent to two hours, at the end of the second year; and being then employed in constructing other instruments, at the end of the fourth year should yield an equivalent to four hours, at the end of the sixth to eight, and so the geometrical series, 2, 4, 8, 16, etc. would arise, which, carried out to the eleventh term at the end of the twenty-second year, is 2,048. It may perhaps serve somewhat to illustrate the matter, to suppose that the individual who applied an hour's labour to planting the bread fruit tree, gave the same portion of time to the cultivation of another sort of plant, yielding its produce, and perishing at the termination of the second year from the time of its being placed in the soil, and the returns made from which are equal to double the labour expended on its culture. Instead of consuming the crop at the termination of the second year, he gives it to some other person or persons, on condition of their applying for his benefit, two hours' labour, its equivalent, to the culture of a second crop; at the end of the fourth year he proceeds in the same manner and, continuing the process, at the termination of the twenty-second year, the produce of the labour of both hours, the one applied to the cultivation of the former plant, and the other, to that of the latter, would be equal. The only difference in the cases would be that the person in question would, in the latter case, have the trouble of making the bargain with one or more individuals every second year, and would then also have the power to apply, if he so chose, to the supply of his wants, the events, in this instance brought about by his previous expenditure; and that, in the latter case, he would have neither the power nor the trouble.

We have assumed, that all instruments are formed at one point of time and exhausted at another. This is the case with but very few. The period of formation almost always spreads over a large space of time, and that of exhaustion, over another. It is evidently, however, to fix on a point to be determined by a consideration of all the periods at which the labour going to the formation was expended, which shall represent the true period of formation; and on another point, determined from a consideration of similar circumstances regarding the times when the capacity was exhausted, which shall represent the true period of exhaustion.

Thus, suppose a small field in some new settlement in North America, were formed by twelve days labour, it would, were it of the order A, return in one year an equivalent to twenty-four days labour and then be completely exhausted and worthless. It might, however, be that it belonged to this order, although it neither yielded so much as twenty-four days labour, nor was exhausted at the end of the year. Say, that the crop sown is wheat and that one bushel wheat is equivalent to one day's labour. Were it at once exhausted, it ought to yield twenty-four bushels wheat; it however only yields eighteen, and is not then exhausted. There is consequently a deficiency of six bushels. Now, six bushels at the end of the second year, at the same rate of doubling in a year, ought to produce twelve. Let us suppose that the next crop is hay and that the net hay yield the second year is one ton, equal to eight bushels wheat, then $12-8 = 4$, there is still a deficiency of four bushels, equivalent, at the end of the third year, to eight. If, therefore, the next crop of hay the third year, be equal to what it was the second, that is to eight bushels wheat, the deficiency will then be made up. Let us suppose that it is so, and that the field is at that time totally exhausted and useless. It is evident, that such a field, though not producing or being exhausted by the supposition, yet producing and being exhausted, in a manner equivalent to the supposition, might, with propriety be said to belong to the order A.

But it is farther probable that such a field, might not produce quite so much grain or hay as we have even by the last hypothesis supposed, and would not even at the end of the third year or for a much longer period, be exhausted; still, if the deficiency in the one, were equivalent to the farther supply in the other, it would evidently properly belong also to the same order.

Again, by the suppositions we have made, the labour, or its equivalent, was expended exactly at the commencement of the period of one year. It might however, have been that some part of the expenditure, going to the formation of this instrument, was made several months before the commencement of the year and some several months after. But, had what was expended before, been proportionably less and what was expended after, proportionably greater, the change would not make any alteration to the relation existing between the time and the expenditure or, consequently, to the place of the instrument.

The spaces over which the several points of time, at which the formation of any instrument is effected, extend, and those over which the several points of time at which its capacity is exhausted also extend, frequently run into each other. Thus according to our system a riding-horse is an instrument. The space of time over which the whole period of his formation extends, commences when his dam is put apart for breeding, continues as long as anything is laid out for the purpose of giving efficiency and durability to him as an instrument, and probably therefore only terminates a few days before the death of the animal. There would be a number of points all along that space, at each of which something had been expended on his account and from the date of which, and the amount expended at each, data would be furnished, to ascertain the whole expenses of his formation and the precise point from whence it might be dated. The whole period of his exhaustion would also extend over a large space. It would commence when he was first ridden for pleasure or business, and would terminate shortly after his death when his hide went to the tanner and his flesh to the dogs. An account of the several items expended, and the times when they were expended, and of the several items yielded, and the times at which they were yielded, would furnish data for determining the total cost of formation and capacity and the points to be fixed on at the periods of formation and exhaustion, and thus the place of the instrument could be determined.

Calculations of this sort would be intricate, and could not be well effected without having recourse to methods, not usually employed in investigations like the present. In point of fact, there is in practice, as we will see afterwards, a system of notation of instruments, which enables us pretty accurately, and very easily to determine their place in such a series as we have supposed. It is sufficient for the end here aimed at, to perceive that when all particulars are known, concerning the formation and exhaustion of any instrument and the periods intervening between these, data are then furnished for placing it in some part of such a series as we have described; and that it may consequently be assumed that every instrument does, in reality, belong to some one order in the series A, B, C, D, etc. or to an order that may be interposed between some two proximate orders of that series.

It may perhaps appear, that though, could instruments be considered apart, the foregoing explications might serve to show, that they might all be reduced to a place in our series, yet as they very commonly act in combination, and as, in such instances, the events in which two or more of them issue are the same, it must be impossible to fix with accuracy the order to which each belongs. Thus, a horse and a cart form together an instrument for the transport of goods. The events therefore in which both issue being the same, we cannot measure the part that may belong to each, in any other manner, than by appropriating to each the proportion indicated by their respective costs of formation, and hence they will both appear to belong to the same order, though perhaps they do in fact, belong to different orders. But our subsequent enquiries will show, that the great mass of the instruments existing in the same society are, in reality, at about the same orders; and, that instruments acting in combination with other instruments, are almost always at the same orders. This objection is therefore removed as all instruments acting in combination may thus be considered as one.

Instruments are frequently repaired. The labour or its equivalent so expended, may be considered either as a partial reformation of the old instrument, or as the addition of a new instrument to be combined in action with the old one. The same rules therefore apply to repairs effected on instruments as to their original formation.

We have assumed hitherto that both formation and exhaustion are properties common to all instruments. There is, however, a class of instruments that forms an exception to this general rule. An extensive and important class exists, of a nature so peculiar, that the instruments belonging to it are never exhausted, unless in consequence of some revolution in the circumstances of the society. That part of the surface of the earth devoted to agricultural purposes composes this class. The peculiarity arises from every portion of land so employed, forming two distinct instruments. A piece of land, that it may do its part in providing a supply for future wants, must first be rendered capable of culture and then be cultivated. It is not necessary that he who renders it fit for culture, should also cultivate it, though it commonly happens that both operations are performed by the same individual. But by whosoever the operation of converting waste land into land bearing crops be performed, two ends are always gained by it, the power of cultivation, and the actual culture. There is this great difference between them, that while the changes produced in a piece of land to fit it for cultivation are lasting, remaining unless some means be taken to do away with them; those that are effected on it by the actual process of cultivation are of short, or at all events, of limited duration. When an individual has converted a portion of morass or forest, into a field fit for the operations of tillage, it does not return again to the state of morass or forest. He has fitted it for being made an instrument of agriculture or rather a succession of instruments of agriculture. The farmer by manuring it, sowing certain seeds in it and tilling it, forms it into such an instrument. The changes he thus effects, however, pass away. The seeds he sows growing into different plants are carried off; the manure yields part of its substance to them and is in part dissipated; the soil that had been loosened and pulverized by the plough and harrow, is gradually again compacted and hardened by the effects of the action of the sun and rain. As far then as it was actually an instrument of agriculture it is exhausted. But its power of being again formed into such an instrument remains and the same operations, the same rotation of crops, may indefinitely succeed one another.

The individual who first forms a portion of land into these combined instruments has probably in view only the ends to be gained by one of them. His motive to expend labour on the formation of the field, is to fit it for immediate culture. But he cannot effect this without also rendering it capable of being cultivated to all succeeding times. The returns, which for this reason it makes in those succeeding times, form what is called rent; and this peculiarity in the nature of this sort of double instrument, is one of the chief causes of the existence of that particular species of revenue. Any portion of land, therefore, which bears a crop, considered as regards its fitness for being cultivated is an instrument of indefinite exhaustion, and will not consequently coincide with the conditions by which the orders in our series are determined. We shall see, that in every instance it may, notwithstanding, be reduced to a determined place in that series. A portion of cultivated land, considered as an instrument actually subject to the operations of the husband-man does not differ from any other instrument.

In conclusion, it may be observed that the position in our series which any instrument will occupy is determined by the following circumstances.

1. The shorter space of time between the period of its formation and that of its exhaustion, the nearer will any instrument be placed to the order A, that is, towards the more quickly returning orders.

2. The greater the capacity and the less the cost of its formation, the nearer will any instrument be to the order A; the less the capacity, the greater the cost of formation, the farther will it be from A.

Generally, the proximity of instruments to A is inversely as the cost and the time, and directly as the capacity.

... Having traced the general nature of instruments and shown that the relations existing among the circumstances by which they are affected, make it practicable to arrange them in a regular series, the object next claiming our attention is to ascertain the causes determining the amount of them which each society possesses, and to mark the more remarkable phenomena which the operation of those causes produces.

The causes determining the amount of instruments formed by any society will, I believe, be found to be four.

1. The quantity and quality of the materials owned by it.
2. The strength of the effective desire of accumulation.
3. The rate of wages.
4. The progress of the inventive faculty.

The nature of the second of these and the circumstances on which its strength depends, will form the subject of the next chapter, but previously to entering on it, it is necessary to establish the following proposition.

The capacity which any people can communicate to the materials they possess, by forming them into instruments cannot be indefinitely increased while their knowledge of their powers and qualities remains stationary, without moving the instruments formed continually onwards in the series A B C etc.; but there is no assignable limit to the extent of the capacity which a people, having attained considerable knowledge of the qualities and powers of the materials they possess can communicate to them, without carrying them out of the series A B C etc., even if that knowledge remain stationary.

The capacity of instruments may be increased by adding to their durability or to their efficiency; that is, by prolonging the time during which they bring to pass the events for the purpose of effecting which, they are formed, or, by increasing the amount of them which they bring to pass within the same time.

A dwelling-house is an instrument, aiding to bring to an issue events of various classes. It more or less completely prevents rain, damp, and the extremes of cold and heat, from penetrating to the space included within the area. It preserves all other instruments contained within it, in comparative safety. It gives those who inhabit it the power of carrying on unmolested various domestic occupations and of enjoying, undisturbed by the gaze of strangers, any of the gratifications or amusements of life, of which they may be able and desirous to partake. Events of these sorts, it may bring to pass, for a longer or shorter time, or to a greater or less extent, within the same time. In the former case, the durability is increased, in the latter, the efficiency; in both, the capacity is augmented. Dwelling-houses are built of different materials, and those materials are wrought with more or less care. A dwelling might be slightly run up of wood, lath, mud, plaster, and paper which would only be habitable for a few months or years, like the unsubstantial villages, that Catharine of

Russia saw in her progress through some parts of her dominions. Another of the same size, accommodation and
appearance that might last for two or three centuries, might
be constructed by employing stone, iron and the most durable
woods, and joining and compacting them together, with
great nicety and accuracy. Between these two extremes, there
are all imaginable varieties. According to that adopted, both
the durability and the efficiency will be greater or less. These
two may be separated from each other, at least in imagination, and therefore we may consider them apart.

If the increased durability that may be given an instrument be considered apart from the increased efficiency, that
will also probably be communicated to it, it must be regarded
simply as an extension of its existence and consequently as a
like extension of its capacity. A dwelling-house lasts, we shall
say sixty years, but in other respects is perfectly similar to one
lasting only thirty years. Considered as an instrument, the
former is, therefore, exactly equal to two of the latter, the one
formed thirty years after the other. A house lasting one
hundred and twenty years would, in like manner, have the
capacity of four houses, one formed now, a second thirty, a
third sixty, and a fourth ninety years hence. The capacity
thus increasing at the same rate as the duration, if the limits
to the power of giving durability be indefinite, the limits to
the power of communicating capacity are also indefinite.

But to give additional durability to the instrument, there
must be additional labour bestowed on its formation. An increase of the durability of an instrument may therefore be
considered as a power communicated to it of giving existence
to a new instrument at the end of a certain period, and purchased by a present expenditure. The effects produced by the
change will be determined by the relations subsisting between
the returns made by the addition, its cost, and the time
elapsing between the expenditure and return. If we suppose
the present expenditure necessary to produce the durability,
to be always equal to the durability produced, then the compound instrument will be moved towards the more slowly
returning orders, because the new instrument is in that case
one of slower return. One dwelling-house lasts thirty years;

another the same as it in other respects, but costing double the expense of formation, lasts sixty years; the former house is an instrument of the order O, doubling in fifteen years. The part of the duration of the latter extending from the thirtieth to the sixtieth year, is to be considered, by our hypothesis as a separate instrument. If we suppose that during the time it is in use it returns as the other, at the end of the sixtieth year it will have returned only four, and therefore, is an instrument of the order C doubling only in thirty years. The compound instrument will, in consequence, be of an order between X and Y doubling in between twenty-four and twenty-five years. The procedure of adding to the durability, by adding equally to the expense of formation, will have greater effect in placing an instrument further from A, the more it is subjected to its operation. Thus, were an instrument of this sort to have its duration prolonged, to one hundred and twenty years, and at the same expense, the last thirty would return only four in one hundred and twenty years, whereas had it formed an instrument of the order O, it ought to have yielded two hundred and fifty-six. Were the durability increased still farther, at the same cost, the divergence would be much greater, going on in a geometrical ratio. If therefore, continual additions having been made to the durability of an instrument, it cannot be preserved at an order of equally quick return, unless the several augmentations be communicated to it, by an expenditure diminishing in a geometrical ratio; that is, in a ratio becoming indefinitely less, as it is continued. This, however, cannot happen for it would imply an absurdity. While instruments are in existence they are either producing events, or giving a new direction to their course. But, mere matter, unless in some very rare instance, is never acting, or acted upon, without undergoing a change. This we term wear and the effects it indicates form consequently a definite power, to counteract which, a definite force must be found. It cannot then be counteracted, by a force indefinitely small.

The same thing may be illustrated in another manner. When events are produced and governed by design, they in turn generate other events of greater powers than themselves, and these others, in a series rapidly increasing. Mere durability in instruments may be considered as a capacity to generate future events lying dormant in them, till the lapse of years exposes its existence and gives it opportunity to act. The greater the time therefore for the expiration of which it must wait, the less the chance of its being on an equality with rivals whose powers are continually and rapidly multiplying either events, or enjoyments, whenever they have a field on which to exert their energies.

While the knowledge of the course of events which the members of any society possess remains unaltered, and the materials they own are the same, the duration of the instruments they form cannot consequently, be indefinitely increased, without their being moved, farther and farther, from the more quickly returning orders.

The durability of instruments refers only to those of gradual exhaustion; their efficiency, or the extent of their power, to bring about events within a certain time, refers both to those of gradual, and of sudden exhaustion. If the knowledge of the course of events, and the amount of the materials remain the same, the efficiency of these materials when formed into instruments cannot be indefinitely increased, without that increase being at length made with additional difficulty, and through means of an amount of labour greater than was required in the earlier stages. The action of matter upon matter always depends on some cause. Those causes,—the inherent qualities and powers of the different matters around him,—are the means man employs to make one material to act so on another as to produce the events he desires, and he does so by applying his labour to give them such a form and position as may bring their powers into play. If we suppose any number of men to be fixed to one situation, and their knowledge of the qualities of the materials around them to remain stationary, they will naturally first make choice of those materials whose powers are most easily brought into action, and which produce the desired events most abundantly and speedily. But as the stock of materials which any society possesses is limited, its members, if we suppose them to acquire no additional knowledge of the powers of those materials, and yet to add continually to the amount of instruments they form out of them, must at length have recourse to such as are either operated on with greater difficulty, or bring about desired events more sparingly or tardily. The efficiency of the instruments produced must therefore be generated by greater cost; that is, they must pass to orders of slower return.

This passage will be rapid or slow, as the amount of knowledge possessed is small or great. When art is in its infancy, and men know but a few of the properties fitting them for becoming instruments, that are inherent in the materials in their possession they cannot much vary their mode of proceeding on them, by combining and giving new turns to their actions on each other. In more advanced stages of society, on the contrary, where the powers of a great number of materials are known, and where consequently their operations on each other, may be combined, and multiplied to a great extent, the means by which the same end may be attained are very numerous. Some of them are more easy or expeditious than others, but they differ by very slight degrees, and the instruments formed by successively adopting them, would occupy positions in one series not widely distant from one another.

If we then consider the capacity that may be given any amount of materials, by a society among whom the progress of art is stationary, as separated into the durability and efficiency, of the instruments its members form, it would appear that they are both subject to similar laws, and that neither can be indefinitely increased, without carrying the instruments constructed continually on, to orders of slower return. The same general conclusions must obviously hold good, concerning the capacity considered as combined of both. There is, however, a circumstance flowing from the consideration of this union, which is deserving of notice, as it has considerable effect in the relations between the cost and capacity of instruments, and consequently on the position to be assigned them. It often happens, that additional labour bestowed on an instrument, to give it greater efficiency, gives it also great durability. Thus the same choice of materials, and the same careful and laborious formation of them, that render the walls of a dwelling-house effective in excluding the inclemency of the weather, give it also solidity and strength, and consequently prolong its duration. A tool, in the fabrication of which good steel has been employed, not only cuts better but lasts longer, than one formed of inferior stuff. In such cases, and they are very numerous, the capacity being increased, both as concerns durability and efficiency, by the same outlay its proportion to the cost is greater and a larger expenditure may be made on the formation of the instrument without moving it at all or moving it but a short distance towards the orders of slower return. Sometimes the same expenditure that gives efficiency to instruments, partly also increases their durability and partly quickens their exhaustion. Thus the majority of roads in North America, and in many other countries, are constructed altogether of the soil of which the surface happens to consist, arranged in a form adapted to the purpose. Such roads, unless in the best of weather are very inefficient instruments in facilitating transport, and their durability is so small that they are probably reconstructed, by repair, every four or five years. A road formed of small fragments of stone, in the manner that is termed macadamization, costs perhaps twenty times as much, but is both a far more efficient and a far more durable instrument. Besides, however, being more durable and efficient, the facility it gives to transport occasions an increase of transport, and its exhaustion is thus quickened. For example, the capacity of a road of this sort may be adequate to the transport of two hundred thousand carriages; if this be spread over twenty years, it will be an instrument of much slower return, than if, in consequence of the annual transport being doubled, that number pass over it in ten years.

As efficiency and durability are frequently produced by the same means, so, it sometimes happens that the means which would add to the one, cannot be employed without diminishing the other, thus there are many tools and utensils that cannot be made very strong, and therefore durable, without being at the same time clumsy and inefficient; and they cannot be made very light and easy to work with, without being also of little durability. The difficulty in the combination of the qualities of durability and efficiency, in the same materials, can only however be considered as absolutely limiting the capacity of those instruments, to support the weight of which, a corporeal exertion is required; and is consequently confined to wearing apparel, and to those tools and utensils which are altogether moved by the hand. When the weight rests on some firm basis, it can be poised and, by the application of sufficient expenditure, friction can be removed. The circumstance of the qualities of durability and efficiency depending on the same materials, has therefore probably, on the whole, the effect of retarding somewhat, though not very greatly, the progress of instruments as greater capacity is given to them, towards the more slowly returning orders.

The various powers of the material would seem to be connected at some common centre, and its several parts to exercise reciprocal influences on each other. Hence, a discovery of new properties in any one material, or more easy modes of bringing the old into play generally extends the power of man over a great range of the other materials which he had been in the habit of before applying to his purposes. When art therefore, has made considerable progress, and comprehends within its dominion a multiplicity of materials, the variety of effects which may be generated, from the action, and reaction on each other of the numerous powers at its disposal, becomes illimitable. As in numbers, every addition multiplies amazingly, the possible antecedent combinations, until at length the amount becomes too great to be ascertained. Hence it is that, though among barbarous nations, the ability of man to increase the amount of instruments he possesses may be bounded, among nations having made considerable advance in art, there seems no assigning any limit to it, other than that indicated in the second part of the proposition, the necessary gradual passage of the instruments constructed, to orders of slower and slower return.

It is hence that, if we turn to any community where art has advanced, we invariably see that however much industry may have already exerted itself on the materials within its reach, the field for its possible future action seems rather increased than diminished, and that the farther we stretch our view over it, to the greater distance, its extreme circumference recedes from us. The industry of the people of Great Britain has probably been as largely supplied to the materials which its limited territory possesses, as that of any other community presently existing; yet certainly, there is no lack of matters on which it might be farther exercised. A large portion of its surface, and which wants not, nevertheless, all the requisites for the sustenance of vegetable life, lies yet uncultivated. With the exception of the mountainous and rocky regions, heat, light, air and water, in sufficient abundance rest on every part of it, nor is the presence of many of the earths, the mixture of which forms a proper shelter for the tender radical fibres, and a commodious storehouse for an important part of their nourishment, anywhere wanting. There is also in general a considerable supply diffused over the surface of the decomposing remains of former vegetables, and animals, the material which constitutes nearly the whole solid food that the organic life of plants requires; and even when this is deficient at one point, there are larger collections of it at some other. The outlay requisite in many instances, to give such form to these materials, as to fit them for the purposes of the agriculturalist would no doubt be very great, still, whatever it might be, as the instrument formed would be of unlimited duration, the annual returns from it would, in time, exceed the cost of formation and bring it within the limits of our series.

Were we to go over the various other instruments, the returns from which supply the wants of this community, we should perceive that everywhere their capacities are capable of being greatly increased. One would not find it very easy to say how much might be added to the durability and efficiency of dwelling-houses alone. The amount of the capacity for the facilitation of future transport, which might be embodied in railroads, returning ultimately much more than the cost of their formation, is incalculable; as is also the degree to which mining operations might be extended. Even supposing all these and many other instruments to have acquired a vastly increased extent, both as concerns durability and efficiency; instead of limiting their farther increase, it would seem likely rather to open up a still wider space, for the exertion of future industry in the formation of others. Were the soil universally cultivated, were railroads extended and ramified throughout the country, and were the riches of the mineral kingdom more fully brought out, the additional facility given to the formation of instruments, by the command afforded of the materials necessary for their construction, and the ease with which they might be transported from point to point, would, it may well be supposed, be sufficient, to give the means of a still greater increased construction of them, and a still farther advance, of the amount of the capacities for the supply of futurity, embodied in the various instruments, spread over the surface of the territory, or lying above or beneath it. In short, the more we consider the subject, the more clearly shall we perceive the impossibility of fixing any limit to the amount of the labour which may be expended in the formation of instruments, in this, or any community, where art has made considerable advance.

This progress, while art itself remains stationary, would however, undoubtedly gradually carry instruments to more and more slowly returning orders, and would not therefore take place, unless the society were inclined to construct instruments of those orders.

4 John Stuart Mill

FUNDAMENTAL PROPOSITIONS RESPECTING CAPITAL

John Stuart Mill (1806–73) was the eldest son of James Mill; the latter's influence, and that of Ricardo, are the most important for understanding his views on capital accumulation which are summarized in the passages below.[1] It is perhaps the clearest, and certainly the most influential, statement of the main constituents of the classical theory of capital accumulation. There is the neglect of the distinction between fixed and circulating capital for the purpose of a long-run analysis that could be more easily discussed in terms of the wage-fund approach. Then the familiar emphasis on saving as the source of capital, together with an unwillingness to contemplate any significant discrepancy between saving and investment decisions. Redundancy of labourers was likely to occur only in the short-run, since over the long-term the supply of savings not only replaces and increases capital, including the wage-fund, but occasions no reduction in consumption. In short, it is the saving of capitalists which is the instrument for translating the consumers' demand for commodities into the capitalists' demand for labour; this proposition is as true for J. S. Mill as it had been for Adam Smith and shows how essentially consistent was the classical analysis of capital accumulation over the period of its development.

1. If the preceding explanations have answered their purpose, they have given not only a sufficiently complete possession of the idea of Capital according to its definition, but a sufficient

[1] From *Principles of Political Economy* (1848), Book 1, Ch. 5.

familiarity with it in the concrete, and amidst the obscurity with which the complication of individual circumstances surrounds it, to have prepared even the unpractised reader for certain elementary propositions or theorems respecting capital, the full comprehension of which is already a considerable step out of darkness into light.

The first of these propositions is, that industry is limited by capital. This is so obvious as to be taken for granted in many common forms of speech; but to see a truth occasionally is one thing, to recognize it habitually, and admit no propositions inconsistent with it, is another. The axiom was until lately almost universally disregarded by legislators and political writers; and doctrines irreconcileable with it are still very commonly professed and inculcated.

The following are common expressions implying its truth. The act of directing industry to a particular employment is described by the phrase 'applying capital' to the employment. To employ industry on the land is to apply capital to the land. To employ labour in a manufacture is to invest capital in the manufacture. This implies that industry cannot be employed to any greater extent than there is capital to invest. The proposition, indeed, must be assented to as soon as it is distinctly apprehended. The expression 'applying capital' is of course metaphorical: what is really applied is labour; capital being an indispensable condition. Again, we often speak of the 'productive powers of capital'. This expression is not literally correct. The only productive powers are those of labour and natural agents; or if any portion of capital can by a stretch of language be said to have a productive power of its own, it is only tools and machinery, which, like wind or water, may be said to co-operate with labour. The food of labourers and the materials of production have no productive power; but labour cannot exert its productive power unless provided with them. There can be no more industry than is supplied with materials to work up and food to eat. Self-evident as the thing is, it is often forgotten that the people of a country are maintained and have their wants supplied, not by the produce of present labour, but of past. They consume what has been produced, not

what is about to be produced. Now, of what has been produced, a part only is allotted to the support of productive
labour; and there will not and cannot be more of that labour
than the portion so allotted (which is the capital of the country)
can feed, and provide with the materials and instruments of
production.

Yet, in disregard of a fact so evident, it long continued to be
believed that laws and governments, without creating capital,
could create industry. Not by making the people more
laborious, or increasing the efficiency of their labour; these
are objects to which the government can, in some degree,
indirectly contribute. But without any increase in the skill or
energy of the labourers, and without causing any persons to
labour who had previously been maintained in idleness, it
was still thought that the government, without providing
additional funds, could create additional employment. A
government would, by prohibitory laws, put a stop to the
importation of some commodity; and when by this it had
caused the commodity to be produced at home, it would
plume itself upon having enriched the country with a new
branch of industry, would parade in statistical tables the
amount of produce yielded and labour employed in the
production, and take credit for the whole of this as a gain to
the country, obtained through the prohibitory law. Although
this sort of political arithmetic has fallen a little into dis-
credit in England, it still flourishes in the nations of Continental Europe. Had legislators been aware that industry is
limited by capital, they would have seen that, the aggregate
capital of the country not having been increased, any portion
of it which they by their laws had caused to be embarked in
the newly-acquired branch of industry must have been withdrawn or withheld from some other; in which it gave, or
would have given, employment to probably about the same
quantity of labour which it employs in its new occupation.*

* An exception must be admitted when the industry created or upheld by
the restrictive law belongs to the class of what are called domestic manufactures. These being carried on by persons already fed—by labouring
families, in the intervals of other employment—no transfer of capital to
the occupation is necessary to its being undertaken, beyond the value of the

2. Because industry is limited by capital, we are not however to infer that it always reaches that limit. Capital may be temporarily unemployed, as in the case of unsold goods, or funds that have not yet found an investment: during this interval it does not set in motion any industry. Or there may not be as many labourers obtainable, as the capital would maintain and employ. This has been known to occur in new colonies, where capital has sometimes perished uselessly for want of labour: the Swan River settlement (now called Western Australia), in the first years after its foundation, was an instance. There are many persons maintained from existing capital, who produce nothing, or who might produce much more than they do. If the labourers are reduced to lower wages, or induced to work more hours for the same wages, or if their families, who are already maintained from capital, were employed to a greater extent than they now are in adding to the produce, a given capital would afford employment to more industry. The unproductive consumption of productive labourers, the whole of which is now supplied by capital, might cease, or be postponed until the produce came in; and additional productive labourers might be maintained with the amount. By such means society might obtain from its existing resources a greater quantity of produce: and to such means it has been driven, when the sudden destruction of some large portion of its capital rendered the employment of

---

materials and tools, which is often inconsiderate. If, therefore, a protecting duty causes this occupation to be carried on, when it otherwise would not, there is in this case a real increase of the production of the country.

In order to render our theoretical proposition invulnerable, this peculiar case must be allowed for; but it does not touch the practical doctrine of free trade. Domestic manufactures cannot, from the very nature of things, require protection, since the subsistence of the labourers being provided from other sources, the price of the product, however much it may be reduced, is nearly all clear gain. If, therefore, the domestic producers retire from the competition, it is never from necessity, but because the product is not worth the labour it costs, in the opinion of the best judges, those who enjoy the one and undergo the other. They prefer the sacrifice of buying their clothing to the labour of making it. They will not continue their labour unless society will give them more for it, than in their own opinion its product is worth.

the remainder with the greatest possible effect a matter of paramount consideration for the time.

When industry has not come up to the limit imposed by capital, governments may, in various ways, for example by importing additional labourers, bring it nearer to that limit: as by the importation of Coolies and free Negroes into the West Indies. There is another way in which governments can create additional industry. They can create capital. They may lay on taxes, and employ the amount productively. They may do what is nearly equivalent; they may lay on taxes on income or expenditure, and apply the proceeds towards paying off the public debts. The fundholder, when paid off, would still desire to draw an income from his property, most of which therefore would find its way into productive employment, while a great part of it would have been drawn from the fund for unproductive expenditure, since people do not wholly pay their taxes from what they have saved, but partly, if not chiefly, from what they would have spent. It may be added, that any increase in the productive power of capital (or, more properly speaking, of labour) by improvements in the arts of life, or otherwise, tends to increase the employment for labour; since, when there is a greater produce altogether, it is always probable that some portion of the increase will be saved and converted into capital; especially when the increased returns to productive industry hold out an additional temptation to the conversion of funds from an unproductive destination to a productive.

3. While, on the other hand, industry is limited by capital, so on the other, every increase of capital gives, or is capable of giving, additional employment to industry; and this without assignable limit. I do not mean to deny that the capital, or part of it, may be so employed as not to support labourers, being fixed in machinery, buildings, improvements of land, and the like. In any large increase of capital a considerable portion will generally be thus employed, and will only co-operate with labourers, not maintain them. What I do intend to assert is, that the portion which is destined to their maintenance, may (supposing no alteration in anything else) be indefinitely increased, without creating an impossibility of

finding them employment: in other words, that if there are human beings capable of work, and food to feed them, they may always be employed in producing something. This proposition requires to be somewhat dwelt upon, being one of those which it is exceedingly easy to assent to when presented in general terms, but somewhat difficult to keep fast hold of, in the crowd and confusion of the actual facts of society. It is also very much opposed to common doctrines. There is not an opinion more general among mankind than this, that the unproductive expenditure of the rich is necessary to the employment of the poor. Before Adam Smith, the doctrine had hardly been questioned; and even since his time, authors of the highest name and of great merit* have contended, that if consumers were to save and convert into capital more than a limited portion of their income, and were not to devote to unproductive consumption an amount of means bearing a certain ratio to the capital of the country, the extra accumulation would be merely so much waste, since there would be no market for the commodities which the capital so created would produce. I conceive this to be one of the many errors arising in political economy, from the practice of not beginning with the examination of simple cases, but rushing at once into the complexity of concrete phenomena.

Every one can see that if a benevolent government possessed all the food, and all the implements and materials, of the community, it could exact productive labour from all capable of it, to whom it allowed a share in the food, and could be in no danger of wanting a field for the employment of this productive labour, since as long as there was a single want unsaturated (which material objects could supply) of any one individual, the labour of the community could be turned to the production of something capable of satisfying that want. Now, the individual possessors of capital, when they add to it by fresh accumulations, are doing precisely the same thing which we suppose to be done by a benevolent government. As it is allowable to put any case by way of hypothesis, let us imagine the most extreme case conceivable. Suppose that

* For example, Mr. Malthus, Dr. Chalmers, M. de Sismondi.

every capitalist came to be of opinion that, not being more meritorious than a well-conducted labourer, he ought not to fare better; and accordingly laid by, from conscientious motives, the surplus of his profits; or suppose this abstinence not spontaneous, but imposed by law or opinion upon all capitalists, and upon landowners likewise. Unproductive expenditure is now reduced to its lowest limit; and it is asked, how is the increased capital to find employment? Who is to buy the goods which it will produce? There are no longer customers even for those which were produced before. The goods, therefore, (it is said) will remain unsold; they will perish in the warehouses; until capital is brought down to what it was originally, or rather to as much less, as the demand of the consumers has lessened. But this is seeing only one-half of the matter. In the case supposed, there would no longer be any demand for luxuries, on the part of capitalists and landowners. But when these classes turn their income into capital, they do not thereby annihilate their power of consumption; they do but transfer it from themselves to the labourers to whom they give employment. Now, there are two possible suppositions in regard to the labourers; either there is, or there is not, an increase of their numbers, proportional to the increase of capital. If there is, the case offers no difficulty. The production of necessaries for the new population, takes the place of the production of luxuries for a portion of the old, and supplies exactly the amount of employment which has been lost. But suppose that there is no increase of population. The whole of what was previously expended in luxuries, by capitalists and landlords, is distributed among the existing labourers, in the form of additional wages. We will assume them to be already sufficiently supplied with necessaries. What follows? That the labourers become consumers of luxuries; and the capital previously employed in the production of luxuries is still able to enjoy itself in the same manner: the difference being, that the luxuries are shared among the community generally, instead of being confined to a few. The increased accumulation and increased production might, rigorously speaking, continue, until every labourer had every indulgence of wealth, consistent with continuing to work; supposing that the power of their labour were physically sufficient to produce all this amount of indulgences for their whole number. Thus the limit of wealth is never deficiency of consumers, but of producers and productive power. Every addition to capital gives to labour either additional employment, or additional remunerations; enriches either the country, or the labouring class. If it finds additional hands to set to work, it increases the aggregate produce; if only the same hands, it gives them a larger share of it; and perhaps even in this case, by stimulating them to greater exertion, augments the produce itself.

4. A second fundamental theorem respecting Capital relates to the source from which it is derived. It is the result of saving. The evidence of this lies abundantly in what has been already said on the subject. But the proposition needs some further illustration.

If all persons were to expend in personal indulgences all that they produce, and all the income they receive from what is produced by others, capital could not increase. All capital, with a trifling exception, was originally the result of saving. I say, with a trifling exception; because a person who labours on his own account may spend on his own account all he produces, without becoming destitute; and the provision of necessaries on which he subsists until he has reaped his harvest, or sold his commodity, though a real capital, cannot be said to have been saved, since it is all used for the supply of his own wants, and perhaps as speedily as if it had been consumed in idleness. We may imagine a number of individuals or families settled on as many separate pieces of land, each living on what their own labour produces, and consuming the whole produce. But even these must save (that is, spare from their personal consumption) as much as is necessary for seed. Some saving, therefore, there must have been, even in this simplest of all states of economical relations; people must have produced more than they used, or used less than they produced. Still more must they do so before they can employ other labourers, or increase their production beyond what can be accomplished by the work of their own hands. All that any one employs in supporting and carrying on any other labour than his own, must have been originally brought together by saving; somebody must have produced it and forborne to consume it. We may say, therefore, without material inaccuracy, that all capital, and especially all addition to capital, is the result of saving.

In a rude and violent state of society, it continually happens that the person who has capital is not the very person who has saved it, but some one who, being stronger, or belonging to a more powerful community, has possessed himself of it by plunder. And even in a state of things in which property was protected, the increase of capital has usually been, for a long time, mainly derived from privations which, though essentially the same with saving, are not generally called by that name, because not voluntary. The actual producers have been slaves, compelled to produce as much as force could extort from them, and to consume as little as the self-interest or the usually very slender humanity of their taskmasters would permit. This kind of compulsory saving, however, would not have caused any increase of capital, unless a part of the amount had been saved over again, voluntarily, by the master. If all that he made his slaves produce and forbear to consume, had been consumed by him on personal indulgences, he would not have increased his capital, nor been enabled to maintain an increasing number of slaves. To maintain any slaves at all, implied a previous saving; a stock, at least of food, provided in advance. This saving may not, however, have been made by any self-imposed privation of the master; but more probably by that of the slaves themselves while free; the rapine or war, which deprived them of their personal liberty, having transferred also their accumulations to the conqueror.

There are other cases in which the term saving, with the associations usually belonging to it, does not exactly fit the operation by which capital is increased. If it were said for instance, that the only way to accelerate the increase of capital is by increase of saving, the idea would probably be suggested of greater abstinence, and increased privation. But it is obvious that whatever increases the productive power of labour creates an additional fund to make savings from, and enables capital to be enlarged not only without additional privation, but concurrently with an increase of personal consumption. Nevertheless, there is here an increase of saving, in the scientific sense. Though there is more consumed, there is also more spared. There is a greater excess of production over consumption. It is consistent with correctness to call this a greater saving. Though the term is not unobjectionable, there is no other which is not liable to as great objections. To consume less than is produced, is saving; and that is the process by which capital is increased; not necessarily by consuming less, absolutely. We must not allow ourselves to be so much the slaves of words, as to be unable to use the word saving in this sense, without being in danger of forgetting that to increase capital there is another way besides consuming less, namely, to produce more.

5. A third fundamental theorem respecting Capital, closely connected with the one last discussed, is, that although saved, and the result of saving, it is nevertheless consumed. The word saving does not imply that what is saved is not consumed, nor even necessarily that its consumption is deferred; but only that, if consumed immediately, it is not consumed by the person who saves it. If merely laid by for future use, it is said to be hoarded; and while hoarded is not consumed at all. But if employed as capital, it is all consumed; though not by the capitalist. Part is exchanged for tools or machinery, which are worn out by use; part for seed or materials, which are destroyed as such by being sown or wrought up, and destroyed altogether by the consumption of the ultimate product. The remainder is paid in wages to productive labourers, who consume it for their daily wants; or if they in their turn save any part, this also is not, generally speaking, hoarded, but (through savings banks, benefit clubs, or some other channel) re-employed as capital, and consumed.

The principle now stated is a strong example of the necessity of attention to the most elementary truths of our subject: for it is one of the most elementary of them all, and yet no one who has not bestowed some thought on the matter is habitually aware of it, and most are not even willing to admit it when first stated. To the vulgar, it is not at all apparent that what is saved is consumed. To them, every one who saves appears in the light of a person who hoards: they may think such conduct permissible, or even laudable, when it is to provide for a family, and the like; but they have no conception of it as doing good to other people: saving is to them another word for keeping a thing to oneself; while spending appears to them to be distributing it among others. The person who expends his fortune in unproductive consumption is looked upon as diffusing benefits all round; and is an object of so much favour, that some portion of the same popularity attaches even to him who spends what does not belong to him; who not only destroys his own capital, if he ever had any, but under pretence of borrowing, and on promise of repayment, possesses himself of capital belonging to others, and destroys that likewise.

This popular error comes from attending to a small portion only of the consequences that flow from the saving or the spending; all the effects of either which are out of sight being out of mind. The eye follows what is saved into an imaginary strong-box, and there loses sight of it; what is spent, it follows into the hands of tradespeople and dependents; but without reaching the ultimate destination in either case. Saving (for productive investment), and spending, coincide very closely in the first stage of their operations. The effects of both begin with consumption; with the destruction of a certain portion of wealth; only the things consumed, and the persons consuming, are different. There is, in the one case, a wearing out of tools, a destruction of material, and a quantity of food and clothing supplied to labourers, which they destroy by use: in the other case, there is a consumption, that is to say, a destruction of wines, equipages, and furniture. Thus far, the consequence to the national wealth has been much the same; an equivalent quantity of it has been destroyed in both cases. But in the spending, this first stage is also the final stage; that particular amount of the produce of labour has disappeared, and there is nothing left; while, on the contrary, the saving person, during the whole time that the destruction was going on, has had labourers at work repairing it; who are ultimately found to have replaced, with an increase, the equivalent of what has been consumed. And as this operation admits of being repeated indefinitely without any fresh act of saving, a saving once made becomes a fund to maintain a corresponding number of labourers in perpetuity, reproducing annually their own maintenance with a profit.

It is the intervention of money which obscures, to an unpractised apprehension, the true character of these phenomena. Almost all expenditure being carried on by means of money, the money comes to be looked upon as the main feature in the transaction; and since that does not perish, but only changes hands, people overlook the destruction which takes place in the case of unproductive expenditure. The money being merely transferred, they think the wealth also has only been handed over from the spendthrift to other people. But this is simply confounding money with wealth. The wealth which has been destroyed was not the money but the wines, equipages, and furniture which the money purchased; and these having been destroyed without return, society collectively is poorer by the amount. It may be said, perhaps, that wines, equipages and furniture, are not subsistence, tools and materials, and could not in any case have been applied to the support of labour; that they are adapted for no other than unproductive consumption, and that the detriment to the wealth of the community was when they were produced, not when they were consumed. I am willing to allow this, as far as is necessary for the argument, and the remark would be very pertinent if these expensive luxuries were drawn from an existing stock, never to be replenished. But since, on the contrary, they continue to be produced as long as there are consumers for them, and are produced in increased quantity to meet an increased demand; the choice made by a consumer to expend five thousand a year in luxuries keeps a corresponding number of labourers employed from year to year in producing things which can be of no use in production; their services being lost so far as regards the increase of the national wealth, and the tools, materials, and food which they annually consume being so much subtracted from the general stock of the community applicable to productive purposes. In proportion as any class is improvident or luxurious, the industry of the country takes the direction of producing luxuries for their use; while not only the employment for productive labourers is diminished, but the subsistence and instruments which are the means of such employment do actually exist in smaller quantity.

Saving, in short, enriches, and spending impoverishes, the community along with the individual; which is but saying in other words, that society at large is richer by what it expends in maintaining and aiding productive labour, but poorer by what it consumes in its enjoyments.*

---

* It is worth while to direct attention to several circumstances which to a certain extent diminish the detriment caused to the general wealth by the prodigality of individuals, or raise up a compensation, more or less ample, as a consequence of the detriment itself. One of these is, that spendthrifts do not usually succeed in consuming all they spend. Their habitual carelessness as to expenditure causes them to be cheated and robbed on all quarters, often by persons of frugal habits. Large accumulations are continually made by the agents, stewards, and even domestic servants, of improvident persons of fortune; and they pay much higher prices for all purchases than people of careful habits, which accounts for their being popular as customers. They are, therefore, actually not able to get into their possession and destroy a quantity of wealth by any means equivalent to the fortune which they dissipate. Much of it is merely transferred to others, by whom a part may be saved. Another thing to be observed is, that the prodigality of some may reduce others to a forced economy. Suppose a sudden demand for some article of luxury, caused by the caprice of a prodigal, which not having been calculated on beforehand, there has been no increase of the usual supply. The price will rise; and may rise beyond the means or the inclinations of some of the habitual consumers, who may in consequence forego their accustomed indulgence, and save the amount. If they do not, but continue to expend as great a value as before on the commodity, the dealers in it obtain, for only the same quantity of the article, a return increased by the whole of what the spendthrift has paid; and thus the amount which he loses is transferred bodily to them, and may be added to their capital; his increased personal consumption being made up by the privations of the other purchasers, who have obtained less than usual of their accustomed gratification for the same equivalent. On the other hand, a counter-process must be going on somewhere, since the prodigal must have diminished his purchases in some other quarter to balance the augmentation in this; he has perhaps called in funds employed in sustaining productive labour, and the dealers in subsistence and in the instruments of production have had commodities left on their hands, or have received, for the usual amount of commodities, a less than usual return. But such losses of income or capital, by industrious

6. To return to our fundamental theorem. Everything which is produced is consumed; both what is saved and what is said to be spent; and the former quite as rapidly as the latter. All the ordinary forms of language tend to disguise this. When people talk of the ancient wealth of a country, of riches inherited from ancestors, and similar expressions, the idea suggested is that the riches so transmitted were produced long ago, at the time when they are said to have been first acquired and that no portion of the capital of the country was produced this year, except as much as may have been this year added to the total amount. The fact is far otherwise. The greater part, in value, of the wealth now existing in England has been produced by human hands within the last twelve months. A very small proportion indeed of that large aggregate was in existence ten years ago;—of the present productive capital of the country scarcely any part, except farmhouses and manufactories, and a few ships and machines; and even these would not in most cases have survived so long, if fresh labour had not been employed within that period in putting them into repair. The land subsists, and the land is almost the only thing that subsists. Everything which is produced perishes, and most things very quickly. Most kinds of capital are not fitted by their nature to be long preserved. There are a few, and but a few productions, capable of a very prolonged existence. Westminster Abbey has lasted many centuries, with occasional repairs; some Grecian sculptures have existed above two thousand years; the Pyramids perhaps double or treble that time. But these were objects devoted to unpro-

---

persons except when of extraordinary amount, are generally made up by increased pinching and privation; so that the capital of the community may not be, on the whole, impaired, and the prodigal may have had his self-indulgence at the expense not of the permanent resources, but of the temporary pleasures and comforts of others. For in every case the community are poorer by what any one spends, unless others are in consequence led to curtail their spending. There are yet other and more recondite ways in which the profusion of some may bring about its compensation in the extra savings of others; but these can only be considered in that part of the Fourth Book, which treats of the limiting principle to the accumulation of capital.

ductive use. If we except bridges and acqueducts (to which may in some countries be added tanks and embankments), there are few instances of any edifice applied to industrial purposes which has been of great duration; such buildings do not hold out against wear and tear, nor is it good economy to construct them of the solidity necessary for permanency. Capital is kept in existence from age to age not by preservation, but by perpetual reproduction; every part of it is used and destroyed, generally very soon after it is produced, but those who consume it are employed meanwhile in producing more. The growth of capital is similar to the growth of population. Every individual who is born, dies, but in each year the number born exceeds the number who die: the population, therefore, always increases, though not one person of those composing it was alive until a very recent date.

7. This perpetual consumption and reproduction of capital affords the explanation of what has so often excited wonder, the great rapidity with which countries recover from a state of devastation; the disappearance, in a short time, of all traces of the mischiefs done by earthquakes, floods, hurricanes, and the ravages of war. An enemy lays waste a country by fire and sword, and destroys or carries away nearly all the moveable wealth existing in it: all the inhabitants are ruined, and yet, in a few years after, everything is much as it was before. This vis medicatrix naturae has been a subject of sterile astonishment, or has been cited to exemplify the wonderful strength of the principle of saving, which can repair such enormous losses in so brief an interval. There is nothing at all wonderful in the matter. What the enemy have destroyed, would have been destroyed in a little time by the inhabitants themselves; the wealth which they so rapidly reproduce, would have needed to be reproduced and would have been reproduced in any case, and probably in as short a time. Nothing is changed, except that during the reproduction they have not now the advantage of consuming what had been produced previously. The possibility of a rapid repair of their disasters mainly depends on whether the country has been depopulated. If its effective population have not been extirpated at the time, and are not starved afterwards; then, with the same skill and

knowledge which they had before, with their land and its permanent improvements undestroyed, and the more durable buildings probably unimpaired, or only partially injured, they have nearly all the requisites for their former amount of production. If there is as much of food left to them, or of valuables to buy food, as enables them by any amount of privation to remain alive and in working condition, they will in a short time have raised as great a produce, and acquired collectively as great wealth and as great a capital, as before; by the mere continuance of that ordinary amount of exertion which they are accustomed to employ in their occupations. Nor does this evince any strength in the principle of saving, in the popular sense of the term, since what takes place is not intentional abstinence, but involuntary privation.

Yet so fatal is the habit of thinking through the medium of only one set of technical phrases, and so little reason have studious men to value themselves on being exempt from the very same mental infirmities which beset the vulgar, that this simple explanation was never given (so far as I am aware) by any political economist before Dr. Chalmers; a writer many of whose opinions I think erroneous, but who has always the merit of studying phenomena at first hand, and expressing them in a language of his own, which often uncovers aspects of the truth that the received phraseologies only tend to hide.

8. The same author carries out this train of thought to some important conclusions on another closely connected subject, that of government loans for war purposes or other un-productive expenditure. These loans, being drawn from capital (in lieu of taxes, which would generally have been paid from income, and made up in part or altogether by increased economy) must, according to the principles we have laid down, tend to impoverish the country: yet the years in which expenditure of this sort has been on the greatest scale have often been years of great apparent prosperity: the wealth and resources of the country, instead of diminishing, have given every sign of rapid increase during the process, and of greatly expanded dimensions after its close. This was confessedly the case with Great Britain during the last long Continental war; and it would take some space to enumerate all the unfounded

theories in political economy to which that fact gave rise, and to which it secured temporary credence; almost all tending to exalt unproductive expenditure, at the expense of productive. Without entering into all the causes which operated, and which commonly do operate, to prevent these extraordinary drafts on the productive resources of a country from being so much felt as it might seem reasonable to expect, we will suppose the most unfavourable case possible: that the whole amount borrowed and destroyed by the government was abstracted by the lender from a productive employment in which it had actually been invested. The capital, therefore, of the country, is this year diminished by so much. But unless the amount abstracted is something enormous, there is no reason in the nature of the case why next year the national capital should not be as great as ever. The loan cannot have been taken from that portion of the capital of the country which consists of tools, machinery, and buildings. It must have been wholly drawn from the portion employed in paying labourers: and the labourers will suffer accordingly. But if none of them are starved; if their wages can bear such an amount of reduction, or if charity interposes between them and absolute destitution, there is no reason that their labour should produce less in the next year than in the year before. If they produce as much as usual, having been paid less by so many millions sterling, these millions are gained by their employers. The breach made in the capital of the country is thus instantly repaired, but repaired by the privations and often the real misery of the labouring class. Here is ample reason why such periods, even in the most unfavourable circumstances, may easily be times of great gain to those whose prosperity usually passes, in the estimation of society, for national prosperity.*

* On the other hand, it must be remembered that war abstracts from productive employment not only capital, but likewise labourers; that the funds withdrawn from the remuneration of productive labourers are partly employed in paying the same or other individuals for unproductive labour; and that by this portion of its effects war expenditure acts in precisely the opposite manner to that which Dr. Chalmers points out, and, so far as it goes, directly counteracts the effects described in the text. So far as labourers are taken from production, to man the army and navy, the labouring

This leads to the vexed question to which Dr. Chalmers has very particularly adverted; whether the funds required by a government for extraordinary unproductive expenditure, are best raised by loans, the interest only being provided by taxes, or whether taxes should be at once laid on to the whole amount; which is called in the financial vocabulary, raising the whole of the supplies within the year. Dr. Chalmers is strongly for the latter method. He says, the common notion is that in calling for the whole amount in one year, you require what is either impossible, or very inconvenient; that the people cannot, without great hardship, pay the whole at once out of their yearly income; and that it is much better to require of them a small payment every year in the shape of interest, than so great a sacrifice once for all. To which his answer is, that the sacrifice is made equally in either case. Whatever is spent, cannot but be drawn from yearly income. The whole and every part of the wealth produced in the country forms, or helps to form, the yearly income of somebody. The privation which it is supposed must result from taking the amount in the shape of taxes is not avoided by taking it in a loan. The suffering is not averted, but only thrown upon the labouring classes, the least able, and who

---

classes are not damaged, the capitalists are not benefited, and the general produce of the country is diminished, by war expenditure. Accordingly, Dr. Chalmers's doctrine, though true of this country, is wholly inapplicable to countries differently circumstanced; to France, for example, during the Napoleon wars. At that period the draught on the labouring population of France, for a long series of years, was enormous, while the funds which supported the war were mostly supplied by contributions levied on the countries overrun by the French arms, a very small proportion alone consisting of French capital. In France, accordingly, the wages of labour did not fall, but rose; the employers of labour were not benefited, but injured; while the wealth of the country was impaired by the suspension or total loss of so vast an amount of its productive labour. In England all this was reversed. England employed comparatively few additional soldiers and sailors of her own, while she diverted hundreds of millions of capital from productive employment, to supply munitions of war and support armies for her Continental allies. Consequently, as shown in the text, her labourers suffered, her capitalists prospered, and her permanent productive resources did not fall off.

least ought, to bear it: while all the inconveniences, physical, moral, and political, produced by maintaining taxes for the perpetual payment of the interest, are incurred in pure loss. Whenever capital is withdrawn from production, or from the fund destined for production, to be lent to the State, and expended unproductively, that whole sum is withheld from the labouring classes: the loan, therefore, is in truth paid off the same year; the whole of the sacrifice necessary for paying it off is actually made: only it is paid to the wrong persons, and therefore does not extinguish the claim; and paid by the very worst of taxes, a tax exclusively on the labouring class. And after having, in this most painful and unjust way, gone through the whole effort necessary for extinguishing the debt, the country remains charged with it, and with the payment of its interest in perpetuity.

These views appear to me strictly just, in so far as the value absorbed in loans would otherwise have been employed in productive industry within the country. The practical state of the case, however, seldom exactly corresponds with this supposition. The loans of the less wealthy countries are made chiefly with foreign capital which would not, perhaps, have been brought in to be invested on any less security than that of the government: while those of rich and prosperous countries are generally made, not with funds withdrawn from productive employment, but with the new accumulations constantly making from income, and often with a part of them which, if not so taken, would have migrated to colonies, or sought other investments abroad. In these cases (which will be more particularly examined hereafter*), the sum wanted may be obtained by loan without detriment to the labourers, or derangement of the national industry, and even perhaps with advantage to both, in comparison with raising the amount by taxation, since taxes, especially when heavy, are almost always partly paid at the expense of what would otherwise have been saved and added to capital. Besides, in a country which makes so great yearly additions to its wealth that a part can be taken and expended unproductively

* Infra. Book IV, Ch. iv and v.

without diminishing capital, or even preventing a considerable increase, it is evident that even if the whole of what is so taken would have become capital, and obtained employment in the country, the effect on the labouring classes is far less prejudicial, and the case against the loan system much less strong, than in the case first supposed. This brief anticipation of a discussion which will find its proper place elsewhere appeared necessary to prevent false inferences from the premises previously laid down.

9. We now pass to a fourth fundamental theorem respecting Capital, which is, perhaps, oftener overlooked or misconceived than even any of the foregoing. What supports and employs productive labour, is the capital expended in setting it to work, and not the demand of purchasers for the produce of the labour when completed. Demand for commodities is not demand for labour. The demand for commodities determines in what particular branch of production the labour and capital shall be employed; it determines the direction of the labour; but not the more or less of the labour itself, or of the maintenance or payment of the labour. These depend on the amount of the capital, or other funds directly devoted to the sustenance and remuneration of labour.

Suppose, for instance, that there is a demand for velvet; a fund ready to be laid out in buying velvet, but no capital to establish the manufacture. It is of no consequence how great the demand may be; unless capital is attracted into the occupation, there will be no velvet made, and consequently none bought; unless, indeed, the desire of the intending purchaser for it is so strong that he employs part of the price he would have paid for it in making advances to work-people, that they may employ themselves in making velvet; that is, unless he converts part of his income into capital, and invests that capital in the manufacture. Let us now reverse the hypothesis, and suppose that there is plenty of capital ready for making velvet, but no demand. Velvet will not be made; but there is no particular preference on the part of capital for making velvet. Manufacturers and their labourers do not produce for the pleasure of their customers, but for the supply of their own wants; and, having still the capital and the labour which are the essentials of production, they can either produce something else which is in demand, or if there be no other demand, they themselves have one, and can produce the things which they want for their own consumption. So that the employment afforded to labour does not depend on the purchasers, but on the capital.[1] I am, of course, not taking into consideration the effects of a sudden change. If the demand ceases unexpectedly, after the commodity to supply it is already produced, this introduces a different element into the question: the capital has actually been consumed in producing something which nobody wants or uses, and it has therefore perished, and the employment which it gave to labour is at an end, not because there is no longer a demand, but because there is no longer a capital. This case therefore does not test the principle. The proper test is, to suppose that the change is gradual and foreseen, and is attended with no waste of capital, the manufacture being discontinued by merely not replacing the machinery as it wears out, and not re-investing the money as it comes in from the sale of the produce. The capital is thus ready for a new employment, in which it will maintain as much labour as before. The manufacturer and his work-people lose the benefit of the skill and knowledge which they had acquired in the particular business, and which can only be partially of use to them in any other; and that is the amount of loss to the community by the change. But the labourers can still work; and the capital which previously employed them will, either in the same hands, or by being lent to others, employ either those labourers or an equivalent number in some other occupation.

This theorem, that to purchase produce is not to employ labour; that the demand for labour is constituted by the wages which precede the production, and not by the demand which may exist for the commodities resulting from the production; is a proposition which greatly needs all the illustration it can receive. It is, to common apprehension, a paradox; and even among political economists of reputation,

[1] This sentence replaced in the third edition (1852) the original text: 'So that the capital cannot be dispensed with—the purchasers can.'

I can hardly point to any, except Mr. Ricardo and M. Say, who have kept it constantly and steadily in view. Almost all others occasionally express themselves as if a person who buys commodities, the produce of labour, was an employer of labour, and created a demand for it as really, and in the same sense, as if he bought the labour itself directly, by the payment of wages. It is no wonder that political economy advances slowly, when such a question as this still remains open at its very threshold.[1] I apprehend, that if by demand for labour be meant the demand by which wages are raised, or the number of labourers in employment increased, demand for commodities does not constitute demand for labour. I conceive that a person who buys commodities and consumes them himself, does no good to the labouring classes; and that it is only by what he abstains from consuming, and expends in direct payments to labourers in exchange for labour, that he benefits the labouring classes, or adds anything to the amount of their employment

For the better illustration of the principle, let us put the following case. A consumer may expend his income either in buying services, or commodities. He may employ part of it in hiring journeymen bricklayers to build a house, or excavators to dig artificial lakes, or labourers to make plantations and lay out pleasure grounds; or, instead of this, he may expend the same value in buying velvet and lace. The question is, whether the difference between these two modes of expending his income affects the interest of the labouring classes. It is plain that in the first of the two cases he employs labourers, who will be out of employment, or at least out of that employment, in the opposite case. But those from whom I differ say that this is of no consequence, because in buying velvet

[1] The rest of this paragraph replaced in the third edition (1852) the original text: 'I am desirous of impressing on the reader that a demand for commodities does not in any manner constitute a demand for labour, but only determines into a particular channel a portion, more or less considerable, of the demand already existing. It determines that a part of the labour and capital of the community shall be employed in producing certain things instead of other things. The demand for labour is constituted solely by the funds directly set apart for the use of labourers.'

and lace he equally employs labourers, namely, those who make the velvet and lace. I contend, however, that in this last case he does not employ labourers; but merely decides in what kind of work some other person shall employ them. The consumer does not with his own funds pay to the weavers and lacemakers their day's wages. He buys the finished commodity, which has been produced by labour and capital, the labour not being paid nor the capital furnished by him, but by the manufacturer. Suppose that he had been in the habit of expending this portion of his income in hiring journeymen bricklayers, who laid out the amount of their wages in food and clothing, which were also produced by labour and capital. He, however, determines to prefer velvet, for which he thus creates an extra demand. This demand cannot be satisfied without an extra supply, nor can the supply be produced without an extra capital: where, then, is the capital to come from? There is nothing in the consumer's change of purpose which makes the capital of the country greater than it otherwise was. It appears, then, that the increased demand for velvet could not for the present be supplied, were it not that the very circumstance which gave rise to it has set at liberty a capital of the exact amount required. The very sum which the consumer now employs in buying velvet, formerly passed into the hands of journeyman bricklayers, who expended it in food and necessaries, which they now either go without, or squeeze by their competition from the shares of other labourers. The labour and capital, therefore, which formerly produced necessaries for the use of these bricklayers, are deprived of their market, and must look out for other employment; and they find it in making velvet for the new demand. I do not mean that the very same labour and capital which produced the necessaries turn themselves to producing the velvet; but, in some one or other of a hundred modes, they take the place of that which does. There was capital in existence to do one of two things—to make the velvet, or to produce necessaries for the journeyman bricklayers; but not to do both. It was at the option of the consumer which of the two should happen; and if he chooses the velvet, they go without the necessaries.

¹ For further illustration, let us suppose the same case reversed. The consumer has been accustomed to buy velvet, but resolves to discontinue that expense, and to employ the same annual sum in hiring bricklayers. On closer inspection, however, it will be seen that there is an increase of the total sum applied to the remuneration of labour. The velvet manufacturer, supposing him aware of the diminished demand for his commodity, diminishes the production, and sets at liberty a corresponding portion of the capital employed in the manufacture. This capital, thus withdrawn from the maintenance of velvet-makers, is not the same fund with that which the customer employs in maintaining bricklayers; it is a second fund. There are, therefore, two funds to be employed in the maintenance and remuneration of labour, where before there was only one. There is not a transfer of employment from velvet-makers to bricklayers; there is a new employment created for bricklayers, and a transfer of employment from velvet-making to some other labourers, most probably those who produce the food and other things which the bricklayers consume.

In answer to this it is said, that though money laid out in buying velvet is not capital, it replaces a capital; that though it does not create a new demand for labour, it is the necessary means of enabling the existing demand to be kept up. The funds (it may be said) of the manufacturer, while locked up in velvet, cannot be directly applied to the maintenance of labour; they do not begin to constitute a demand for labour until the velvet is sold, and the capital which made it replaced from the outlay of the purchaser; and thus, it may be said, the velvet-maker and the velvet-buyer have not two capitals, but only one capital between them, which by the act of purchase the buyer transfers to the manufacturer, and if instead of buying velvet he buys labour, he simply transfers this capital elsewhere, extinguishing as much demand for labour in one quarter as he creates in another.

¹ In the second edition (1849) there was here inserted 'a different mode of stating the argument'. In the third edition (1852) this became the long footnote of this section; and five new paragraphs were inserted at this point.

The premises of this argument are not denied. To set free a capital which would otherwise be locked up in a form useless for the support of labour, is, no doubt, the same thing to the interests of labourers as the creation of a new capital. It is perfectly true that if I expend 1,000l. in buying velvet, I enable the manufacturer to employ 1,000l. in the maintenance of labour, which could not have been so employed while the velvet remained unsold: and if it would have remained unsold for ever unless I bought it, then by changing my purpose, and hiring bricklayers instead, I undoubtedly create no new demand for labour: for while I employ 1,000l. in hiring labour on the one hand, I annihilate for ever 1,000l. of the velvet-maker's capital on the other. But this is confounding the effects arising from the mere suddenness of a change with the effects of the change itself. If when the buyer ceased to purchase, the capital employed in making velvet for his use necessarily perished, then his expending the same amount in hiring bricklayers would be no creation, but merely a transfer, of employment. The increased employment which I contend is given to labour, would not be given unless the capital of the velvet-maker could be liberated, and would not be given until it was liberated. But every one knows that the capital invested in an employment can be withdrawn from it, if sufficient time be allowed. If the velvet-maker had previous notice, by not receiving the usual order, he will have produced 1,000l. less velvet, and an equivalent portion of his capital will have been already set free. If he had no previous notice, and the article consequently remains on his hands, the increase of his stock will induce him next year to suspend or diminish his production until the surplus is carried off. When this process is complete, the manufacturer will find himself as rich as before, with undiminished power of employing labour in general, though a portion of his capital will now be employed in maintaining some other kind of it. Until this adjustment has taken place, the demand for labour will be merely changed, not increased: but as soon as it has taken place, the demand for labour is increased. Where there was formerly only one capital employed in maintaining weavers to make 1,000l. worth of velvet, there is

now that same capital employed in making something else,
and 1,000l. distributed among bricklayers besides. There
are now two capitals employed in remunerating two sets of
labourers; while before, one of those capitals, that of the
customer, only served as a wheel in the machinery by which
the other capital, that of the manufacturer, carried on its
employment of labour from year to year.

The proposition for which I am contending is in reality
equivalent to the following, which to some minds will appear a
truism, though to others it is a paradox: that a person does
good to labourers, not by what he consumes on himself, but
solely by what he does not so consume. If instead of laying
out 100l. in wine or silk, I expend it in wages, the demand
for commodities is precisely equal in both cases: in the one,
it is a demand for 100l. worth of wine or silk, in the other for
the same value of bread, beer, labourers' clothing, fuel, and
indulgences: but the labourers of the community have in the
latter case the value of 100l. more of the produce of the
community distributed among them. I have consumed that
much less, and made over my consuming power to them. If it
were not so, my having consumed less would not leave more
to be consumed by others; which is a manifest contradiction.
When less is not produced, what one person forbears to
consume is necessarily added to the share of those to whom
he transfers his power of purchase. In the case supposed I do
not necessarily consume less ultimately, since the labourers
whom I pay may build a house for me, or make something
else for my future consumption. But I have at all events
postponed my consumption, and have turned over part of my
share of the present produce of the community to the labourers. If after an interval I am indemnified, it is not from the
existing produce, but from a subsequent addition made to it.
I have therefore left more of the existing produce to be consumed by others; and have put into the possession of labourers
the power to consume it.

[1] There cannot be a better reductio ad absurdum of the
opposite doctrine than that afforded by the Poor Law. If it be

---

[1] This paragraph was inserted in the sixth edition (1865).

equally for the benefit of the labouring classes whether I consume my means in the form of things purchased for my own use, or set aside a portion in the shape of wages or alms for their direct consumption, on what ground can the policy be justified of taking my money from me to support paupers? since my unproductive expenditure would have equally benefited them, while I should have enjoyed it too. If society can both eat its cake and have it, why should it not be allowed the double indulgence? But common sense tells every one in his own case (though he does not see it on the larger scale), that the poor rate which he pays is really subtracted from his own consumption, and that no shifting of payment backwards and forwards will enable two persons to eat the same food. If he had not been required to pay the rate, and had consequently laid out the amount on himself, the poor would have had as much less for their share of the total produce of the country, as he himself would have consumed more.*

* [1849] The following case, which presents the argument in a somewhat different shape, may serve for still further illustration.

Suppose that a rich individual A, expends a certain amount daily in wages or alms, which, as soon as received, is expended and consumed in the form of coarse food, by the receivers. A dies, leaving his property to B, who discontinues this item of expenditure, and expends in lieu of it the same sum each day in delicacies for his own table. I have chosen this supposition, in order that the two cases may be similar in all their circumstances, except that which is the subject of comparison. In order not to obscure the essential facts of the case by exhibiting them through the hazy medium of a money transaction, let us further suppose that A, and B after him, are landlords of the estate on which both the food consumed by the recipients of A's disbursements, and the articles of luxury supplied for B's table, are produced; and that their rent is paid to them in kind, they giving previous notice what description of produce they shall require. The question is, whether B's expenditure gives as much employment or as much food to his poorer neighbours as A's gave.

From the case as stated, it seems to follow that while A lived, that portion of his income which he expended in wages or alms, would be drawn by him from the farm in the shape of food for labourers, and would be used as such; while B, who came after him, would require, instead of this, an equivalent value in expensive articles of food, to be consumed in his own household: that the farmer, therefore, would, under B's regime, produce that much less, of ordinary food, and more of expensive delicacies, for each day of the year than was produced in A's time, and that there would be

It appears, then, that a demand delayed until the work is completed, and furnishing no advances, but only reimbursing advances made by others, contributes nothing to the demand for labour; and that what is so expended, is, in all its effects, so far as regards the employment of the labouring class, a mere nullity; it does not and cannot create any employment except at the expense of other employment which existed before.

But though a demand for velvet does nothing more in regard to the employment for labour and capital, than to determine so much of the employment which already existed, into that particular channel instead of any other; still, to the producers already engaged in the velvet manufacture, and not intending to quit it, this is of the utmost importance. To them, a falling off in the demand is a real loss, and one which, even if none of their goods finally perish unsold, may mount to any height, up to that which would make them choose, as the smaller evil, to retire from the business. On

---

that amount less of food shared, throughout the year, among the labouring and poorer classes. This is what would be conformable to the principles laid down in the text. Those who think differently, must, on the other hand, suppose that the luxuries required by B would be produced, not instead of, but in addition to, the food previously supplied to A's labourers, and that the aggregate produce of the country would be increased in amount. But when it is asked, how this double production would be effected—how the farmer, whose capital and labour were already fully employed, would be enabled to supply the new wants of B, without producing less of other things; the only mode which presents itself is, that he should first produce the food, and then, giving that food to the labourers whom A formerly fed, should by means of their labour, produce the luxuries wanted by B. This, accordingly, when the objectors are hard pressed, appears to be really their meaning. But it is an obvious answer, that, on this supposition, B must wait for his luxuries till the second year, and they are wanted this year. By the original hypothesis, he consumes his luxurious dinner by day, pari passu with the rations of bread and potatoes formerly served out by A to his labourers. There is not time to feed the labourers first, and supply B afterwards; he and they cannot both have their wants ministered to: he can only satisfy his own demand for commodities, by leaving as much of theirs, as was formerly supplied from that fund, unsatisfied.

It may, indeed, be rejoined by an objector, that since, on the present showing, time is the only thing wanting to render the expenditure of B

the contrary, an increased demand enables them to extend their transactions – to make a profit on a larger capital, if they have it, or can borrow it; and, turning over their capital more rapidly, they will employ their labourers more constantly, or employ a greater number than before. So that an increased demand for a commodity does really, in the particular department, often cause a greater employment to be given to labour by the same capital. The mistake lies in not perceiving that, in the cases supposed, this advantage is given to labour and capital in one department, only by being withdrawn from another; and that, when the change has produced its natural effect of attracting into the employment additional capital proportional to the increased demand, the advantage itself ceases.

The grounds of a proposition, when well understood, usually give a tolerable indication of the limitations of it. The general principle, now stated, is that demand for commodities determines merely the direction of labour, and the kind of wealth

---

consistent with as large an employment to labour as was given by A, why may we not suppose that B postpones his increased consumption of personal luxuries until they can be furnished to him by the labour of the persons whom A employed? In that case, it may be said, he would employ and feed as much labour as his predecessors. Undoubtedly he would; but why? Because his income would be expended in exactly the same manner as his predecessor's; it would be expended in wages. A reserved from his personal consumption a fund which he paid away directly to labourers; B does the same, only instead of paying it to them himself, he leaves it in the hands of the farmer who pays it to them for him. On this supposition, B, in the first year, neither expending the amount, as far as he is personally concerned, in A's manner nor his own, really saves that portion of his income, and lends it to the farmer. And if, in subsequent years, confining himself within the year's income, he leaves the farmer in arrears to that amount, it becomes an additional capital, with which the farmer may permanently employ and feed A's labourers. Nobody pretends that such a change as this, a change from spending an income in wages of labour to saving it for investment, deprives any labourers of employment. What is affirmed to have that effect is, the change from hiring labourers to buying commodities for personal use; as represented by our original hypothesis.

In our illustration we have supposed no buying and selling, or use of money. But the case as we have put it, corresponds with actual fact in everything except the details of the mechanism. The whole of any country is virtually a single farm and manufactory, from which every member of

produced, but not the quantity or efficiency of the labour, or
the aggregate of wealth. But to this there are two exceptions.
First, when labour is supported, but not fully occupied, a new
demand for something which it can produce may stimulate
the labour thus supported to increased exertions, of which
the result may be an increase of wealth, to the advantage of
the labourers themselves and of others. Work which can be
done in the spare hours of persons subsisted from some other
source, can (as before remarked) be undertaken without
withdrawing capital from other occupations, beyond the
amount (often very small) required to cover the expense of
tools and materials, and even this will often be provided by
savings made expressly for the purpose. The reason of our
theorem thus failing, the theorem itself fails, and employment of this kind may by the springing up of a demand for
the commodity, be called into existence without depriving
labour of an equivalent amount of employment in any other
quarter. The demand does not, even in this case, operate on
labour any otherwise than through the medium of an existing
capital, but it affords an inducement which causes that capital
to set in motion a greater amount of labour than it did
before.

[1] The second exception, of which I shall speak at length in a
subsequent chapter, consists in the known effect of an ex-

---

the community draws his appointed share of the produce, having a certain
number of counters, called pounds sterling, put into his hands, which, at
his convenience, he brings back and exchanges for such goods as he pre-
fers, up to the limit of the amount. He does not, as in our imaginary case,
give notice beforehand what things he shall require; but the dealers and
producers are quite capable of finding it out by observation, and any change
in the demand is promptly followed by an adaptation of the supply to it.
If a consumer changes from paying away a part of his income in wages,
to spending it that same day (not some subsequent and distant day) in
things for his own consumption, and perseveres in this altered practice
until production has had time to adapt itself to the alteration of demand,
there will from that time be less food and other articles for the use of
labourers, produced in the country, by exactly the value of the extra
luxuries now demanded; and the labourers, as a class, will be worse off by
the precise amount.

[1] This paragraph was inserted in the sixth edition (1865).

tension of the market for a commodity, in rendering possible
an increased development of the division of labour, and hence
a more effective distribution of the productive forces of
society. This, like the former, is more an exception in appearance than it is in reality. It is not the money paid by the
purchaser, which remunerates the labour; it is the capital of
the producer: the demand only determines in what manner
that capital shall be employed, and what kind of labour it
shall remunerate; but if it determines that the commodity
shall be produced on a large scale, it enables the same capital
to produce more of the commodity, and may, by an indirect
effect in causing an increase of capital, produce an eventual
increase of the remuneration of the labourer.

The demand for commodities is a consideration of importance, rather in the theory of exchange, than in that of production. Looking at things in the aggregate, and permanently,
the remuneration of the producer is derived from the productive power of his own capital. The sale of the produce for
money, and the subsequent expenditure of the money in
buying other commodities, are a mean exchange of equivalent
values for mutual accommodation. It is true that, the division
of employments being one of the principal means of increasing the productive power of labour, the power of
exchanging gives rise to a great increase of the produce; but
even then it is production, not exchange, which remunerates
labour and capital. We cannot too strictly represent to ourselves the operation of exchange, whether conducted by
barter or through the medium of money, as the mere mechanism by which each person transforms the remuneration of
his labour or of his capital into the particular shape in which it
is most convenient to him to possess it; but in no wise the
source of the remuneration itself.

10. The preceding principles demonstrate the fallacy of
many popular arguments and doctrines, which are continually reproducing themselves in new forms. For example,
it has been contended, and by some from whom better things
might have been expected, that the argument for the income-
tax, grounded on its falling on the higher and middle classes
only, and sparing the poor, is in error; some have gone so far

as to say, an imposture; because in taking from the rich
what they would have expended among the poor, the tax
injures the poor as much as if it had been directly levied from
them. Of this doctrine we now know what to think. So far,
indeed, as what is taken from the rich in taxes, would, if not
so taken, have been saved and converted into capital, or
even expended in the maintenance and wages of servants or
of any class of unproductive labourers, to that extent the
demand for labour is no doubt diminished, and the poor
injuriously affected, by the tax on the rich; and as these
effects are almost always produced in a greater or less degree,
it is impossible so to tax the rich as that no portion of the tax
can fall on the poor. But even here the question arises, whether
the government, after receiving the amount, will not lay out
as great a portion of it in the direct purchase of labour, as the
taxpayers would have done. In regard to all that portion of
the tax, which, if not paid to the government, would have
been consumed in the form of commodities (or even expended
in services if the payment has been advanced by a capitalist),
this, according to the principles we have investigated, falls
definitely on the rich, and not at all on the poor. There is
exactly the same demand for labour, so far as this portion is
concerned, after the tax, as before it. The capital which
hitherto employed the labourers of the country remains, and
is still capable of employing the same number. There is the
same amount of produce paid in wages, or allotted to defray
the feeding and clothing of labourers.

If those against whom I am now contending were in the
right, it would be impossible to tax anybody except the poor.
If it is taxing the labourers, to tax what is laid out in the produce of labour, the labouring classes pay all the taxes. The
same argument, however, equally proves, that it is impossible
to tax the labourers at all; since the tax, being laid out either
in labour or in commodities, comes all back to them; so that
taxation has the singular property of falling on nobody. On
the same showing, it would do the labourers no harm to
take from them all they have, and distribute it among the
other members of the community. It would all be 'spent
among them,' which on this theory comes to the same thing.

The error is produced by not looking directly at the realities of the phenomena, but attending only to the outward mechanism of paying and spending. If we look at the effects produced not on the money, which merely changes hands, but on the commodities which are used and consumed, we see that, in consequence of the income-tax, the classes who pay it do really diminish their consumption. Exactly so far as they do this, they are the persons on whom the tax falls. It is defrayed out of what they would otherwise have used and enjoyed. So far, on the other hand, as the burthen falls, not on what they would have consumed, but on what they would have saved to maintain production, or spent in maintaining or paying unproductive labourers, to that extent the tax forms a deduction from what would have been used and enjoyed by the labouring classes. But if the government, as is probably the fact, expends fully as much of the amount as the tax-payers would have done in the direct employment of labour, as in hiring sailors, soldiers, and policemen, or in paying off debt, by which last operation it even increases capital; the labouring classes not only do not lose any employment by the tax, but may possibly gain some, and the whole of the tax falls exclusively where it was intended.

All that portion of the produce of the country which any one, not a labourer,[1] actually and literally consumes for his own use, does not contribute in the smallest degree to the maintenance of labour. No one is benefited by mere consumption, except the person who consumes. And a person cannot both consume his income himself, and make it over to be consumed by others. Taking away a certain portion by taxation cannot deprive both him and them of it, but only him or them. To know which is the sufferer, we must understand whose consumption will have to be retrenched in consequence: this, whoever it be, is the person on whom the tax really falls.[2]

---

[1] 'Not a labourer' was inserted in the third edition (1852).
[2] See Appendix F, *Fundamental Propositions on Capital*.

Further Reading for Part 1

M. Blaug, *Ricardian Economics* (1958.)

M. E. A. Bowley, *Nassau Senior and Classical Economics* (1937).

E. Cannan, *History of the Theories of Production and Distribution in English Political Economy, 1776–1848* (1953).

B. A. Corry, *Money, Saving and Investment in English Economics, 1800–1850* (1962).

V. Edelberg, 'The Ricardian Theory of Profits', *Economica*, Feb. 1933.

I. Fisher, 'What is Capital', *Economic Journal*, VI, 1896.

C. D. W. Goodwin, *Canadian Economic Thought. The Political Economy of a Developing Nation, 1814–1914* (1961).

B. F. Hoselitz (ed.), *Theories of Economic Growth* (1960).

R. W. James, *The Life and Works of John Rae, Political Economist* (1965).

R. L. Meek, 'Physiocracy and Classicism in England', *Economic Journal*, March 1951; *The Economics of Physiocracy* (1962).

C. W. Mixter, *The Sociological Theory of Capital* (1905).

D. P. O'Brien, *J. R. McCulloch. A Study in Classical Economics* (1970).

Lord Robbins, *Robert Torrens and the Evolution of Classical Economics* (1958).

J. S. Schumpeter, *History of Economic Analysis* (1954).

W. R. Scott, *Adam Smith as Student and Professor* (1937).

J. J. Spengler, 'John Rae on Economic Development: A Note', *Quarterly Journal of Economics*, LXXIII, 1959.

O. St. Clair, *A Key to Ricardo* (1957).

G. S. L. Tucker, *Progress and Profits in British Economic Thought* (1960).

Unsigned, 'John Rae and John Stuart Mill: A Correspondence', *Economica*, X, 1943.

Part Two

THE ACCUMULATION OF CAPITAL

5 Anon.

FEES, WAGES AND INITIAL CAPITAL REQUIREMENTS IN THE EIGHTEENTH-CENTURY TRADES[1]

Trade or Occupation	Apprentice-ship Fees (£'s)	Journeyman's Wages (shillings per week)	Master's Capital (£'s)
Apothecary	20–300	5–15+b	100–200
Appraisers	See Upholsterers and Brokers		
Armourers	15–20	15–20	50
Attorneys	50–300 gns	25 gns+	100–200 gns
Back-makers	5–10	15	200–300
Bakers	5–20	7–8	100
Barber-surgeons	1–20	2–5+b	50
Basket-makers	5–10	10–20	100
Bellows-makers	5–10	10	50–100
Bird-cage-makers	5–10	15–20	100+
Birmingham hardwaremen	40–100	7/6–10+b	500–2,000
Blacksmiths	5–20	8	500+
Block-makers	10+	15–18	400+
Blue-makers	10–20	2–5+b	100–500
Boat-builders	10	15	300
Bodice-makers	—	7–8	50
Book-binders	5–20	12	50–100
Booksellers	40–100 gns	7/6–15+b	500–1,000+
Box-makers	10	12–15	100
Braziers	10	12–15	100–1,000
Breeches-makers	10	12–15	50
Brewers (common)	50–200 gns	20–80+b	very large

[1] Abstracted from *A General Description of all Trades, digested in Alphabetical Order* (1747) by an unknown author. A plus sign after a figure indicates a minimum amount and 'b' shows that board and lodging were given in addition to wages.

Trade or Occupation	Apprenticeship Fees (£'s)	Journeyman's Wages (shillings per week)	Master's Capital (£'s)
Bricklayers	5–20	15–20	100+
Brickmakers	—	25+	500+
Brokers	10–20	10–18	100–200
Broom-makers	—	8–16	500
Brush-makers	5–10	15–18	100
Buckle-makers	5–10	12–18	very small
Buckram-stiffeners	5–10	10	200+
Butchers (various)	5–10	5–7/6+b	50
Button-makers	5	8–12	50–1,000
Button-mould-makers	5	12–15	20
Button-sellers	20–30	—	500+
Cabinet-makers	10–20	12–15	100–3,000
Calenders	10	10–12	100
Cap-makers	5–10	9–12	50–100
Card-makers	40–50	18–20	500
Carmen	5	12	100
Carpenters	10–20	15	—
Carvers	10–20	18–30	100–200
Chain-makers	5–10	8–10	50–100
Chair-makers (various)	10	12	300–500
Chandlers (various)	—	—	300–500
Chemists	100–200	—	very small
China-men	20–50	7/6–10+b	500+
Chocolate makers	—	24–30	50
Clock-makers	10	10–30	50–1,000
Clothiers	5–10	10–15	500
Coach-makers	20	15+	500
Coal-crimps	100 gns	20	very large
Coffee-men	10	—	100
Coffin-makers	See Box-makers		
Collar-makers	10	3–5+b	100–200
Colour-men	10–30	5–10+b	200–500
Comb-makers	5–10	10–15	100
Confectioners	20–40	15–25	300
Cooks	10–20	5+b	—
Coopers (various)	10–20	15	200–500
Coppersmiths	See Braziers		
Cordwainers	5–10	9–24	100–300
Curriers	10–15	few	200–500
Cutlers	10–15	15	50+
Distillers	20–30	5–7/6+b	500+
Drapers	30–100	10–20+b	1,000+

Trade or Occupation	Apprentice-ship Fees (£'s)	Journeyman's Wages (shillings per week)	Master's Capital (£'s)
Druggists	50–100	5–7/6+b	500–1,000
Dyers (various)	10	10–12	500
Enamellers	10	18–24	very small
Engine-makers	10–20	8–20	500
Engravers (various)	10	—	very small
Factors (various)	60–100 gns	7/6–20+b	very large
Fan-makers	10	18–24	20–100
Farriers	5	9	50
Fell-mongers	5–20	10–12	1,000+
Felt-makers	10	—	100–1,000
Fine-drawers	5	15–18	very small
Fish-hook and Fishing-tackle-makers	5–10	15	20–100
Fishermen	—	⅓ of profits	50–60
Fishmongers	20+	7/6+b	50–1,000
Flatters	See Gold and Silver wire-drawers		
Flax-dressers	—	15	30
Founders (various)	10–15	18	50–very large
Frame-making	5–10	10–20	50
Frame-work knitters	5	10–20	100
Fruiterers	10	12	500
Fullers	5	10–12	50–200
Gardeners and Nurserymen	5	10	100–500
Gilders	10	18–24	100
Glass-blowers	—	high	very large
Glass-grinders	5	15–20	50
Glass-sellers	20	7/6+b	100–500
Glaziers	10–20	12–15	100–500
Globe-makers	5	15–18	20–100
Glovers	5–40	15–18	200–500
Gold and Silver wire-drawers	5	18–20	100
Gold-beaters	5–10	18	50–100
Goldsmiths (non-banking)	20	10–40+b	30+
Grinders	5	—	50
Grocers	20–100	7/6+b	500+
Gunsmiths (various)	20	20–30+	500–1,000
Hair-curlers and wig-makers	20	8–15	100+
Hoop-Petticoat-makers	5–20	7	20
Horners	10	15	100–500
Horse-milliners	20–50	7/6+b	1,000+
Hosiers	50–200	7/6–12/6+b	1,000–8,000
Hot-pressers	5–10	12–15	100

Trade or Occupation	Apprentice-ship Fees (£'s)	Journeyman's Wages (shillings per week)	Master's Capital (£'s)
Hour-glass-makers	5	12	50
Husbandmen	—	seasonal	200–300
Jewellers	20–50	20–40+b	very large
Joiners	See Carpenters		
Inholders	See Vintners		
Iron-mongers	30–100	7/6–20+b	500+
Lace-men	5–10	18–20	500–2,000
Last-makers	5	18–20	50
Leather-cutters	20	7/6–12/6+b	300–500
Leather-dressers	See Curriers		
Leather-sellers	30–40	7/6–12/6+b	300–500
Lighter-builders	10	15	300–500
Lightermen	—	12–15	very large
Loom-makers	5–10	12–15	50–100
Lorinors	5	18	100
Mantua-makers	5–20 gns	7–9	—
Mariners	—	5–12/6	—
Masons	10	15–18	200
Mast-makers	5–10	15–18	300
Mathematical instrument-makers	5–20	21	50–500
Mercers	30–100	7/6–40+b	500–2,000
Merchants (various)	100–300	—	very large
Millers	5	10	100–200
Milliners	20–30 gns	7/6+b	100–300
Mill-makers	5–10	7–8	100
Mill-wrights	5–10	12–15	100–150
Musical-instrument makers	20	21	300
Needlemakers	5	12–15	50–200
Net-makers	20	7/6+b	300–500
Oil-men	20–50	7/6+b	500–1,000
Packers	10–20	12–14	300–400
Painters	5–20	15–20	very small–200
Paper-makers	5–10	15–18	300+
Parchment-makers	5	10–12	—
Patten-makers	10	10–12	100+
Pattern-drawers	10–20	18–24	100+
Paviors	5	15	50–100
Pawnbrokers	20–30	7/6–12/6	500
Perfumers	—	10–12	100–200
Pewterers	20	15–20	500
Pin-makers	5–10	12–15	50–1,000

Trade or Occupation	Apprentice-ship Fees (£'s)	Journeyman's Wages (shillings per week)	Master's Capital (£'s)
Pipe-makers	5	16–18	50
Plaisterers	5–10	15–30	50+
Plane-makers	5	16–18	50
Plumbers	10–20	15	100–200
Potters	5–10	15–20	1,000–3,000
Poulters	5–10	10–12	20+
Printers (book)	10–30	16	500
Printers (calico)	5	10–40	1,300+
Print-sellers	20	5–7/6+b	50–1,000
Pump-makers	5–10	12–15	50–100
Refiners	10	18–24	500–8,000
Robe-makers	See Tailors		
Rope-makers	5–10	24–30	2,000+
Sadlers	20	15–18+b	100
Sailmakers	10	18–20	500+
Salesmen and clothes brokers	20	10+b	300
Salters	50–100 gns	—	1,000+
Sawyers	5–10	18	—
Scale-makers	10–15	15–20	100–500
Scriveners	See Attorneys		
Setters	5–10	12	100
Shipwrights	10	18	very large
Silk-men	100	—	very large
Silk-throwers	5	9–10	400
Skinners	50–100	7/6+b	1,000
Skreen-makers	15–20	12–15	50–500
Snuff-box makers	5	12	20
Snuff-makers	—	10–12	50
Soap-boilers	200–300	20–40+b	very large
Spectacle-makers	20–30	15	50–200
Starch-makers	—	—	very large
Stationers	50	—	100–500
Stay-makers	5–10	12–15	50
Stuff-men	40–100	7/6–12/6+b	300–1,000
Sugar-bakers	100+	—	very large
Surgeons	50–500	—	300
Tallow-chandlers	10–20	15–20+b	200
Tanners	5	10	500
Taylors	5–10	12+	100+
Tea-men	—	—	300–3,000
Thread-men	50	7/6–12/6+b	500–1,000
Tin-men	10–20	12–15	50–500

Trade or Occupation	Apprentice-ship Fees (£'s)	Journeyman's Wages (shillings per week)	Master's Capital (£'s)
Tobacconists	30–100	7/6–12/6+b	5,000–10,000
Toy-men	50–100	—	200–2,000
Trunk-makers	5–10	12–15	200+
Turners	5–10	18–20	100–300
Vinegar-makers	See Brewers		
Vintners	20	—	500
Upholsterers	20–50	15–18	100–500
Warehouse-men	—	—	very large
Watermen	—	—	15
Wax-chandlers	50	7/6+b	500
Weavers	5	10–30	100–5,000
Whalebone-men	50–100	7/6–20+b	500–1,000
Wheelwrights	10	15–18	200
Whip-makers	5–20	10–12	100–500
Wood-mongers	See Carmen		
Wool-combers	5	12–18	100–1,000
Wool-men	20–100	5–15	500
Woolsted-men	20–50	7/6+b	200–500

6 Andrew Hooke

THE NATIONAL DEBT AND THE NATIONAL CAPITAL[1]

The estimates of national capital given by Andrew Hooke are a typical example of the statistical standards of the eighteenth-century pamphleteer. In this case the author presents a set of crude estimates, claiming that he has corrected and updated those originally computed by Gregory King for 1688 with the express purpose of demonstrating that the recent growth of the national debt represented a small burden on the country, when compared with the size of the national capital. Hooke arranged his estimates under three headings, the first two of which were particularly fallacious, namely cash stock and personal stock. Beginning with the quite unjustified assumption, common to other writers at the time, that cash in circulation bore a fixed relation to total income and increased by fixed increments over time, Hooke seems to have arbitrarily settled on a multiplier of twenty to arrive at a figure for personal capital. The estimate given for land stock was perhaps more nearly correct, but less original, and leaned heavily on King's earlier valuation.[2] It is useful to recall that King had put the value of land and buildings at £234 million on the basis of 18 years' purchase, while Hooke makes them £370 million on the basis of $18\frac{1}{2}$ years' purchase. According to Giffen in his discussion of these earlier efforts at assessing the national capital, a more objective estimate is that of Vivant de Mezagues, because his assessment distinguished between land itself, to which a capital value of 22 years' purchase was given, and houses, which were capitalized at only 12 years' purchase. In total, however, the French

[1] From *An Essay on the National Debt and National Capital* (1750).
[2] In *The Natural and Political Observations and Conclusions* ... (1696).

observer's estimate for landed capital was, at £385 million, little different from Hooke's at £370 million. It is clear also that neither pamphlet was free from bias. Just as Hooke was concerned to show 'that the paying off the National Debt is not a Matter of that Importance to the Community, as is generally imagined; that it may subsist many years longer without Prejudice to the Constitution, and even be increased to double the Sum, without any real danger of a National Bankruptcy . . ,'[1] in the same manner Vivant de Mezagues was at pains to show the landed classes of England '. . . that all she has mortgaged to foreigners, is so much dead loss to her, and that all she has mortgaged to her own subjects, has only served to increase the evil. In short, this last measure has given birth at home to a race of men known by the name of "money jobbers"; a race, always labouring to imitate the wasps that devour the honey of the industrious bees; a race of men, sworn enemies of the plough, the landed interest, and the only beneficial trade of the nation.'[2] Vivant de Mezagues confined his remarks to the land and stock only, whereas Hooke's estimate, notwithstanding its gross errors, does distinguish the main items which constituted the pre-classical concept of capital. Before Smith, most eighteenth-century writers still adhered to the mercantilist idea of the 'national stock' as being the total of real and personal estates in the country; the latter included, of course, the money stock of the nation which tended to fluctuate with changes in the balance of trade.

Without entering minutely into the State of the National Debt, which would be of no Service to the Reader, with regard to the present dissertation, we shall take the Amount of it, or the whole Sum for which the publick Faith is become Surety to Individuals, to be, as 'tis generally asserted, about Eighty Millions. This, it must be own'd, is a large sounding Sum, and, by artful Management, has been too successfully

[1] Op. cit., p. 44.
[2] *A General View of England . . . from the Year 1600 to 1762 . . .* (1762, Eng. trans., 1766), pp. 78–9.

employed to make false impressions; but, as in private Life, a Man can never know the true State of his Affairs, by inspecting one side of his Accounts only, so in this Case, the Knowledge of what we owe, without knowing, at the same Time, the Value of our whole Capital, will be of no Use towards the Discovery of the real State of the Nation; but, if we can, by any proper Means, come at the intrinsic Value of the NATIONAL STOCK, real and personal, we may then be able, by comparing the Debtor and Creditor Side of the Account together, to strike a BALANCE that will give us a pretty just Idea of our present Situation and Abilities.

The Difficulty and Hazard of so bold an Undertaking, and the Impracticability of arriving at an Arithmetical Exactness, in estimates relative to such intricate and complicated Subjects, are obvious to every Reader; and the ill Success of the Few who have gone before us, in this yet unbeaten Track, may be thought sufficient to discourage any future Attempt of the like Nature; However, as nothing is too hard for Resolution and Industry and as in other Things, so in this, the Miscarriages of our Predecessors, if rightly improved, may, like Lighthouses, serve to caution us against splitting on the same dangerous Rocks, and put us on shaping a new Course that may at length bring us in Safety to the appointed Port, we shall boldly venture to discard all Implicitism, to lay an entire new Foundation for our future Building, and endeavour to raise the Superstructure on such solid Principles as may abide the Test of the most critical Examination.

IN Order to this we shall first enquire into the Quantity of our Coin; 2. Into the Amount of the rest of the personal Stock of the Nation, viz. of Wrought Plate, Bullion, Jewels, Rings, Furniture, Apparel, Shipping, Stock in Trade, Stock for Consumption, and Live Stock of Cattle, etc. and, 3. Into the Value of all the Lands of the Kingdom. These three Articles, comprising the total Intrinsic Value of the Nation, when clearly and fully explained, will, we doubt not, dispel the Clouds that have been too artfully thrown over this Subject, fully satisfy every candid Enquiry after Truth, and serve to silence, at least, if not convince, all Gainsayers.

AS to the present quantity of our COIN, we have these

Facts to reason upon, which, in our Apprehension, will sufficiently ascertain this Article. Dr. DAVENANT in his Discourses on the Publick Revenues has, from the Mint Accounts, and some other Evidences, determined the Coin of England to have been, in 1600 about four Millions, in 1660 about fourteen Millions, and in 1688 about eighteen Millions and an half.* Now this being taken here for granted, if we divide the Surplus fourteen Millions and half, (Difference of the Quantity of the COIN, according to this Account, in the Years 1600 and 1688) by eighty-eight, the Number of Years intervening those two Periods, the Quotient one hundred sixty-four thousand, seven hundred, seventy-two Pounds will be, at a Medium, the annual Increment of the National COIN during that Interval.

$$
\begin{array}{lll}
88) & 14{,}500{,}000 & (164{,}772 \\
    & \cdots\cdots & \\
    & \overline{5\ 70} & \\
    & \quad\overline{420} & \\
    & \quad\ \overline{680} & \\
    & \qquad\overline{640} & \\
    & \qquad\ \overline{240} & \\
    & \qquad\quad\overline{64}\quad \text{Rem.} &
\end{array}
$$

AND if we suppose but a like annual Increment from 1688 to the present Year, 1749, it will clearly follow that the current Coin of the Nation is, at this day upon this State of the Case, more than seven times its Quantity in 1600, upwards of double its Quantity at the RESTORATION, and near ten Millions more than it actually was at the REVOLUTION. —— For, by multiplying 164,772, the medium annual Increment of the COIN, upon this Supposition, from A.D. 1600 to the present Year, 1749, by one hundred and forty

* I think the Dr. is apparently mistaken, even according to his own Account, when he states the whole National COIN A.D. 1600 at four Millions only, and that it should rather have been about six Millions and an half, as will appear afterwards, in its proper Place, beyond all contradiction.

eight, the number of Years intervening those two Periods, the product will be twenty-four Millions three hundred eighty six thousand two hundred fifty-six: to which if you add the four Millions COIN at the former of the two Periods, the total Amount will be twenty eight millions three hundred eighty six thousand two hundred fifty six Pounds for the present Quantity of the National COIN, q.e.d.

Annual Increment	164772
Multiplied by	148
	1318176
	659088
	164772
TOTAL	£24,386,256
To which add the Coin A.D. 1600	4,000,000
	£28,386,256

OR, if we take it from the second Period A.D. 1660 (when, according to Dr. DAVENANT's more accurate Account, the National COIN was about fourteen Millions) and divide the surplus four Millions and an half (Difference of the Quantity of the COIN in the years 1660 and 1688) by twenty eight, the Number of Years intervening these two last Periods, the Quotient will be 160,714.

$$
\begin{array}{r}
28)\quad 4,500,000 \quad (160,714 \\
\cdots\ \cdots \\
\hline
170 \\
\hline
200 \\
\hline
40 \\
\hline
120 \\
\hline
8 \quad \text{Rem.}
\end{array}
$$

AND if we suppose, as in the former case, but an equal
Increment of the COIN from 1688 to the present Year 1749,
the Consequence will be, as clear, that the National Cash,
at this Day, is also upwards of double its Quantity at the
Restoration, and more than nine Millions greater than it was
at the Revolution. —— For by multiplying the Medium
annual Increment of the COIN, upon this Supposition, by
eighty eight, the number of Years intervening those two
Periods, the Product will be fourteen millions one hundred
forty two thousand, eight hundred thirty two Pounds, which
differs not a Quarter of a Million from the like Amount on
the former Supposition; so that, in either Case, the present
Quantity of the National COIN turns out nearly the same.

Annual Increment on the last supposition	160,714
Multiplied by	88
	1285712
	1285712
	14,142,832.
To which add the Coin in 1660	14,000,000
	28,142,832
Difference	243,424
Former Amount	£28,386,256

THAT these would be the States of the National COIN,
upon the supposition before-mentioned, respectively, is
Arithmetically demonstrated; but, as 'tis notorious that our
Commerce has been increasing since the Revolution, and,
consequently, that our Coin must have proportionally
increased also, so if we could possibly add the Surplus
annual Increments of the Coin, from that Period to the
present Time, which must be considerable, they would
respectively amount to a great deal more. Upon the whole,
then, from these premises we may venture to conclude, with a
sufficient Degree of Certainty, and without fear of Con-

tradiction, that the current Cash of the Nation, at this Day, cannot reasonably be estimated at less than thirty Millions.

THIS Point then being gained, let us secondly enquire into the Value of the rest of the personal Stock of the Kingdom; and endeavour to settle the probable Ratio, or Proportion, of the Sum of the Coin to the Amount of the other personal Stock, in order to facilitate the following Estimates. And here the two great Masters of Political Arithmetick, Sir WILLIAM PETTY and Dr. DAVENANT, differ from each other, and both from the Truth, so widely, that we have little or no Assistance from either of those Gentlemen. Instead, therefore, of remarking on the Error and Insufficiency of their respective Principles, which would lead us into too large a field, and be but of little Use to the Generality of our Readers, we shall set out on an entire new Foundation, and, by throwing some brighter Lights on this obscure Subject, endeavour so to illustrate it, that Persons of moderate Sagacity, who do not readily perceive the Justness of Consequences drawn from abstract Principles, (which appear evident enough to others who are conversant with that sort of Reasoning) may, notwithstanding, have a sufficient degree of Evidence, to remove all doubting, and to induce a free rational Assent to the Truth of the following Propositions.

It shall suffice, therefore, to observe, for the present, that Sir WM. PETTY makes the Amount of the whole Personal Stock, exclusive of our Coin, to be to our Coin alone as 70 to 6, or, nearly, as 12 to 1 which Dr. DAVENANT computes to be only as 42 to 14, or, as three to 1, tho' he had all the Evidence of the Mint Accounts to correct himself by, which made him certain of one Article of the utmost Consequence. An Advantage, says an ingenious Author, which if Sir WM. PETTY had enjoyed and seen his Mistake in Under-estimating the Amount of our Coin, he would easily have rectified himself with regard to the Value of our whole Stock likewise, and have assigned for it a much larger Amount than seventy six Millions.*

* Sir WM. PETTY, although he was greatly mistaken in his Opinion of the Quantity of our Coin or Capital, which he makes to amount to scarcely six Millions, yet he reckons, about the Year 1660

HOW these two learned Gentlemen came to differ so widely from one another is not very mysterious; a small Difference in the first Principles (especially of Hypothetical Arguments) always making a vast Disagreement in the Conclusion; And then tho' the former, in his conjectural Estimates, approaches much nearer the Truth than the latter, yet 'tis no difficult matter to prove that Sir Wm. Petty, himself, must have been greatly mistaken, in making the Ratio of the Coin to the other personal Stock, in 1660, to be as 1 to 12 nearly, when undoubtedly it must have been in a much less proportion, and probably, as at this Day, not above a twentieth part of the value of the whole; as will apear pretty evident from the following Remarks, of a certain author, which are notorious Facts, and open to everybody's observation.

'IF you go into the House, says he, of the meanest cottager, you will find some sort of Furniture within, besides his own Tools; and generally some little Stock without Doors; all which together may amount to three or four Pounds, or probably much more, tho' this man shall never have five Shillings at once by him throughout the Year. If you go into a Farmer's House, and examine his Circumstances, you will find he has seldom more by him at once, than thirty or forty Shillings, if so much, except for a few Days

---

The Value of our Shipping to be	3,000,000
Of our Live Stock	36,000,000
Of the other personal Stock	31,000,000
	70,000,000

whereas, according to Dr. DAVENANT, the whole personal Stock of the Kingdom, in 1600, amounted to but fifty-six Millions, and, in 1688, to no more than eighty-eight Millions, altho' he allows the Coin alone to be at this last Period eighteen Millions and an half; so that, by his Account, all the other personal Stock must have been no more than sixty-nine Millions and an half, or not much above one Year's Income, according to his own conjecture concerning this Income, which he makes to amount to fifty-eight Millions Sterling; That is, in effect, saying, that upon every eighty-eight Pounds ten shillings invested in Stock, fifty-eight Pounds at least should be the annual Profit.

after a Fair, and till he has carried it to his Landlord; whereas his constant Stock in his House, Barton Barns and Grounds, of all Kinds, shall be worth upwards of two hundred Pounds. If you survey a common shopkeeper's House, you will rarely meet with more than ten or twelve Pounds in the Till, tho', at the same time, the Stock in his Shop alone is worth three or four hundred Pounds. If you examine the Houses of Wholesale Dealers, you will find such, as are worth ten or twelve thousand Pounds and upwards, have seldom above two or three hundred Pounds in Specie lying by them; and Merchants worth twenty or thirty thousand Pounds, who have most occasion for Money at Command, will not often keep more in Cash at their Bankers than a thousand or fifteen hundred Pounds, and much less than this Sum in general; and 'tis well-known that the Bankers themselves are so far from keeping any of their own Money by them, that they keep but a part, only, of what is deposited in their Hands by other Persons; without which they would have no advantage. And, lastly, if you enquire into the State of Gentlemen's Houses, from Peers or those of the lowest Rank, it will be found that the ready Money by them, is a very small part of their Plate, Jewels, Furniture, and Stock of all kinds; So that in the whole Circle of People of all Degrees, the sum lying by them, in ready Cash, does not appear to be one-twentieth part of their whole Stock, i.e. of the whole Stock of the Kingdom;'

and consequently the total Value or Amount of the personal Stock, exclusive of the Coin, at this Day, cannot be reasonably estimated at less than six hundred Millions; For if we multiply thirty Millions, the present Cash Capital, according to our Account, by twenty, the lowest Rate of Proportion between that and the other personal Stock, the Product will be exactly six hundred Millions as aforesaid.

$$\begin{array}{r} 30,000,000 \\ 20 \\ \hline 600,000,000 \end{array}$$

THE second Article being thus unexceptionably, as we apprehend, settled and adjusted, at least so far as not to exceed the Truth in its Valuation, we shall have but little Difficulty with the third and last, viz. The Value in Fee of all the Lands in the Kingdom. 'Tis well-known that the Land Tax, at 4 Shillings in the Pound, produces annually into the Exchequer two Millions; and 'tis as well known that Lands, in general, thro'out the Kingdom, are not assessed at above half their Value, or a twentieth part of their Rack-Rents; and, consequently, the Amount of the yearly Rents of the real Estates of the Nation, must be, at least, twenty Millions, which, in Fee, at eighteen and an half Year's Purchase (and surely this is not over-rating) makes three hundred and seventy Millions.

$$
\begin{array}{r}
20,000,000 \\
18 \cdot 5 \\
\hline
100000000 \\
160000000 \\
20000000 \\
\hline
370,000,000
\end{array}
$$

NOW, as this settles the Proportion of the Cash Stock to the Land Capital, in the Instance before us, to be as 1 to $12\frac{1}{3}d.$, and as the Proportion of the said Cash Stock to the other personal Stock was before settled as 1 to 20, so these Ratios of 1, 20, $12\frac{1}{3}d.$ may be reasonably considered, in all preceding Times (or at least since we became a considerable trading Nation) as the establish'd Proportions that the Cash Stock, the other Personal Stock, and the Land Capital, of the Kingdom bear to one another.

UPON these Principles, which we apprehend cannot reasonably be disputed, the following Estimates are made, which, at one view, exhibits to the Reader a pretty just idea of the State of the Nation, in this regard, at these four Periods, viz. A.D. 1600, 1660, 1688, and 1749, and opens a new Scene that may throw some farther Lights on this Subject, and, if rightly improved, will greatly assist us in our future Calculations.

ESTIMATES OF THE NATIONAL STOCK
A.D. 1600

Cash Stock	..	..	..	6,500,000
Personal Stock..	..	..	..	130,000,000
Land Stock	..	..	..	80,166,666
				216,666,666

A.D. 1660

Cash Stock	..	..	..	14,000,000
Personal Stock..	..	..	..	280,000,000
Land Stock	..	..	..	172,666,666
				466,666,666

A.D. 1688

Cash Stock	..	..	..	18,500,000
Personal Stock..	..	..	..	370,000,000
Land Stock	..	..	..	228,166,666
				616,666,666

A.D. 1749

Cash Stock	..	..	..	30,000,000
Personal Stock..	..	..	..	600,000,000
Land Stock	..	..	..	370,000,000
				1,000,000,000

THAT this is a fair Representation of Matters, nobody can deny, and, if the Facts and Reasonings be admitted, the whole Capital Stock of the Kingdom appears, on solid Principles, to be not only vastly superior in Value to what it has been usually estimated, but, in Fact, upwards of three hundred thirty three Millions more than quadruple its Quantity in 1600, upwards of sixty six Millions more than double to what it was in 1660, and no less than three hundred and eighty three Millions and one-third of a Million higher than it was at the Revolution: From which if you deduct the eighty Millions National Debt, the remaining three hundred three Millions and one third of a Million will be the Net improved Capital Stock of the Kingdom since that Period; which two last Sums, viz. three hundred eighty three Millions and one third of a Million, and three hundred and three Millions and one third of a Million, being severally divided by 60, the number of Years since the Revolution, gives in the first case six Millions three hundred eighty eight thousand eight hundred eighty nine Pounds, nearly, for the Gross, and, in the last case, upwards of five Millions fifty five thousand five hundred fifty five Pounds for the Net, annual Increment of the National Capital, at a Medium, from the Revolution to the present time; And by deducting the lesser Quotient from the greater, the remaining one Million and one third of a Million will be the mean Proportion of the Debt annually contracted, according to this account, since that Period.

$$
\begin{array}{lll}
60) & 383,333,333 & (6,388,888 \\
& \quad\cdots & \\
& 233 & \\
& \overline{} & \\
& 533 & \\
& \overline{} & \\
& 53 \quad \text{Rem.} & \\
\\
60) & 303,333,333 & (5,055,555 \\
& \quad\cdots & \\
& 333 & \\
& \overline{} & \\
& 33 \quad \text{Rem.} & \\
& & \overline{} \\
& & 1,333,333
\end{array}
$$

AND here we might safely rest the Matter, and trust the candid Reader's Judgment with the Success of our Enquiry, but as we desire to give all possible Satisfaction on this Head, we shall spend a few pages in comparing our Estimates with those made by Sir William Petty, and Dr. Davenant, which stand as under, viz.

SIR WILLIAM PETTY'S ESTIMATES IN 1660

Cash Stock	6,000,000
Personal Stock	70,000,000
Land Capital	174,000,000
	250,000,000

DR. DAVENANT'S ESTIMATES A.D. 1600

Cash Stock	4,000,000
Personal Stock	13,000,000
Land Stock	72,000,000
	89,000,000

A.D. 1660

Cash Stock	14,000,000
Personal Stock	42,000,000
Land Stock*	237,000,000
	293,000,000

A.D. 1688

Cash Stock	18,500,000
Personal Stock	69,500,000
Land Stock	252,000,000
	340,000,000

BY these Accounts it appears, that we differ vastly in our Estimates from those learned Gentlemen. From Sir Wm. Petty in 1660, upwards of TWO HUNDRED AND SIXTEEN MILLIONS. From Dr. Davenant, in 1600, ONE HUNDRED TWENTY SEVEN MILLIONS and upwards; in 1660 ONE

* Dr. Davenant having omitted to estimate the Land Stock in 1660, we have no other Way to supply that Defect, but by observing the same proportion between that and the whole Personal Stock, as he has done in his former Estimate in 1600.

HUNDRED SEVENTY THREE MILLIONS and upwards; and in 1688 TWO HUNDRED SEVENTY SIX
MILLIONS and upwards: Variations so very considerable,
that unless we are able rationally to account for them, our
Credit, we fear, notwithstanding the Solidity of our Principles, will have little Force against the opinion of two such
establish'd Authorities.

As to Sir Wm. Petty, it is obvious, his Error lay in mis-
taking an Article of the greatest Consequence, by which the
rest are apparently govern'd; as he had no proper Means of
coming at the Knowledge of the Quantity of the current
Coin at that time, it is not to be wondered that he should guess
that to be scarcely six Millions, which was, in fact, (as appeared afterwards according to Dr. Davenant) FOURTEEN
MILLIONS; and that he should estimate the other Personal
Stock at but SEVENTY MILLIONS, which, according to
his own Rate of Proportion, if he had been right in his Cash
Article, would have amounted to ONE HUNDRED SIXTY
EIGHT MILLIONS (twelve times 14 being just the Sum)
and, in consequence, his Total to THREE HUNDRED AND
FIFTY SIX MILLIONS, viz.

Cash Stock	..	..	..	14,000,000
Personal Stock ..	..	..	..	168,000,000
Land Stock	..	..	..	174,000,000

356,000,000

THUS then we have clearly accounted for ONE HUN-
DRED & SIX MILLIONS Deficiency in Sir Wm. Petty's
Estimate viz. EIGHT MILLIONS in the Coin Article and
NINETY EIGHT MILLIONS in the other personal Stock
Article; but as to the remaining ONE HUNDRED AND
TEN MILLIONS Excess in our Estimate, which is wholly
in the Personal Stock Article (Sir William being TWO
Millions above us in that of the Land) we cannot promise
ourselves the same success, for want of knowing the Principles
upon which that Gentleman grounded his Calculations; but
if we should suppose that, as in his Cash Article so in this, he
was govern'd too much by Conjecture, there are not wanting

Reasons, in the Performance itself, by comparing the several Parts of it together, to render it highly probable. For, taking the Number of People in England and Wales to be at that Time, according to his own Estimate, Seven Millions and that they spent Yearly one with another £6.13s.4d. a Head it necessarily follows that the Fund for their Maintenance, or, the annual Income of the Nation, supposing no Increment of Stock, must have been at least FORTY SIX MILLIONS and TWO THIRDS of a Million, which, upon TWO HUN-DRED and FIFTY MILLIONS Capital, according to his mistaken Account is upwards of eighteen and an half per Cent, or, upon THREE HUNDRED FIFTY SIX Millions, according to his Account rectify'd, upwards of thirteen per Cent Profit; the lowest of which Sums is certainly a Super-lucration much too large upon a Trading Stock, where great Part of it lies dead and unprofitable, and where upwards of two thirds was, by his own Account, invested in Husbandry, the least advantagious of any of the Trading Articles.

AS to Dr. Davenant, he was as certainly mistaken in the Quantity of the Coin A.D. 1600 which he states at FOUR MILLIONS only, as Sir Wm. Petty was in the same Article in 1660, but with this remarkable difference, that the Latter had no Facts to go upon; whereas the Former, who had the best Means of Knowledge, absurdly sets up Conjecture in Oppo-sition to his own Facts.

HE says, There was coined during the Reign of
   Q. Elizabeth, in Silver 4,632,932
And suppose that the Gold of former Princes
   and of her Stamp, was 1,500,000

                  In all .. £6,132,932

And yet at the same time, presumes that there
   were not co-existing of her Stamp at any 2,500,000
   one time, in Silver, above Which with the
   Gold before-mentioned 1,500,000

Makes his Coin upon the whole amount to
   (as aforesaid) 4,000,000

and this without assigning any other Reasons for so large a Deduction, than that Q. Elizabeth recoined all the Silver Species that had been debased in the three former Reigns, which is no Reason at all, unless we suppose Money coin'd out of old Silver Species to be less durable, and subject to more casualties, than that made from new Bullion, which is absurd; and that she fabricated her own COIN a-new, on Account of an Alteration of the Standard which is absolutely false in Fact, there being no such Alteration during her whole Reign; So that according to the Doctor's own Account (and with making sufficient Allowance for Waste) there must have been at least SIX Millions COIN about the Beginning of the 17th Century.

Besides all the Silver Coin, that had been fabricated, from the Conquest to the 34.H.8 being 476 Years, was STERLING Standard, i.e. in every Pound wt. there were eleven Ounces two penny wt. fine Silver and eighteen penny wt. Allay, which in that Year was altered to ten Ounces Fine and two Ounces Allay and afterwards debased at times 'till it was reduced, 5.E.6 so low as to have but three Ounces FINE and nine Ounces Allay. The next Years Coinage brought it up to eleven Ounces one penny-wt. FINE and nineteen penny wt. Allay, which, in the following, was again reduced to eleven Ounces FINE and one Ounce Allay, but 2 Eliz. it was fully restored to its Original STERLING Purity, at which it has continued, without any Alteration, to this Day.

NOW, as there was no other Reason for recoining the old Sterling Money than its Waste by Wear and Clipping, and even then it was passable by Weight, (which in those Ages was a common Way) 'tis highly probable that a very considerable Quantity of that Money was remaining at the End of Elizabeth's Reign of which the Doctor has taken no notice at all; and if we allow but HALF a Million for this Article (and surely this cannot be too much, considering the Quantity that, in all probability, was hoarded during the Reigns of Henry and Edward, to prevent Debasement) and add that to the former Account, the Sum total of the Coin at the end of Q. Elizabeth's Reign, must have been, at least, SIX MILLIONS and an HALF, at which, for the Reasons aforesaid, we shall venture to state it.

AS to Dr. Davenant's Rules of POLITICAL ARITH-METICK, of which he boasts so much, and which, he says, was his Guide in the Estimates he made of the National Stock, in the Years 1600, 1660 and 1688, and his Averment that every article might be justified by as plain Demonstration as any Thing of that Nature was capable of; and altho' he was pretty certain of his Cash Articles, at the two last of those Periods, from inspecting the Mint Accounts, (an Advantage which Sir Wm. Petty never enjoy'd) yet he seems to have been in a worse Situation than if he had no Rule at all. His whole system, as far as we can dive into it, is nothing but a Jumble of erroneous and inconfident Principles, devoid of all Foundation and Connection in Nature; No wonder, then, the Conclusions which must necessarily partake of the Quality of his Premisis, are so various and contradictory. Thus his Proportions of the personal Stock, exclusive of Coin, to the Coin alone are in 1600, as $3\frac{1}{4}$th to 1 in 1660 as 3 to 1 and in 1688 to $3\frac{22}{100}$ to 1 nearly; And of the LAND Capital to the COIN, in 1600 as 18 to 1 and in 1688 as 13 to 1 nearly and yet he assigns no Reasons for such remarkable and essential Variations. So again he says, the whole Stock of the Kingdom doubles itself in about 30 Years; whereas the total Super-lucration, i.e. the National Gain over and above the National Expence (which is the only Fund for increasing the National Stock) will not, at 10 per Cent simple Interest, amount, within that Time, to much above one third Part of the Value of the whole Stock of the Nation, as any body who will take the Trouble to go thro' the necessary Calculations, at any one Period of Time, from the beginning of the last Century to this Day, may readily find. In short, all his Estimates, abstracted from Facts, carry such apparent Absurdities on the Face of them, that 'tis amazing any Regard should ever have been paid to any of them; and we are confident, the Reader would think it an Impertinence and Waste of Time to enter farther into Particulars; His facts are the only Things to be depended upon, and when he leaves them, you must leave him, or render yourself ridiculous.

HAVING a little digressed here, in order to supersede the Force of Authority, which too often passes for Argument, to the Prejudice of Truth, and which as often has nothing but Chimaera and Confidence to support it, we shall return to the main Argument, and proceed to enquire what further Practical Uses may be made of the foregoing well-established Principles.

IN the first Place, then, from the Plain Rules laid down, for finding the Annual Increment of Stock, at a Medium, for any Period of Time, where the Quantity of the Coin is ascertained at the Beginning and End of such Period, we have, by the Rule of Proportion, an easy Process of coming at the present annual Increment of the whole Capital Stock of the Kingdom; For the whole Capital being considered as a joint Trading Stock, it must necessarily follow, that the Increments of the respective Branches are proportionally equal, i.e. that the annual Increment of the Cash, Personal and Land Stock, will have the same Ratio to each other as their respective Capitals, and if so, then the present Cash annual Increment will be THREE HUNDRED FORTY FOUR THOUSAND THREE HUNDRED EIGHTY SEVEN POUNDS; the present personal Stock annual Increment (exclusive of the COIN) will be twenty times that Sum, or, SIX MILLIONS EIGHT HUNDRED EIGHTY SEVEN THOUSAND SEVEN HUNDRED FORTY THREE POUNDS: and the present Land annual Increment twelve and one third times that Sum, or FOUR MILLIONS TWO HUNDRED FORTY SEVEN THOUSAND FOUR HUNDRED FORTY ONE POUNDS; making in all ELEVEN MILLIONS FOUR HUNDRED SEVENTY NINE THOUSAND FIVE HUNDRED SEVENTY ONE POUNDS for the annual Augmentation of the whole Capital Stock of the Kingdom. For if FOURTEEN MILLIONS produces ONE HUNDRED SIXTY THOUSAND SEVEN HUNDRED AND FOURTEEN POUNDS annual Increment of Cash (as has been shown to be the case in fact) then the annual Increment of CASH upon THIRTY MILLIONS present CASH STOCK, will be THREE HUNDRED FORTY FOUR THOUSAND THREE HUNDRED EIGHTY SEVEN POUNDS: upon SIX HUNDRED MILLIONS present PERSONAL STOCK, SIX MIL-

LIONS EIGHT HUNDRED EIGHTY SEVEN THOU-
SAND SEVEN HUNDRED FORTY THREE POUNDS
nearly; and upon THREE HUNDRED AND SEVENTY
MILLIONS present LAND CAPITAL, FOUR MILLIONS
TWO HUNDRED FORTY SEVEN THOUSAND FOUR
HUNDRED FORTY ONE POUNDS, as aforesaid, q.e.d.
as may appear by the following Operations.

CASE I

As 14 M. is to   160,714, so is 30 M. to 344,387,
                          30
                        ─────
    14)   4821420   (344,387
                 . . . . .
                 62
                 ──
                 61
                 ──
                 54
                 ───
                 122
                 ───
                 100
                 ───
                  2   Rem.

CASE II

As 14 M. is to   160,714, so is 600 M. to 6,887,743,
                         600
                       ───────
    14)   96428400   (6,887,743
                 . . . . . .
                124
                ───
                122
                ───
                108
                ───
                104
                ──
                 60
                 ──
                 40
                 ──
                 12   Rem.

CASE III

As 14 M. is to   160,714, so is 370 M. to 4,247,441
                              370
                           _____
                           11249980
                           482142
                           _____
14)   59464180   (4,247,441
                           . . . . .
                           34
                           ___
                           66
                           ___
                           104
                           ___
                           61
                           ___
                           58   £11,479,571
                           ___
                           20
                           ___
                        8 Rem.

IF we should prosecute our enquiries further, and attempt
to ascertain the annual Income and Expences of the Kingdom, we have this Principle for our Guide that cannot
greatly mislead us, at least we are sure not to exceed in our
Estimate. The whole CAPITAL of the Kingdom being, in
fact, a Trading Stock, may be reasonably presumed to produce, communibus annis, ten per Cent. That the LAND
CAPITAL does so, and more, is certain, otherwise the
Farmer could never pay his Rent, his Charges in Husbandry,
and maintain his Family; and, I imagine that every Gentleman, who is versed in Trade, will readily admit that the
Personal Stock of the Nation (altho' a considerable Part of it
lies dead and unprofitable) connected with the Labour of
the People, does not come one Jot behind the Land, with
regard to its Annual Profit; and, if so, then by consequence,
the present annual Income of the Kingdom must be a Tenth

Part of the whole Capital, and amount to, at least ONE HUNDRED MILLIONS; from which if we deduct the annual Increase of our Wealth, over and above our Expences, as stated at ELEVEN MILLIONS FOUR HUNDRED SEVENTY NINE THOUSAND FIVE HUNDRED SEVENTY ONE POUNDS, the Remainder, or EIGHTY EIGHT MILLIONS FIVE HUNDRED TWENTY THOUSAND FOUR HUNDRED TWENTY NINE POUNDS, will be the amount of our whole present Expence; And, if the whole Number of the People of GREAT BRITAIN be (as 'tis generally computed) Ten Millions, the aforesaid Sum of EIGHTY EIGHT MILLIONS FIVE HUNDRED TWENTY THOUSAND FOUR HUNDRED AND TWENTY NINE Pounds divided among them all will amount to about EIGHT POUNDS SEVENTEEN SHILLINGS, upon a Medium, for the annual Expence of each Person.

$$100,000,000$$
$$11,479,571$$

$$100) \qquad 8,852042/9$$

THESE Estimates of the annual Income and Expences of Great Britain, compared with those made by Sir Wm. Petty about A.D. 1660, upon different Principles, discover such an Harmony and Agreement, in general, between them, as is no contemptible Proof of their Truth and Exactness, or, at least, of the Modesty of our Computations* and we agree so nearly with the Estimates made, by another Gentleman, of the annual Income of the Nation, and of each Person's Expences, in 1688, calculated upon Sir Wm. Petty's principles, the

* Sir William, from the Number of Inhabitants in England and Wales which he states, about the year 1660, at Seven Millions and their annual Expence at Six Pounds thirteen Shillings and four Pence each, makes, in consequence, the annual Income of the Nation, at that Period to be Forty-Six-Millions and two-thirds of a Million; which is precisely the same Sum as it turns out upon our Principles; and if he had taken Scotland into the Account, as we have done the Number of whose Inhabitants he computes at about a Million, it must have amounted to upwards of Six Millions more, which is an Evidence of the Modesty of our Computations.

former being stated by him at SIXTY ONE MILLIONS
SEVEN HUNDRED TEN THOUSAND SEVEN HUN-
DRED AND FOURTEEN POUNDS, and the latter at
EIGHT POUNDS a Head, that, in the first instance, we
are but FORTY FOUR THOUSAND FORTY EIGHT
POUNDS short, and in the last but SEVENTEEN SHIL-
LINGS per Annum higher, which Variations are in our
Favour.

TO apply this to the Purpose of the present Speculation

THE Facts as stated and proved in the preceding Essay
are these,

The National Debt	About	80,000,000
The National Capital	„	1,000,000,000
The Annual Income	„	100,000,000
The Annual Increment of Stock	„	11,500,000

UPON this View of the Case (which in our Opinion
approaches as near the Truth as the Nature of such an intricate and complicated Subject will admit) it appears that
the National Debt, taking it in round Number, is to the
National Capital but as 1 to 12: to the National Income as 4
to 5; and to the Annual Increment of the National Stock as
7 to 1. Now we appeal to every candid and impartial Judge,
whether that Man may not be justly reputed in most flourishing Circumstances whose Debts do not amount to a twelfth
part of his Capital, or to four fifths of his annual Income and
whose Yearly Profits in Trade will, if appropriated to that
Purpose, actually discharge the whole within the Space of
Seven Years in Simple Interest?

OR to state it in another Light.

THE annual Interest paid by the Government for EIGHTY
MILLIONS at four per Cent, is Three Millions two hundred
thousand Pounds; the Annual National Income has been
shewn to be ONE HUNDRED MILLIONS, or upwards of
thirty that Sum; the Question, then, on this State of the Case,
will be Whether a Man can, with any Propriety, be said to
have an incumbered Estate, whose annual Payment of
Interest, for Money borrowed, is not a Thirtieth Part of his
Yearly Income, or even a Third Part of the Value in Fee of

his annual improved Rents? And that this is the exact State of the Nation, at present, has been shewn in this Essay; as will most evidently appear to any one who will give himself the Trouble to go through the particular Operations.

THE Sum of all is this,

IT has been shewn from Dr. Davenant corrected that the National Cash was in the Year 1600 about SIX MILLIONS and an half; at the recoinage soon after the RESTORATION about FOURTEEN MILLIONS; and at the REVO-LUTION about EIGHTEEN and half Millions; and from these established Facts we have, by just Deductions, esti-mated the present current Cash of the Kingdom to be at least THIRTY Millions.

WE have shown, by just Remarks made on the Condition and Circumstances of People of all Ranks in the Kingdom, from the Peer to the Peasant that the Plate, Jewels, Furni-ture, Equipage and other personal Stock of all Kinds, for State Trade and Consumption, both dead and alive, must be at least twenty times the Value of the Cash Stock in every private Family; and from thence have fairly concluded the whole Personal Estate of the Nation, exclusive of the Coin, to be at least Six Hundred Millions.

WE have shewn, from the present Annual Produce of the Land Tax, into the Exchequer, compared with the well known Rates of Assessment, that the Yearly Rents of all the Houses and Lands in the Kingdom is twelve one third times the Value of the Coin and cannot amount to less than THREE HUNDRED AND SEVENTY MILLIONS; and by adding these several Sums together, have clearly evinced that the present actual Value of the whole Capital Stock of GREAT BRITAIN cannot be less than a THOUSAND Millions.

WE have also shown, that the Proportions which the national Cash Stock, Personal Stock, and Land Stock bear to each other, at present, may reasonably be presumed to have been, in preceding times, nearly the same; so that we cannot greatly err by establishing 1, 20 and $12\frac{1}{3}d.$ as the settled fix'd Ratios to be used in all Computations, of the like Kind; and, upon these Principles, we have proceeded to

estimate the Value of the several Articles above mentioned
at these four Periods, viz. A.D. 1600, 1660, 1688 and 1749;
which, in the first instance, comes out to be TWO HUN-
DRED SIXTEEN MILLIONS and two thirds of a Million,
in the second, four hundred sixty six Millions and two thirds
of a Million; in the Third Six Hundred Sixteen Millions and
two thirds of a Million; and in the last a Thousand Millions;
i.e. the Amount of the whole Capital Stock of the Kingdom
is to the same Amount at the Beginning of the last Century
as four and an half to 1; at the Restoration, as ten to four and
an half; and at the Revolution as ten to six, nearly; Or more
exactly, in 1600 as 1000 to 216⅔ds; in 1660, as 1000 to
466⅔ds; and in 1688, as 1000 to 616⅔ds. That is, in other
Words, and taking it in round Numbers, the Nation is at
present richer than it was in 1600 by SEVEN HUNDRED
EIGHTY THREE MILLIONS; than it was at the RESTO-
RATION, by FIVE HUNDRED THIRTY THREE
MILLIONS; and than it was at the REVOLUTION, by
THREE HUNDRED EIGHTY THREE MILLIONS.

We have shewn you farther, that at this Day, the annual
Increment of the Capital Stock of the Kingdom is near
ELEVEN AND HALF MILLIONS; that the annual In-
come cannot be less than a HUNDRED MILLIONS; that
the National Debt is not a twelfth Part of the national
Capital, nor the Interest of it a thirtieth Part of the national
Income; and that the annual Increment of the national
Stock alone, would, if appropriated and appli'd to that
Purpose, pay off the whole publick Debt, within the Space
of seven Years at Simple Interest. From all these Premises,
then, we think it may be justly concluded, agreeable to our
first Petition, 'that the Nation is so little impaired by the
publick Debt, that it stands at present in as full Vigour both
for Defence and Offence, as it ever did in the most flourishing
Times of any of the Reigns of His Majesty's Royal Predecessors'; and that all the Fears and Clamours, of the weak
and the wicked, raised on this Topick, are destitute of any
real Foundation, in the Nature of Things, and ought not to
give a single Person one Moment's Uneasiness, with Regard
to the prognosticated Consequences.

7 Growth of Steam Power in the Borough of Birmingham, 1780–1838

Period of Erection	Engines		Grinding Flour	Working Metals	Glass Works	Wood Sawing, etc.	Paper Making and Working	Colours, Chemicals, etc.	Clay Grinding	Pumping	Sundries	Void and Removed	High Pressure Engines, included in first and second Columns	
	No.	Horse-Power											No.	Power
1780	1	14	..	..	..	..	..	..	..	..	..	14	..	..
1783	1	25	25	..	..	..	..	..	..	..	..	..	..	..
1787	1	18	..	..	..	..	..	..	..	..	..	18	..	..
1788	1	18	..	..	..	..	..	..	..	..	..	18	..	..
1791	1	14	..	..	..	..	..	..	..	..	..	14	..	..
1792	1	16	..	16	..	..	..	..	..	..	..	..	..	..
1796	2	70	..	24	..	..	..	..	..	46	..	..	..	..
1797	1	24	24	..	..	..	..	..	..	..	..	..	..	..
1798	1	4	..	..	..	..	..	..	..	..	..	4	..	..
1800	1	60	..	60	..	..	..	..	..	..	..	..	..	..
1803	4	184	24	160	..	..	..	..	..	..	..	..	..	..
1804	1	30	..	30	..	..	..	..	..	..	..	..	..	..
1805	1	30	..	30	..	..	..	..	..	..	..	..	..	..
1807	3	151	..	97	4	..	..	..	..	..	..	50	1	4
1808	2	36	..	30	..	..	..	..	..	..	6	..	..	..
1809	4	89	..	83	..	6	..	..	..	..	..	..	1	6
1810	3	18	..	18	..	..	..	..	..	..	..	..	..	..
1811	3	33	..	28	..	..	..	..	5	..	..	..	..	..
1812	3	39	..	39	..	..	..	..	..	..	..	..	1	6
1813	5	82	28	54	..	..	..	..	..	..	..	..	..	..
1814	2	42	..	26	..	16	..	..	..	..	..	..	..	..
1815	1	3	..	..	..	..	..	..	3	..	..	..	..	..
1816	10	101	..	53	..	3	20	..	25	..	..	..	..	..
1817	1	8	..	8	..	..	..	..	..	..	..	..	..	..
1818	3	28	18	4	6	..	..	..	..	..	..	..	..	..
1819	4	67	17	46	4	..	..	..	..	..	..	..	..	..
1820	5	58	16	13	..	..	..	13	..	..	..	16	..	..

Period of Erection	Engines		Grinding Flour	Working Metals	Glass Works	Wood Sawing, etc.	Paper Making and Working	Colours, Chemicals, etc.	Clay Grinding	Pumping	Sundries	Void and Removed	High Pressure Engines, included in first and second Columns	
	No.	Horse-Power											No.	Power
1821	3	55	..	55	..	..	..	..	..	..	..	..	..	..
1822	4	62	..	48	4	..	..	10	..	..	..	..	..	..
1823	2	14	..	..	..	..	14	..	..	..	..	..	..	..
1824	7	103	21	62	8	12	..	..	..	..	..	..	..	..
1825	6	149	..	142	..	7	..	..	..	..	..	..	..	..
1826	13	162	12	93	16	13	..	12	..	..	16	..	..	..
1827	6	164	8	150	..	..	..	..	..	..	6	..	..	..
1828	3	30	..	20	6	..	4	..	..	..	..	..	..	..
1829	5	45	..	22	4	9	..	4	6	..	..	..	..	..
1830	5	53	..	50	..	..	..	..	..	..	3	..	..	..
1831	7	90	40	18	..	12	..	17	..	3	..	..	..	..
1832	12	325	..	65	13	..	6	..	12	200	4	25	..	..
1833	9	61	24	29	..	..	..	4	..	..	4	..	..	..
1834	17	157	..	113	4	22	..	..	6	..	12	..	7	35
1835	24	217	..	159	18	12	..	3	8	..	17	..	13	78
1836	21	274	..	76	..	24	..	..	6	162	6	..	18	97
1837	12	96	..	70	4	..	16	..	..	..	6	..	10	66
1838	18	276	..	164	4	16	..	65	..	..	27	..	14	157
At Work in Dec. 1 '38	240	3595	257	2155	95	152	60	128	38	444	107	159	65	449

Estimated Consumption of Coal by the above Engines, 240 tons per day. Estimated number of Persons employed—Males 5200; Females 1762. Estimated amount of Power hired out, 530 horses.

SOURCE: *Journal of the Statistical Society*, Vol. 2, January 1840.

8 Patrick Colquhoun

AN ATTEMPT TO ESTIMATE THE PUBLIC AND PRIVATE PROPERTY OF THE UNITED KINGDOM[1]

Patrick Colquhoun (1745–1820) was an extremely active publicist; he was a provost of Glasgow and a police magistrate in London, where he wrote factual treatises on the *Police of the Metropolis* (1795) and on *Indigence* (1806). But it was his great statistical manual, the *Treatise of the British Empire*, which rightly became his best-known work; it alone, out of a number of similar exercises published at the time, can bear comparison with Gregory King's extensive calculations of more than a century earlier. While Colquhoun owed something to the previous efforts of Sir F. M. Eden, Henry Beeke, Benjamin Bell and, of course, Pitt, all of whom made assessments of the nation's taxable incomes, many of his estimates appear to have been arrived at independently. The capital estimates, which were quite unique for the time, came to provide the basis for most of the subsequent work in the field. Joseph Lowe in *The Present State of England . . .* (1822) took over many of the estimates without question, while in the next decade Pablo de Pebrer in his *Taxation, Expenditure, Power, Statistics, and Debt of the Whole British Empire* (1833) consciously set out to bring them up to date. Later in the century, when Giffen was at work, they continued to be well regarded. But a basic weakness of Colquhoun's figures, and one that vitiated most nineteenth-century measurement of capital accumulation, was their tendency to identify capital with wealth. As was the case with Andrew Hooke, half a

[1] From *A Treatise on the Wealth, Power, and Resources, of the British Empire . . .* (1814), II.

century before, Colquhoun's intention was to help in countering current fears over the level of the national debt, so that broad definitions suited his purposes; in the process, however, his inclusion of such items as fisheries, household goods and military establishments, diminished the usefulness of his estimates for assessing the capital stock, even assuming that he had correctly calculated the raw data from which the estimates were built up.

In all civilized countries the individuals comprising the body politic are distinguished from the population in savage life by the wealth or property which they possess, and which is more or less rendered secure by the power and efficacy of the Law. In the British dominions this security is more firmly established than perhaps in any country in the world. The protection thus afforded to every species of property, acquired in a course of ages, has given a spring or impetus to industry, which has certainly never been equalled in any other nation or empire in ancient or modern times.

An era has arrived in the affairs of the British Empire, discovering resources which have excited the wonder, the astonishment, and perhaps the envy of the civilized world. The accumulation of property, extensive beyond all credibility, and (during a war of unexampled expence) rapid in its growth beyond what the most sanguine mind could have conceived, renders it an interesting subject of inquiry with a view to discover the nature, extent, and component parts of the property of the British dominions, by which the nation has been placed in so elevated a situation in the scale of Europe.

In contemplating the affairs of nations, it will be found that the same principles and rules will apply as those to which individuals resort on all emergencies, where, in extensive and complicated transactions, recourse is had to an accurate view of the resources in possession and to the means of rendering these resources as productive as possible.

The resources of nations are derived from the productive labour of the people; and this labour is augmented or diminished according to forms of government, and the intelligence, ability, and zeal,—or the want of these qualities in those to whom it is assigned to direct the affairs of states and empires.

When the limited population and territory of the British islands are considered in relation to many other states and kingdoms in the world, it is fair to conclude that, the rapid strides which this nation has made in the course of the last and present century towards wealth and power may fairly be imputed to the form of its government, and the wisdom of its councils.

It is by no means however to be inferred that the government is either in its nature absolutely perfect, or that the councils of this as well as other nations have not erred on many occasions. It is the lot of humanity to err. It is sufficient to say that it possesses advantages over all other governments, and that the purity of those intrusted with the highest offices of the state greatly exceeds those in similar situations in other countries.

It is scarcely necessary to enter into details for the purpose of proving that the prosperity of the British nation has been rapid beyond all example, particularly within the last sixty years, notwithstanding the calamities of our successive wars of unexampled expence. Opposed until recently not only by a most formidable and inveterate enemy, but also through his machinations and the influence of his conquests by all the most powerful nations of Europe; yet with a population which cannot be estimated at more than between seventeen and eighteen millions, this country has stood the shock against a population of more than one hundred millions, while it has possessed itself of all the colonies and territories of the enemy which are not continental, besides annihilating or at least rendering useless the once numerous and powerful navies of all the belligerent powers in Europe.

It becomes an interesting enquiry, by what means these great and extraordinary events have taken place. Who could have supposed that from sixty to seventy millions of money have been raised annually, exclusive of loans, for the expences of the state, in the last three years, with much greater ease than thirty millions could have been raised twenty years ago?—Who could have believed it possible that the surplus property of individuals could have furnished successive loans to government from year to year during the last twenty years to the amount of about £453,617,455 sterling (calculated to the 5th of January, 1813), and that still competitors exist eager to grasp at new loans?—Was it possible to conceive that the nation should be able to sustain a burthen now equal to £22,680,872 sterling additional interest on the national debt since the war of the French revolution first commenced, besides raising a fund during this period, and redeeming the land tax for the reduction of the national debt equal to £156,636,746, and that under all this pressure the increase of individual opulence has been progressive and rapid, while the comforts of the middling and lower classes of the community, if they have not increased, have certainly not diminished?

This paradox can only be solved by attributing it to the progressive and growing opulence of the country. Or in other words, that the surplus savings beyond the actual expenditure of the property, created by the labour of the people in each year, has been more than equal to the demands of government for the exigencies of the state.

Notwithstanding these prominent features, exhibiting in strong colours the power, wealth, and resources of the empire, great uneasiness has been excited in consequence of the rapidity with which the national debt has been increased, under an apprehension that there is a point beyond which the resources of the country cannot be extended, and that a general bankruptcy must ensue.

To discover how far these apprehensions are well or ill founded, it will be here necessary to do that which has never heretofore been done, namely to see what these resources are— of what elements they consist, and to estimate their value upon the same principle as commercial men estimate their stock in trade,—in fine, to examine, as accurately as the nature of the case will permit, the value of that property which is pledged for the security of the national debt and the annual revenue arising from it.

The attempt is bold, and the task is arduous. It is a ground that has not been heretofore at least systematically trod; while in the nature of things accuracy to a point in so extensive and complicated a range is impracticable. Yet if the labour which has been bestowed in the investigation of this extensive and important subject shall be found to approximate to the truth, or shall rather be within the truth (which is what has been throughout the aim of the Author), the advantages resulting from the important details in the interesting Table No. 2, annexed to this Chapter, will be incalculable, since under all the unexampled pressures arising from a long protracted war, generating an enormous public debt, these details will tend in an eminent degree to tranquillize the public mind; producing a confidence in the power and the resources of the country beyond any other nation in the world, while at the same time they tend to cherish a well grounded hope that this great nation is equal to any exigency which may occur in consequence of the complicated and extensive wars which have so long afflicted the world.

It is with nations as it is with individuals who are in the train of acquiring property. At first the progress is slow until a certain amount is obtained, after which, as wealth has a creative power under skilful and judicious management, the accumulation becomes more and more rapid, increasing often beyond a geometrical ratio, expanding in all directions, diffusing its influence wherever talents and industry prevail, and thereby extending the resources by which riches are obtained by communicating the power of acquiring it to thousands, who must have remained without wealth in countries less opulent.

And hence it is, that in proportion to the population of Great Britain and Ireland and the Colonies there will be found a much greater number of individuals possessing wealth than in any other country in Europe—and the result is, that there are more labourers possessing the means of acquiring riches and the power of communicating aid to others who have not yet acquired it.

The insular situation of the British nation, affording great scope for commercial enterprise,—the advantages derived from the salubrity of the climate, and in general from the fertility of the soil, joined to the benefits conferred by the richer and more valuable productions of the tropical colonies, combined with the immense and almost incalculable sources of industry which have burst upon the country by the improvements in manufactures and ingenious machinery,—all contribute in affording profitable employment for the capitals which are in the progress of accumulation; while this industry has acquired, and will continue to acquire, considerable aid from the funding system, which will hereafter be explained in its proper place.

From these combined causes are to be traced the splendid view, which is now attempted to be given, of the public and private property of the British Empire at the present period.

In forming the estimates which are exhibited in the Tables annexed, the ablest writers on this branch of political economy have been consulted, and copious notes have been introduced, calculated to elucidate as far as elucidation has been practicable, the grounds upon which the Author has proceeded.[1] From the paucity however of materials much has been left to the exertion of the mind and to laborious and intricate calculations, where information could not be derived from books or public documents.

As the estimates extend to national and individual property in every quarter of the world where the British flag flies; from such a mass of information brought within so narrow a compass, where every table may be considered as in itself a history, a confident hope is entertained that they cannot fail to prove highly interesting to every British subject, contemplating as he must do the power and resources of the empire with exultation; while to foreign nations it must prove a matter of wonder and astonishment, calculated to produce the most exalted ideas of the wealth, power, and grandeur of the British Empire; since these estimates show

[1] These informative explanatory notes have had to be omitted here.

1st	That the value of landed and other public and private property in	Great Britain and Ireland	in sterling money amounts to	£2,736,640,000
2nd	„	9 Dependencies in Europe	„	£22,161,330
3rd	„	7 Colonies and Settlements in North America	„	£46,575,360
4th	„	14 Colonies and Settlements in the West Indies	„	£100,014,864
5th	„	14 Conquered Colonies in the West Indies	„	£75,220,000
6th	„	4 Settlements in Africa	„	£4,770,500
7th	„	5 Settlements and Colonies in Asia	„	£38,721,090
	Total Colonies and Dependencies	53		£3,009,103,144

8th	That the territory of India under the control and management of the East India Company, when the estimated value of the lands in cultivation is added to the public and private property, cannot amount to less than	£1,072,427,751

Total estimated value of the landed and public and private property of the British Empire in all parts of the world   £4,081,530,895

Of this immense property the Colonies and Dependencies taken from the enemy during the present war, exclusive of ships and other floating property captured since 1792, amount by estimate to £106,917,190! The captures on sea and land may probably amount to fifty or sixty millions more.

Such are the resources which the subjects of His Majesty in every part of the British Empire possess by which property may be acquired. The parent state however enjoys (as she ought to do since she bears the burthen) great advantages over all the dependencies of the Crown; which is rendered manifest by the pecuniary aids which she affords for the exigencies of the State with an ease and facility, and to an extent which astonishes the civilized world.*

If the cause is attentively examined which has produced this extraordinary effect, it will be found in the growing prosperity of the nation, commencing about the year 1787, since which period, but particularly during the last fifteen years, the progress has been most rapid. In agriculture, considerable advances have been made, by new discoveries and improvements in economizing labour and in ameliorating the soil, so as to render it more productive.

In every species of manufacture the improvements have been still more extensive. Ingenious machinery, applicable almost to every purpose of productive industry, have at an enormous expence been erected in every part of the country, not only giving force and efficacy to the labour of man, but in producing valuable articles of commerce from raw materials in many instances of comparatively little value, matured into marketable articles, comprising masses of property to an immense value, created to a considerable extent by inanimated mechanical organizations requiring neither *rest, food,* or *wages.*

Through this medium the national property has acquired a gradual and rapid augmentation, affording collateral aid to agriculture not only by the increased consumption of the produce of the soil, but by the surplus capitals which have been generated by this species of industry and turned to the cultivation and improvement of the land, which has also

* After a war of twenty years, during which period a public debt, funded and unfunded, of £453,617,455 in sterling money has been incurred up to January 1813, in addition to immense sums raised by the War Taxes on Trade and the Property Tax on individuals, estimated during ten years at about £200,000,000 more, the facility with which a loan of £42,000,000 was obtained in 1813, when it might reasonably be supposed the country was exhausted and its resources crippled by the numerous bankruptcies and the obstructions to commercial enterprise, *is truly astonishing*; while it exhibits another strong proof of the vast opulence of the country, and its growing prosperity under every difficulty and distress which the nature and extent of the war had brought upon the people. Within the present year an additional loan of £22,000,000 sterling has been obtained with even greater facility than the former, making in the whole £64,000,000 sterling in the course of the year 1813!

acquired additional impetus from the capitals of individuals, returning yearly from the East Indies and other countries, invested in landed and other property.

In fact, nearly the whole produce of the Colonies and extensive Dependencies of the Crown may be said to center in the parent State. From these and other sources may be traced the vast accumulation of houses built in the metropolis, and other parts of Great Britain and Ireland;* and the vast influx of wealth, arising from improved agriculture, from mines, manufactures, commerce, navigation, and shipping—we may further trace the increased value of the national property in profitable machinery, inland navigations, bridges, docks, and other valuable and productive erections. To which may be added, the vast augmentation of the value of landed property, rendered exceedingly more productive in consequence of the capitals employed in improvements, assisted and stimulated by the new discoveries which have been made in the science of agriculture.

In manufactures the progress has been even more rapid. New improvements and valuable discoveries have given a new and progressive value to these inestimable establishments, which for the last twenty years have added so much to the national wealth.

The increase of wealth is rendered no less manifest by the great augmentation of commercial shipping and the vast capitals employed in navigation, as exhibited in the Tables annexed, being facts well established from public documents, which shew that notwithstanding the exclusion of British shipping from the continental ports of Europe, and the necessity of employing foreign ships in the exports and imports to and from foreign countries, the British shipping, which amounted in 1801 to 1,725,949 tons, had increased to 2,163,094 tons in 1812. Had the trade been open, this in-

---

* According to the Census for Great Britain in 1811, the

number of houses amounted to	2,163,946
And the houses building in Great Britain in 1811 amounts to	18,548
	2,182,494
The houses returned by the Census of 1801	1,937,489
Increase of houses in 10 years	245,005

crease would probably have now been double the present amount.

The immense sums expended in barracks, fortifications, docks, arsenals, ships of war, and military and ordnance stores have greatly augmented the value of the public property, which is estimated on what is presumed to exist at the present time at not above one fourth of the actual cost.

Upon the whole, a confident hope is entertained, that on the strictest examination the aggregate property of the British Empire, amounting to the enormous sum of £4,081,530,895, will be found to fall considerably short of its real value.

It exhibits in glowing colours the proud height to which this great empire has arrived in the scale of nations. It proves incontestably the incalculable resources of the State, and the rapid growth of the wealth of the people. And what is of more importance, the facility and power of rendering this wealth productive to a greater extent than prevails in any other nation in the world.

TABLE No. 2

AN ATTEMPT TO ESTIMATE THE PUBLIC AND PRIVATE PROPERTY IN GREAT BRITAIN AND IRELAND

Being the Result of much Consideration, after consulting the ablest Writers on Political Economy, and the latest Authorities that bear upon the Subject. (1812)

PRODUCTIVE PRIVATE PROPERTY	England and Wales	Scotland	Ireland	Gt. Britain and Ireland
	£ (000's)	£ (000's)	£ (000's)	£ (000's)
Lands cultivated in Grain of all sorts, Grass, Hops, Nurseries, Gardens, etc.	750,400	150,080	300,160	1,200,640
Tithes belonging to the Laity, exclusive of those in possession of the Clergy	80,000	*	*	80,000
Mines, and Minerals	68,000	5,000	2,000	75,000

* The Tithes for Scotland and Ireland are included in the value of the lands.

PRODUCTIVE PRIVATE PROPERTY	England and Wales	Scotland	Ireland	Gt. Britain and Ireland
	£ (000's)	£ (000's)	£ (000's)	£ (000's)
Canals, Tolls, and Timber ..	46,000	2,000	2,000	50,000
Dwelling Houses, not included in the Rent of Lands, including Warehouses, and Manufactories	300,000	30,000	70,000	400,000
Manufactured Goods in progress to maturity, and in a finished state, deposited in Manufactories, Warehouses, and Shops for Sale	100,000	16,000	24,000	140,000
Foreign Merchandise, deposited in Warehouses, Shops, etc. either paid for, or virtually paid by Debts owing to this Country by Foreigners ..	33,000	4,000	3,000	40,000
British Shipping of every description, employed in Trade, including Vessels on the Stocks	20,000	4,000	3,000	27,000
Agricultural Property, consisting of Grain, Hay, Straw, Cheese, Butter, and other Productions of Farms, including Implements of Husbandry	30,000	5,000	10,000	45,000
Animals, viz. Horses, Horned Cattle, Sheep, Hogs, Goats, Asses, Deer, Wild Animals, and Poultry	113,000	20,000	50,000	183,000
Fisheries round the Coasts of Great Britain and Ireland, including inland Fisheries ..	3,000	3,500	3,500	10,000
	£1,543,400	239,580	467,660	2,250,640

UNPRODUCTIVE PRIVATE PROPERTY

Waste Lands at present unproductive, after excluding all such as are incapable of any improvement adequate to the Expence, including Ways and Waters..	82,500	16,500	33,000	132,000

UNPRODUCTIVE PRIVATE PROPERTY	England and Wales	Scotland	Ireland	Gt. Britain and Ireland
	£ (000's)	£ (000's)	£ (000's)	£ (000's)
Household Furniture in Dwelling Houses..	130,000	15,000	40,000	185,000
Wearing Apparel, Idem. ..	16,000	1,600	3,200	20,800
Plate, Jewels, and other Ornamental Articles, in Dwelling Houses..	34,000	3,400	6,800	44,200
Specie in Circulation and hoarded, viz. Gold, Silver, and Copper Coin, including Bank Dollars and Tokens	9,000	2,000	4,000	15,000
	£1,814,900	278,080	554,660	2,647,640
PUBLIC PROPERTY				
Public Buildings, as Palaces, Churches, Hospitals, Prisons, Bridges, etc.	20,000	2,000	5,000	27,000
Public Arsenals, Castles, Forts, and all other places of Defence, with the Artillery, Stores, etc. thereto belonging	12,000	1,000	4,000	17,000
Dock Yards, and all Materials for Shipbuilding and Repairs	—	—	—	10,000
Ships of War, in number about 1000, of which 261 are Ships of the Line, in Employment, including those in Ordinary and building	—	—	—	25,000
Military and Naval Ordnance, and other Public Stores ..	—	—	—	10,000
Totals	£1,846,900	281,080	563,660	2,736,640

AGGREGATE VALUE OF PROPERTY
IN
GREAT BRITAIN AND IRELAND

					£(000's)
Productive Private Property	..	..	..	..	2,250,640
Unproductive, Idem. ..	..	..	..	..	397,000
					2,647,640
Public Property ..	..	..	..	..	89,000
				Total	£2,736,640

SUMMARY RECAPITULATION

	£(000's)	£(000's)
ENGLAND AND WALES—		
Productive Private Property	1,543,400	
Unproductive, Idem	271,500	1,814,900
SCOTLAND—		
Productive Private Property	239,580	
Unproductive, Idem	38,500	278,080
IRELAND—		
Productive Private Property	467,660	
Unproductive, Idem	87,000	554,660
PUBLIC PROPERTY—		
In England and Wales	32,000	
In Scotland	3,000	
In Ireland	9,000	
In common to Great Britain and Ireland, as, the Navy, Military and Ordnance Stores, etc.	45,000	89,000
	Grand Total	£2,736,640

9 Statement of the Income, Expenditure, Debts, and Assets of the Turnpike Trusts in each County of England, and in Wales, during the Year 1836, with the proportion which the Debts bear to the Annual Income, and the Per-Centage Proportion of Unpaid Interest to the Total Debt.

Counties	Income, including Money borrowed	Expenditure, including Debts paid off	Debts	Assets, Arrears of Income	Prop. of Debts, after deducting Assets, to Annual Income	Prop. of Unpaid Interest to Total Debts
	£	£	£	£	No. of Years	Per cent
▌ford	14,021	13,937	56,890	4,562	3·87	23
ks	17,671	16,847	58,630	5,731	2·99	3
ːks	19,258	19,656	60,342	4,195	2·91	27
ꞏnbridge	10,717	11,746	3,726	6,487	3·10	12
ꞏester	64,417	64,285	329,129	12,114	4·92	5
ꞏnwall	27,319	27,410	121,289	4,302	4·28	5
ꞏmberland	15,448	14,568	135,810	1,771	8·67	17
ꞏby	44,810	40,412	432,085	13,713	9·33	22
ꞏon	62,024	62,702	505,333	19,900	7·82	8
ꞏset	22,475	21,914	125,706	7,977	5·23	4
ꞏham	35,756	41,105	138,527	9,353	3·61	2
ꞏ×x	34,109	33,462	32,098	4,564	0·80	nil
ꞏucester	82,144	81,234	390,604	17,715	4·54	7
ꞏnts	27,610	28,590	153,621	10,613	5·18	20
ꞏeford	27,261	27,031	76,673	6,607	2·96	6
ꞏtford	30,257	31,426	68,912	6,171	2·07	9
ꞏtingdon	11,699	11,282	25,167	2,175	1·96	1
ꞏt	71,165	73,729	313,157	22,562	4·09	19
ꞏcaster	154,285	155,348	967,819	26,762	6·09	8
ꞏcester	28,325	27,638	98,355	4,885	3·30	10
ꞏcoln	34,370	39,136	123,347	11,890	3·24	11
ꞏddlesex	98,608	96,508	150,717	6,333	1·46	9
ꞏnmouth	18,805	15,688	97,719	6,398	4·85	4
ꞏfolk	16,016	15,821	61,337	6,122	3·44	3
ꞏthampton	37,990	36,701	142,320	8,614	3·52	26
ꞏthumberland	20,091	22,635	166,641	3,388	8·15	38
ꞏtingham	17,885	18,073	128,887	5,964	6·86	7
ꞏord	24,784	24,826	107,047	9,132	3·95	9

Counties	Income, including Money borrowed	Expenditure, including Debts paid off	Debts	Assets, Arrears of Income	Prop. of Debts, after deducting Assets, to Annual Income	Prop. of Unpaid Interest to Total Debts
	£	£	£	£	No. of Years	Per cent
Rutland	5,804	5,610	11,763	564	1·93	3
Salop	34,784	37,322	130,302	11,418	3·41	3
Somerset	65,078	63,315	350,570	13,548	5·17	6
Stafford	63,527	65,568	298,547	16,992	4·43	20
Suffolk	10,972	12,035	34,277	3,402	2·81	16
Surrey	63,134	63,776	193,295	9,023	2·91	17
Sussex	61,530	54,751	366,612	16,026	5·69	24
Warwick	34,685	34,742	112,838	7,813	3·02	8
Westmorland	7,158	7,084	62,297	1,565	8·48	3
Wilts	38,529	38,349	144,577	12,842	3·41	13
Worcester	42,251	40,837	132,778	8,244	2·94	9
York	182,733	186,632	1,119,363	41,235	5·90	11
Total	1,679,524	1,683,752	8,065,145	392,692	4·56	12
Wales	97,061	96,596	511,986	25,129	5·01	8
Total	1,776,586	1,780,349	8,577,132	417,821	4·59	12

SOURCE: *Journal of the Statistical Society*, Vol. 1, January 1839.

10 G. R. Porter

ON THE ACCUMULATION OF CAPITAL BY THE DIFFERENT CLASSES OF SOCIETY[1]

G. R. Porter (1792–1852) was head of the Statistical Department of the Board of Trade from 1832 and one of the founder members of the Statistical Society of London in the following year. His most famous work, *The Progress of the Nation, in its Various Social and Economical Relations* ... (1836–1843), was the first major attempt to provide the recent economical and social changes that had taken place in Britain with a comprehensive, empirical foundation. As such it stands with Tooke's and Newmarch's *History of Prices* as one of the great statistical achievements of the nineteenth century; indeed these three figures dominated the earliest years of the London Statistical Society. Porter, in particular, was responsible for the first organized efforts to bring regular economic and social information to the attention of government. He was also a convinced free trader, a close associate of James Wilson, the founder-editor of *The Economist,* and one of that influential group who propagated a belief in the essential harmony of economic interests under a regime of laissez-faire during the 1840s and early 1850s.[2] This was the background to Porter's article on the accumulation of capital which, in this respect, was similar to an earlier pamphlet of his entitled *The Effect of the Restrictions on the Importation of Corn* ... (1839). He was also responsible for translating the works of Bastiat, the prominent French free-trader, into English. Clearly underlying Porter's findings with regard to capital accumula-

[1] *Quarterly Journal of the Statistical Society of London*, Sept. 1851.
[2] See S. Gordon, 'The London Economist and the High Tide of Laissez-Faire', *Journal of Political Economy*, LXIII (1955).

tion is the belief that free trade not only ensured continued economic progress for the community as a whole, but that its unfettered operation did not in fact result in an unjust distribution of income and capital. Yet while his analysis was plainly important in seeming to provide a factual basis for the doctrine of social harmony, it also shows how the concept of accumulation as saving and saving as the necessary requisite for the creation of capital, was as much a part of the classical statistician's equipment as it was of the theorist's. In *The Progress of the Nation* . . . , Porter had included a section on Accumulation, with chapters discussing the detrimental effects of heavy public expenditure and itemizing the national capital under real and personal property, and public and commercial (including industrial) investment. But the data provided were largely based on stamp and probate duty returns and the statistics of savings institutions. There is little attempt to show what the structure of the nation's capital looked like, or in what ways and at what rate it had changed in the previous half-century. As Ashley remarked, it was a 'prolonged statistical paean of triumph over the results of growing enlightenment. The blessings of the new era having thus been displayed, it might seem as if it were hardly worth while to learn anything more about the past'.[1] By the time of the paper on accumulation of capital, Porter's findings depended even more completely on the still narrow range of official statistics.

Among the advantages attendant upon the collection and registration of statistical records, perhaps the most important is found in the assistance which they afford for the confirmation or correction of opinions, upon matters that from time to time agitate the public mind, and thus are apt to influence the progress of legislation and to affect the condition of society.

Among such opinions, there is one which is confidently

[1] W. J. Ashley, 'A Survey of the Past History and Present Position of Political Economy', *Essays in Economic Method, 1860–1913* (1962), ed. R. L. Smythe, XII, p. 238.

held by a great number of persons—it might perhaps be said by a majority of those whose word can have any authority upon such a subject—namely, that there is and has for some time been a constant tendency under the social institutions which generally prevail in this and in the other more advanced countries of Europe, for wealth to be accumulated in a fewer number of hands, or, to use a common mode of expression, that the rich are continually becoming richer, and the poor poorer, and that this is especially the case in England. It must be needless to add that such a belief, if generally held, is calculated to create among the people a wide-spread discontent with the order of things under which that result is experienced; and that every benevolent mind which may have arrived at such a conclusion, must be anxious to find a remedy for it. The bare idea of such a condition of society could not be other than distressing, and if there were any true grounds for believing in its existence, we could not too early, nor too strenuously, set ourselves to reform our institutions, and to bring them more into agreement with the better feelings of our nature. This subject having recently been forced upon my consideration in a manner which indicated the existence of a conviction to the effect already stated, on the part of several men whose opinions are deserving of the highest respect, I have been led to quit in regard to it the region of mere opinion, and to enter upon the examination of facts with a view to the confirmation of such fears, or to their rejection, if happily I should find myself justified in adopting the latter result.

The sources of information bearing upon this interesting social question which are open to us are not many. To avoid, as far as possible, all question concerning their accuracy, I shall confine myself in this examination to documents stamped with official authority.

The statement which I shall first bring forward will serve only to show that there has been, and continues to be, a power of saving on the part of the working classes in this country. It does not pretend to afford any comparison between the accumulations of different classes.

The number of depositors and the amount of deposits in

savings banks in the different divisions of the United Kingdom, on the 20th November, 1830, were—

England	367,812	depositors	£12,287,606	deposits
Wales	10,204	,,	314,903	,,
Ireland	34,201	,,	905,056	,,
Total	412,217	,,	£13,507,565	,,

On the 20th November, 1848, the number and amount of
depositors and deposits were—

England	899,606	depositors	£24,985,730	deposits
Wales	21,195	,,	692,495	,,
Ireland	50,024	,,	1,355,801	,,
Total	970,825	,,	£27,034,026	,,
Scotland	86,056	,,	1,080,110	,,
	1,056,881	,,	£28,114,136	,,

showing an increase during 18 years in England, Wales, and
Ireland, of 558,608 depositors, and £13,536,461 deposits.

A closer examination of the accounts of savings banks will
show that the deposits in England, Wales, and Ireland, proportioned to the population, amounted—

In 1831, to 12s. 8d. per head   In 1841, to 19s. 10d. per head
  1836, to 16s. 4d. ,,   1848, to 20s. 11d. ,,

In Scotland the deposits were—

  In 1836   7d. per head
    1841   4s. 8d. ,,
    1848   7s. 5d. ,,

The largest amount of these savings occurred in 1846, when
they reached—

In England	£26,759,817
Wales	674,657
Scotland	1,383,866
Ireland	2,924,910
	£31,743,850

being equal to 24*s*. per head of the population of England, Wales and Ireland, and 10*s*. 1*d*. per head of that of Scotland. The diminution in 1847 and 1848 is clearly the result of the high prices of provisions, and consequent falling-off in wages, caused by the potato rot and its attendant circumstances; and these are too recent, and too strongly impressed on the memories of all who hear me, to render it necessary to offer any further explanation concerning them.

The comparative smallness of the deposits in Scotland arises from two causes. First, the system of allowing interest upon very small sums deposited in private and joint-stock banks; and secondly, the more recent connection of savings banks with the government in that division of the kingdom. There is no reason for supposing that the labouring classes of Scotland are less saving than those of England or Ireland; and presuming that the disposition to save is naturally as great in each part of the kingdom, the workmen of Scotland have, until very recently, had a much stronger incentive than their English fellow subjects to set aside a part of their earnings, because of the absence of any legal provision for the wants of their old age, and against the occurrence of sickness or accident.

The next test to which I would direct attention varies essentially from that afforded by the progress of savings banks; inasmuch as it excludes all evidence of present saving or accumulation, while it offers a strictly comparative view of such saving as between different classes of the community.

The accounts furnished to parliament of the number of persons entitled to dividends upon portions of the public debt, divide the fund-holders into ten classes, according to the amount to which they are so entitled. The figures shown in the table overleaf exhibit the numbers in each class as they stood on the 5th April and 5th July of the years 1831 and 1848 respectively.

It will be seen that there has been a very large addition between 1831 and 1848 to the number of persons receiving 5l. at each payment of dividends, and a small increase upon the number receiving between 5l. and 10l. while, with the exceptions of the largest holders—those whose dividends exceed 2,000l. at each payment, and of whom there has been

	1831			1848		
	April	July	Total	April	July	Total
Not exceeding						
£5	29,414	58,756	88,170	53,985	42,430	96,415
10	14,962	29,828	44,790	25,814	19,123	44,937
50	33,816	64,504	98,320	54,500	41,525	96,025
100	8,961	16,733	25,694	13,069	11,393	24,462
200	5,104	9,668	14,772	6,911	6,971	13,882
300	1,554	2,973	4,527	1,918	2,114	4,032
500	964	1,926	2,890	1,189	1,458	2,647
1000	445	953	1,398	540	682	1,222
2000	134	278	412	155	173	328
Exceeding £2000	66	106	172	97	80	177
	95,420	185,725	281,145	158,178	125,949	284,127

an increase of 5—every other class has experienced a considerable decrease in its numbers. Thus:—

Persons receiving under £5 increase 8,245 or 9·35 per cent

,,	£5	and under	10	,,	147	0·33	,,
,,	10	,,	50	decrease	2,295	2·33	,,
,,	50	,,	100	,,	1,232	4·79	,,
,,	100	,,	200	,,	890	6·02	,,
,,	200	,,	300	,,	495	10·93	,,
,,	300	,,	500	,,	243	8·41	,,
,,	500	,,	1000	,,	176	12·59	,,
,,	1000	,,	2000	,,	84	20·38	,,
,,		above	£2000	increase	5	2·90	,,

As respects this last class, those receiving above 2000l. at each payment of dividends, it must be borne in mind that it includes Insurance offices, which generally have large investments in the public funds, and whose accumulations of this kind are almost certain to increase from year to year, a fact which makes it somewhat surprising that the number has not been augmented in a greater degree than is shown by the tables. A diminution of more than 8 per cent, in the numbers receiving between 300l. and 500l.; of 12½ per cent of those receiving between 500l. and 100l., and of more than 20 per cent among holders of stock, yielding dividends between 1000l. and 2000l. would seem conclusively to show, that at least as respects this mode of disposing of accumulations, there is not any reason to believe that the already rich are acquiring greater wealth at the expense of the rest of the community.

The branch of this inquiry to which my attention was next directed, was that which is elucidated by returns showing the sums assessed to the Income-tax in respect of income derived from trades and professions, in 1812, compared with the like returns in 1848, excluding from the former period the incomes below 150 which under existing law are allowed to pass untaxed.

The total amount thus assessed, after deducting exemptions, was—in 1812, 21,247,621l. while in 1848, the amount was 56,990,223l., showing an increase in 36 years, of 35,742,602l. or 168·21 per cent, being at the rate of 4·67 per cent yearly, an increase very nearly three-fold greater than the increase during the same period of the population of that part of the United Kingdom which is subject to the Income-tax.

The object now in view is not that of showing the increased wealth of the country at large, but in what degree such increase has been experienced among different classes of the people, or occasion might be taken to express the satisfaction which every Englishman must feel at this unmistakeable evidence of the material well-being and continued progress of our country, which feeling is shown by the results to which I thus venture upon calling attention, to be unalloyed by any well-founded fears, concerning the oft-alleged deteriorated condition of the bulk of the people.

The returns examined give the sums assessed to Income-tax in various classes, and for the purposes of the present examination, I have distinguished the incomes thus given:—

Between £150 and £500   Between £1000 and £2000
   „   £500 „ £1000   „   £2000 „ £5000
            and above £5000

In the first of these classes, viz. between 150l. and 500l. per annum, I find a positive increase in 1848, of 13,724,949l.

upon the incomes assessed in 1812. In the next class, embracing incomes between 500l. and 1000l. per annum, the increase since 1812, has been 5,100,540l. On incomes between 1000l. and 2000l. the increase has amounted to 4,078,095l. In the next class, including incomes between 2000l. and 5000l., there is an increase of 4,059,743l. while in the highest class, which includes all incomes above 5000l. per annum, the increase is found to be 8,779,275l. Comparing the lowest with the highest of these classes, it is shown that the increase has been greater in the lowest class by 4,945,674l. or 56·33 per cent.

The returns relating to the property-tax which was replaced in 1815, do not show the number of persons assessed in each class, as is the case with recent returns, and as, under the influence of a childish feeling of exultation, the House of Commons was led to follow up the vote which repealed the tax in 1815, by another vote which directed the destruction of all the documents connected therewith, it is not possible now to make any precise comparison between the two periods in this respect.

By means of the information given in the return for 1848, we are able to ascertain the average amount of the incomes, during that year, of individuals in each of the foregoing classes, and assuming that the average in each of the same classes, was the same in 1812 as now, we may arrive at a reasonable approximation to the actual number then assessed, and to the increase since made to the number in each class.

Incomes			Number in 1812	Number in 1848	Increase
	£	£			
Between	150 and	500	30,732	91,101	60,369
,,	500 ,,	1,000	5,334	13,287	7,953
,,	1,000 ,,	2,000	2,110	5,234	3,124
,,	2,000 ,,	5,000	1,180	2,586	1,406
,,	5,000 ,,	10,000	—	788 ⎫	—
,,	10,000 ,,	50,000	409	371 ⎬	772
,,	50,000 ,,	upwards	—	22 ⎭	—
			39,765	113,389	73,624

The only remaining documents bearing an official character, to which recourse can be had in order to throw light upon this subject, are the returns made from the office of the Commissioners for Inland Revenue, showing the sums upon which probate duty has been paid in respect of personal property left by persons deceased. Considerable reliance may be placed on the accuracy of these returns which, at least in England, include all cases where the property left is of any value, which would make it worth the while of survivors to question the propriety of its distribution. The accounts will, at all events, be strictly comparative between one period and another, since any possible motives which might lead to the evasion of the probate duty will have been equally operative at all times. The growth of the capital thus subject to probate duty is truly remarkable. Stated at intervals of five years beginning with the present century, it has been as follows:—

1801	£3,541,931	1826	£31,024,593
1806	7,039,031	1831	39,532,397
1811	14,757,420	1836	41,768,806
1816	24,073,456	1841	41,476,521
1821	33,023,060	1848	44,348,721

After making a liberal allowance for evasion of the tax in the early years following its first imposition in 1797, and for the collection of arrears in 1848, the increase during less than half a century, of property thus brought under the operation of the probate duty is such as must strike us with astonishment. Our present business, however, is with the comparative amount of estates in different classes, for which purpose a calculation has been made of their value in 1833, the earliest year for which the returns enable us to make the same, and in 1848.

The amount assessed on estates amounting to various sums up to £1,500 was—

| In 1833 | £4,692,825 |
| 1848 | 5,423,200 |

Increase £730,375 or 15·56 per cent

On estates between £1,500 and £5,000 the amounts were—

| In 1833 | £6,821,750 |
| 1848 | 7,450,000 |

Increase   £628,250 or 9·21 per cent

Between £5,000 and £10,000, the difference has been—

| In 1833 | £5,155,500 |
| 1848 | 6,000,000 |

Increase   £844,500 or 16·38 per cent

From £10,000 to £15,000, the amounts were—

| In 1833 | £4,258,000 |
| 1848 | 4,529,000 |

Increase   £271,000 or 6·36 per cent

The estates between £15,000 and £30,000 were estimated—

| In 1833, at | £5,760,500 |
| 1848 | 6,822,000 |

Increase   1,061,500 or 18·42 per cent

Above £30,000, the valuations were—

| In 1833 | £10,637,500 |
| 1848 | 10,757,500 |

Increase   £120,000 or 1·13 per cent

It may reasonably be thought, that the calculation of the value of estates in the various classes is liable to disturbance from year to year, and especially as respects the higher amounts, the number of persons dying in any one year and leaving very large fortunes, being necessarily limited. It would have called for a laborious calculation, and have occupied a longer time than I could well afford, to go through the examination of the official returns year by year, from 1833, to the present time. That such an examination would not, however, much (if at all) disturb the result already shown, may be safely inferred from the fact, that the amount of probate duty received during that period upon all wills where the property has amounted to 30,000l. and upwards, has not increased, but on the contrary has rather diminished. Dividing the 16 years from 1833 to 1848, into equal periods of 4 years each, and ascertaining the average duty paid on estates of 30,000 and upwards in each year of such division, it appears, that the sum received in the 4 years

1833 to 1836,	averaged	£238,306
1837 „ 1840,	„	230,388
1841 „ 1844,	„	229,162
1845 „ 1848,	„	223,962

while the average receipts from the probate duty generally have been steadily and progressively advancing with the increasing wealth of the country.

Having thus examined all the official returns which afford means for arriving at the truth upon this really important subject, we observe the most perfect agreement in their results; and it cannot but be satisfactory to every one to find, that the fears entertained and expressed by many, as to the probable disappearance of the middle classes from among us, are unfounded; that it is far from being true that the rich are growing richer and the poor are becoming poorer; but on the contrary, those who occupy a middle station, (perhaps the safest station as regards personal respectability, and that which offers the surest guarantee for the progress and continued well-being of the country) are progressively increasing in number and in the proportion which they bear relatively to the population of the kingdom.

11 Sir Robert Giffen

RECENT ACCUMULATIONS OF CAPITAL IN THE UNITED KINGDOM

The career and activities of Sir Robert Giffen (1837–1910) closely resemble those of Porter before him, whose civil service background and concern with the formulation of economic policy he shared. Giffen made important statistical contributions to two of the most widely discussed policy questions of the 1870s and 1880s—the condition of the working classes and the debate on the gold standard, of which he was a staunch defender. His most influential works were his *Essays in Finance* (1886) and *The Growth of Capital* (1889), the latter being the culmination of his attempt to chart the progress of the national wealth over the previous century. Giffen's first major effort at assessing the accumulation of capital, which he clearly regarded as a product of industrialization and a measure of the national progress which accompanied it, is reprinted below.[1] His capital estimates for the years 1856, 1875 and 1885 were later continued by F. W. Hirst, the editor of *The Economist*, for 1895, 1905 and 1909. As with most of the estimates that have been considered, the level of accuracy that was regarded as reasonable, and indeed feasible, given the quality of statistical information, was much lower then than now. Giffen, who entertained few doubts about the underlying strength of the Victorian economy, was more concerned with providing a broad indication that the growth of capital in his own day had exceeded anything known in the recent past. For the accuracy of specific figures, he relied very largely on the labours of others, especially Leone Levi and Dudley Baxter, and on his own familiarity

[1] *Journal of the Statistical Society,* XLI (1878).

with the revenue data. Like all nineteenth-century inquiries into the growth of capital before his time, the lack of any official necessity for reliable figures on this economic category meant that Giffen could only avail himself of the income tax returns in order to capitalize property incomes. For those types of property not covered by the statistics, the estimates were crude in the extreme. Another possible method of assessing the national wealth was to make use of the estate duty returns, and probate and succession statistics; this was first done by W. J. Harris in a paper to the Royal Statistical Society in 1894, but the problem remained that a multiplier to the amount bequeathed still had to be decided on. M. G. Mulhall was one of the first to move away from income statistics and to use output and sales data for similar purposes.

I. Introduction

The members of this Society will readily understand that the subject of this paper is not one on which very exact statements are possible. It would only be by a careful inventory of the national wealth made on a specified date by competent valuers, with all the appliances of a national census and ordnance survey at their command, that a near approximation to an absolutely correct account could be obtained; and it would only be by comparing two such statements at different dates that we could get a similarly exact account of the increase or decrease in a given period. That any such valuation is ever likely to be made in any country may well be doubted. The minuteness of inquiry which would be needed to avoid cross entries, the obstacles presented by the difficulty of finding sufficiently numerous and competent valuers, and by the opposition of individual owners of property, the doubt which would exist about even the best valuation, owing to the frequency and magnitude of the mistakes which are discovered when valuations are brought to the test of actual sales, are all reasons against the attempt at any such valuation. In the United States, it is true, such valuations are apparently attempted for the purpose of State taxation, and there is a valuation at every census, but it is quite certain that no small amount of personal property escapes the notice of the valuers, and the result is unsatisfactory. Even if such valuations could be made at given dates, comparisons between the valuations at two different dates would be liable to be thrown out by changes in the interval in the level of prices through the increase and decrease of money, changes in the instruments and forms of credit, which alter the effectiveness of the same amount of money, and changes in the amount of credit itself, apart from the instruments it uses. In the United States, for instance, it would be very important in comparing the valuations of 1860 and 1870, to allow for the depreciation of the standard in the interval, through the large increase of paper money. These are all reasons for being content with approximations only in such a question, and for treating the whole subject with the utmost care and caution. They must also be my excuse in part for avoiding anything like elaboration and minute treatment of certain points. My object is not to treat the subject exhaustively, but rather to bring together and continue certain well known data which have been made use of in similar inquiries previously, and which will justify some broad conclusions, although a great deal must be left in doubt.

The uses of such an inquiry, if conclusions sufficiently trustworthy are obtainable, are obvious enough. It is one of the means of taking stock of national progress or the reverse. We compare at different times the numbers of the population and the amounts of crime and pauperism in a country as some test of its moral progress; or the numbers of the population and particulars of certain home and foreign trades, or of the consumption of certain articles, as a test of material progress. In the same way we may compare the population at different times with the accumulated wealth or the rate of increase of population with the rate of increase of wealth as a test of progress, partly moral and partly material. The particular advantage of this last comparison will also be that it answers directly some important public questions as to what the margin of taxation is in a country, and whether and how much it is increasing or diminishing. There are other questions, as we shall see, on which such inquiries throw light, but the direct information to be expected as to the increase or decrease of wealth, and as to national resources and burdens, may be kept primarily in view.

II. The Present Valuation of the United Kingdom

Before estimating what the recent accumulations have been, it will be expedient to have some view of what the existing capital or property is. We can then compare this sum with similar estimates at former periods, and the rate of increase apparent with such indirect evidence as we may procure as to what the rate of increase must have been.

The most convenient basis for such a proceeding appears now to be the income tax assessments. This is the plan adopted by a writer in the *Economist* in 1863 (see *Economist*, December, 1863), who is believed to be an eminent member of this Society, and whose contributions on this head have, at any rate, obtained wide circulation and acceptance. The method is to discriminate as far as possible in these returns the different sources of income, capitalize these at a suitable number of years' purchase, and then make an allowance or conjecture for the capital of the income not liable to income tax or which otherwise escapes assessment, and for capital which is not treated in the income tax returns as income yielding. The result, up to a point, if we proceed with care, is apparently trustworthy enough. We are quite sure in the first place of the existence of the income returned, whatever balance unreturned there may be; we can be tolerably safe also in not assigning too high a number of years' purchase to the particular descriptions of property; we can arrive in this way at a minimum sum, which cannot be more than the actual property in the country, though it may be much under the true amount. The conjecture as to the remainder may also be of such a kind as to command some confidence in its not being excessive.

Proceeding in this way, we find that the gross annual value of the income tax assessments in the year ended 31st March, 1875, the latest year for which we have particulars, was 571 millions. The details under each schedule for the United

Kingdom since 1853, when Ireland was subjected to the income tax, and for Great Britain previous to that date, will be found in one of the tables in the Appendix; but for the present purpose we must discriminate even more minutely than by schedules. Schedules A and D in particular require to be analysed. Various returns of the Inland Revenue Department have of late years enabled us to do this as to 'lands' and 'houses' under Schedule A, and 'mines,' 'iron-works,' 'railways,' 'canals,' 'gasworks,' 'quarries,' and what are called 'other profits' under Schedule D. These returns are also summarized in one of the tables in the Appendix.[1] Still more a return, printed in the Nineteenth Report of the Inland Revenue Department (Appendix, p. xviii), gives a more minute classification of Schedule D. Using these sources of information, I have drawn up a table (p. 184), showing the amount of income in the property and income tax returns for 1874–5, which is presumably derived from capital, the number of years' purchase in each case at which it appears safe to capitalize the income, and the approximate amount of capital thus deduced, adding an estimate for the remaining property and capital of the country.

The first point I would observe upon in explanation of this table, is the proportion between the income returned to the income tax and the amount here capitalized. The income assessed, as has been stated, is 571 millions, and the amount now capitalized is 378 millions. The difference is 183 millions, and is accounted for (1) by the large amount of the income from trades and professions under Schedule D which is not capitalized. The total income is 175 millions, and the amount capitalized is 35 millions, or only one-fifth, leaving 140 millions, which is not considered to be derived from capital; (2) by the deduction from Schedule C of the amount of the permanent charge of our own national debt in 1875–6, viz., 21,737,000l.; and (3) by the omission of Schedule E, amounting to 32,540,000l. These three sums make up the 183 millions of difference between the total income assessed to the income tax and the amount which is treated as derived from capital. As regards the first of these deductions, I have been guided by

[1] This Appendix has had to be excluded here.

A. Amount of Income in Income Tax Returns, derived from Capital, Number of Years' Purchase at which the same may be Capitalized, and Approximate Amount of Capital; together with Estimate of remaining Income and Capital in the Country.

(ooo's omitted in amount columns)

	Income	Years' Purchase	Capital
	£		£
Under Schedule A—			
Lands	66,911	30	2,007,330
Houses..	94,638	15	1,419,570
Other profits	883	30	26,490
Schedule B—			
(Farmers' profits)	66,752	10	667,520
Schedule C—			
(Public funds less home funds)	20,767	25	519,175
Under Schedule D—			
Quarries	916	4	3,664
Mines	14,108	4	56,432
Ironworks	7,261	4	29,044
Gasworks	2,630	20	52,600
Waterworks	1,869	20	37,380
Canals, etc.	1,007	20	20,140
Fishings	207	20	4,140
Market tolls, etc.	842	20	16,840
Other public companies	25,647	15	384,705
Foreign and colonial securities, etc.	6,836	15	102,540
Railways in United Kingdom	26,215	25	655,375
Railways out of United Kingdom	1,330	20	26,600
Interest paid out of rates, etc.	2,647	25	66,175
Other profits	1,120	20	22,400
Trades and professions—one-fifth of total income of 175 millions	35,000	15	525,000
Total under income tax	377,586	—	6,643,120
Trades and professions omitted, 20 per cent of amount assessed, or 35 millions, of which one-fifth is	7,000	15	105,000
Income of non-income tax paying classes derived from capital	60,000	5	300,000
Foreign investments not in Schedules C or D	40,000	10	400,000
Movable property not yielding income, e.g. furniture of houses, etc., works of art, etc. ..	—	—	700,000
Government and local property, say	—	—	400,000
	484,586	—	8,548,120

the practice of Mr. Dudley Baxter, whose great loss to the study of statistics we have still to regret. In his paper on 'National Income', which was read exactly ten years ago to-night to this Society, he stated: 'Trades and professions require working capital, the interest on which, in the opinion of competent judges, amounts to one-fifth of their gross income.' Perhaps we should credit 'trades and professions' with a larger working capital, but I should be willing in such a matter to be guided by so high an authority, while I have been desirous at every point to avoid too high an estimate.

As regards the second deduction, it will only be proper, I think, that in such a computation as this, we should not reckon the national debt twice over, and that would be the effect of our capitalizing the whole of Schedule C. The national debt is a mortgage upon the aggregate fortune of the country. As we may assume it to be practically all held at home, we may reckon up our whole estate without deducting the debt, whereas we should have to deduct it if it were held by foreigners; but while we do not deduct the debt from the total of our estate, neither can we add it without falling into error.

As regards the third deduction, the whole of Schedule E, there can be little question. Schedule E consists eo nomine of salaries, pensions, and annuities, and is not earned by capital. Perhaps we should deduct the capital value of pensions and annuities on the same principle that we omit the capital value of the interest of the debt; but as pensions and annuities are payments in the nature of salaries, though for past not present services, it would perhaps be unfair to treat them as dead weight and a mortgage on the national resources. The amount in any case would not much affect the aggregate income, which would still be very large.

The next point I would draw attention to is the number of years' purchase of the principal items of income. I do not think anything need be said in explanation of the estimate for the largest item of all, viz., thirty years' purchase as the rate for capitalizing land. Some may think that even a greater number of years' purchase might have been employed; but we must again carefully guard against excessive figures.

The estimate for houses, again, will be considered, I trust, very moderate. The same number of years' purchase was employed for some calculations in the last census report, although other authorities have reckoned twenty years' purchase. I should say that at the present time twenty years' purchase would not be too high, though I hesitate to take so high a number of years, especially as the figures are to be used in comparison with former periods, when house property may not at all times have commanded so great a number of years' purchase as it does now. At any rate, by taking a low number of years, we avoid difficult questions about deductions for repairs and the like, and, in a question of accumulation, the difference between the cost price of building houses and the sums at which we capitalize the income from them.

The next large item, that of farmers' profits, is taken at ten years' purchase only. The resulting total is rather less than 700 millions, which again is less than the value of the three years' gross produce of our agriculture, which is estimated, I believe, by the best authorities at 250 millions annually. Whether this figure is sufficient for farming capital as distinguished from that of the landlord, it will be for those well acquainted with the subject to judge. I have been desirous again to take a low figure.

Coming to the next item, Schedule C, here again I believe there will be no question of the propriety of twenty-five years' purchase. Looking at the price of Indian securities and Colonial Government loans, the income from which, no doubt, forms a large part of Schedule C, exclusive of home funds, we can hardly be far wrong in reckoning that the capital invested in these securities brings in on the average about 4 per cent.

Of the remaining items little need be said. The estimates of twenty-five years' purchase for railways, twenty years' purchase for gas works and water works, four years' purchase for mines, ironworks, and the like can in no case, I should think, be thought excessive. The same with the estimate of fifteen years' purchase for miscellaneous public companies, which would include banks, telegraph companies, insurance companies and the like; and with the estimate of fifteen years' purchase for that small portion of the income of trades and professions which is considered to be derived from capital. By speaking of a fifth of trade and professional income as being interest on capital, we in fact imply that only a usual or legal rate of interest is considered to be derived from capital, and the remainder of the income is due to professional exertions. In this view we should capitalize the trade and professional income derived from capital at perhaps twenty years purchase, and we are therefore moderate in capitalizing at fifteen years' purchase only.

There will be more doubt, perhaps, about the last five items, where we have not the advantage of working from the income tax assessments, and which I have put in a smaller type than the rest of the table to distinguish the difference of basis in the estimate. But we cannot avoid making an estimate of some kind in these cases. The first case, that of trade and professional incomes, not returned under Schedule D, which I estimate to be 20 per cent of what is returned, is, unfortunately, as we all know from the Inland Revenue Reports, a 'true bill.' In this category a certain amount of income liable to be taxed, does escape the officials of the Inland Revenue Department. The loss in this way has been estimated as high as one-third; Mr. Dudley Baxter reckoned it at 16 per cent, from which the present estimate of 20 per cent does not vary materially. I have capitalized this income at the same number of years' purchase as the similar income returned under Schedule D.

The next item, that of the income of the classes who are not charged to income tax derived from capital, is necessarily very conjectural. Mr. Dudley Baxter considered this capital so small that it might be disregarded. Perhaps this would be going too far, considering the large amounts which must be invested in workmen's tools, and also the large number of small retail dealers there are throughout the country, the costermongers, greengrocers, and the like, who have all some capital, but who cannot be got hold of by tax collectors, or whose incomes are really under the minimum. Taking the income of the non-income tax paying classes at about 600 millions, which is about the amount, if we apply Mr. Dudley

Baxter's method of estimating the nation's income at the present time, I have reckoned a tenth as derived from capital, and capitalized at five years' purchase only. The sum thus obtained is again a small one in comparison with the aggregate.

The next item, that of foreign investments, not included in Schedules C and D, will perhaps excite more question. I have put the income thus omitted at 40 millions and capitalized it at ten years' purchase only, which I believe to be underestimated. That there is something omitted is evident from the small amount of income from foreign investments which is dealt with in Schedules C and D. The sums are:—

(ooo's omitted)

	£
Schedule C, less home funds	20,767
Foreign and colonial securities and possessions, and other profits (Cases 4 and 5 under rules in Schedule D to Act 5 and 6 Vict., cap. 35) ..	6,836
Railways out of United Kingdom	1,330
Total	28,933

Now, it is impossible to believe that this 29 millions is the total income derived from the investment of British capital abroad. One has only to go over a stock and share list, like that of the 'Investor's Manual,' jot down the capital of the foreign issues brought out in this country, and which are wholly or mainly held here, to perceive that there is something wrong. We have also to consider that there is a large British capital invested abroad privately, through mercantile houses having dependent houses abroad, through insurance companies doing business abroad, through Anglo-colonial banks receiving deposits here and investing them abroad. In a table in the Appendix I have attempted a computation of the income from the visible part of this great capital. The result is that we cannot put at less than 65,000,000l. the income so derived, leaving out of account altogether the investments of private capital, which we know to be very large. In what way the income tax authorities are to get at the income which now escapes them, it would be out of place here to consider, but apart from the evidence above adduced, I believe I shall be confirmed by those who know the city, in the opinion that much income comes home from abroad which is not returned to the income tax authorities. These estimates fully warrant me in setting down 40 millions as the foreign income omitted from the income tax returns.

The next item on the list, that of movable property not yielding income, such as pictures, works of art, furniture of houses, old china, etc. is put at the capital sum of 700 millions, which is half the amount of the capitalized value of houses. Porter estimates a third for this item in his 'Progress of the Nation', but considering the material advance since his time, I do not think we can be far wrong in placing the contents of houses at something like half the value of the houses themselves. In any case, if we valued the houses at twenty years' purchase, as some authorities do, one-third of the capital sum so arrived at would come to about the figure here stated. My own impression is, that the figure is under the mark, although I have stated it in preference to using a larger figure, in order to have former precedent in my favour.

The last item of all, that of the value of property belonging to Government and local authorities, is necessarily very speculative. There is no property, however, which ought more properly to come into such a valuation. It is the property of the community which is enjoyed in common, and the possession of which has often been bought out of taxes. It includes the value of the land of dockyards and other Government establishments, the plant employed in them, the public buildings and furniture, and the waterworks, gasworks, public parks, embankments, and other possessions of local authorities. The difficulty of valuation arises, however, from the circumstance that we have no statement even of the area of the lands possessed by local bodies, or of what is in Government possession. But the item must be very large. Apart from the local income from property, which is probably included in the income tax returns, there is an income from harbour dues and the like sources which is really a species of property, and there are large possessions which are devoted to some useful purpose, though not yielding a revenue. The municipal debts still outstanding amount to about 100 millions in England and Wales alone, and this is represented by an equivalent outlay for improvements in the localities. We thus arrive at a sum of between 200 and 300 millions as the value of local property; and Government property, although Crown lands only bring in 350,000l. a year, must be something over 100 millions. It would be useless to attempt detail on a matter like this.

In this way the total capital of the people of the United Kingdom may be reckoned as a minimum at 8,500 millions sterling. This is the capitalized value of the income derived from capital, using as far as possible the data of the income tax returns as the basis of the estimate, and with the addition of an estimate of the amount of capital in use not yielding an income. It is a bewildering figure, about eleven times the amount of our national debt, which may thus be reckoned with all soberness as a fleabite. Nearly 7,500 millions out of this amount besides must be reckoned as income-yielding, only the remaining 1,000 millions being set down as the value of movable property or the direct property of imperial or local authorities, which does not yield any individual revenue. The suggestion may perhaps be made that to some extent these are only figures in an account—that the capital outlay on the soil, plant, machinery, factories, and houses of the United Kingdom, or on the circulating capital of our industry, would not come to so much. But in reply I would say that while there is no evidence one way or the other as to what the outlay has been, while we shall never know what it has cost from generation to generation, to give us all this inheritance, there is some justification for thinking that the values are stable and not transitory. They represent an estate on which thirty-four millions of people have facilities for production and distribution, which must be equal all in all to the facilities existing anywhere else, because they are constantly tried in the furnace of free trade, and not sustained by any adventitious means. If certain properties have acquired what is called a monopoly value, it is because actual workers are able to pay the corresponding rent out of their first earnings, and have ample wages and profit besides. In such matters the property of a great country, like a factory or business, must be valued as that of a going concern, and the monopoly value which certain things acquire only enters into the question of the distribution of the estate and its income.

It would be additionally satisfactory if we could compare these figures with an account of the actual accumulation year by year in the shape of a statement of the capital outlay by public companies in adding to their stock and plant; the actual expenditure on new building, ships, and the like; the annual investments abroad, and so on. On some points I have made a few notes of this kind, which satisfy me that in this way also very large totals would be brought out. But the obvious difficulty with the method would be that the outlay by private individuals cannot be got at by means of it at all, and this outlay represents the greater part of the increase of capital in the country. At the same time, the account, if it could be given, would be subject to great deductions, on account of the improvident investment of capital, as in foreign loans, whereby the savings are not really accumulated but wasted. The method pursued in the present paper seems accordingly the safest and the likeliest to yield a moderate result, although it is liable to the observation that some property may increase in income-yielding capacity from decade to decade, and its capitalized value will proportionally increase, without any actual accumulation.

III. The Growth of Capital

Our special business to-night is not, however, with the actual capital at the present time, but with the recent accumulations, though a statement of the present amount appeared to be a necessary preliminary. It is evident almost at the outset that the growth must have been very rapid. If we look at the income tax returns, we perceive that the gross income assessed rose in Great Britain from 115 millions at the beginning of the century, to 130 millions in 1815, 251 millions

B.   Amount of Income in Income Tax Returns derived from Capital in
1865, and Approximate Amount of Capital, assuming the same Number
of Years' Purchase as in Table A; together with Estimate of remaining
Income and Capital in the Country.

(000's omitted)

	Income	Capital
	£	£
Under Schedule A—		
Lands	62,127	1,863,810
Houses	68,757	1,031,355
Schedule B—		
(Farmers' profits)	56,181*	620,000
Schedule C—		
(Public funds less home funds)	8,426	210,650
Under Schedule D—		
Mines	4,829	19,316
Ironworks	1,798	7,192
Railways	16,576	414,400
Canals	900	18,000
Gasworks	1,840	36,980
Quarries	590	2,360
Other profits	3,012†	55,000†
Other income tax, income detailed in Table A –		
estimate	42,000	660,000‡
Total under income tax	267,045	4,939,063
Trades and professions omitted, one-fifth of about		
100 millions of which one-fifth is	5,000	75,000
Income of non-income tax paying classes derived		
from capital, say	40,000	200,000
Foreign investments not in Schedules C and D ..	10,000	100,000
Movable property not yielding income, e.g. furni-		
ture of houses, works of art, etc.	—	500,000
Government and local property, say	—	300,000
	322,045	6,114,063

* This is the amount stated in 1865. Previous to 1875 only the net amount
was entered in the returns for Ireland, and in working out the capital an
allowance has been made for the difference this made in 1875, about 6
millions.

† These include the other profits of Schedule A, and waterworks, fishings,
market tolls, &c in Table A.

‡ In these two cases where we have not the same detail as in 1875, the
capital is assumed to bear the same proportion to the income in 1865 as in
1875.

in 1843, and 262 millions in 1853; and then, in the United Kingdom, from 308 millions in 1855, to 396 millions in 1865, and 571 millions in 1875. If the capital of the portion of the income derived from capital has only progressed at the same rate, the annual increase of capital all through, and especially of recent years, must have been enormous. The increase in the income assessed between 1865 and 1875 amounts to 175 millions, which is equal to 44 per cent of the income assessed in 1865. Leaving out altogether the capital not yielding income, and dealing only with the capital yielding income, a similar increase of capital, assuming the present amount to be what we have stated, would give us for 1865 a total capital of about 2,500 millions, on which the increase at 44 per cent would be 2,288 millions, or in round figures 230 millions per annum. If our estimate is moderate, and any cause would justify a higher figure for the present capital, then the increase between 1865 and 1875 would be even more than we state. But the increase on each description of capital may not have been uniform, and we must look a little into detail to see what kinds of income, and therefore what kinds of capital, have increased.

Comparing 1865 with the present time in this way, we are met by the difficulty that we have not the full details we now have as to the various schedules, especially Schedules A and D. We can compare certain particulars, however, as far back as 1862, which is one reason amongst others why I have selected a ten years' period only as the principal subject of comparison. In this manner we get a table (opposite) for 1865 similar to what we have above compiled for the present time.

In this way, following for 1865 the method of estimating we have used for the present time, though we have not quite so full data, we arrive at a sum of 6,114 millions as the total capital of that period:—

		Mlns. £
The estimate at present being	..	8,500
That of 1865, say ..	.. ..	6,100
The increase is	.. ..	2,400

which corresponds nearly with the increase of 44 per cent in the income tax returns themselves. The national estate has thus improved in the ten years at the rate of 240 millions per annum.

The following table compares the details of the increase:—

C. Approximate Account of Capital as Property in United Kingdom in 1865 and 1875 compared.

	1865	1875	Increase in 1875	
			Amount	Per Cent
	Mlns.	Mlns.	Mlns.	
Lands	1,864	2,007	143	8
Houses	1,031	1,420	389	38
Farmers' profits	620	668	48	8
Public funds less home funds	211	519	308	146
Mines	19	56	37	195
Ironworks	7	29	22	314
Railways	414	655	241	58
Canals	18	20	2	11
Gasworks	37	53	16	43
Quarries	2	4	2	100
Other profits	55	84	29	53
Other income tax, income principally trades and professions and public companies	659	1,128	469	71
	4,938	6,643	1,706	35
Trades and professions omitted	75	105	30	40
Income from capital of non-income tax paying classes	200	300	100	50
Foreign investments not in Schedules C and D	100	420	300	300
Movable property not yielding income ..	500	700	200	40
Government and local property, say ..	300	400	100	33
	6,113	8,548	2,436	40

Generally, I believe, it will be admitted these details correspond with what we should expect to find. The small increase in lands and farmers' profits is what we should expect to find from the comparative stationariness of agricultural industry, while there is a comparatively large increase in railways, somewhat above the average, and an enormous increase in mines and iron works, corresponding to the rapid development of iron and coal mining under the influence of the inflated prices of 1871–3. In the latter case probably part of the increase may be due to improved valuations, but it is in this direction certainly we should have looked for a great increase. So far as it goes, also, the increase of 'Public Funds', Schedule C, is in correspondence with the fact of immense public loans to foreign countries in recent years, though it does not indicate, we believe, the full amount of the increased lending to foreign countries, which we have endeavoured to allow for otherwise. The item which will perhaps excite most surprise is the increase of other income tax returns, principally trades and professions, and 'public companies'. The estimated increase amounts to 469 millions, on a total of 659 millions in 1865, or 71 per cent. It would have been very interesting if it had been possible to give as full details for 1865 as for 1875, and thus show how much of the increase is due to 'public companies', and how much to 'trades and professions'. It is obvious, at all events, that great as the increase is, and in whatever way it has occurred, one of the conspicuous facts of the income tax returns is the rapid increase of Schedule D, and principally of this part of it, in recent years. We can well believe that no such increase of income could have occurred without a corresponding or even greater increase of capital. Here, too, I believe city opinion will confirm me in the statement that something like this is what we should have expected to find. I have often heard it remarked, at least, in explanation of the scarcity of bills in Lombard Street, that the trading classes were believed as a rule to have become richer of late years than they were in proportion. They have had more capital, and so did not require to borrow. Probably enough, therefore, the increase of capital corresponding to trades and professions, that is, of stock-in-trade and tenants' fixtures mainly, has been even larger than the increase of the income itself.

Having formed this estimate as to the increase of property during the last decennial period, it may be useful to corroborate it by an examination of the results that would be yielded by different methods. The comparison seems to bring out the very great moderation of the present method. I have already referred to the calculations of the writer in the *Economist* in 1863, who also took for his basis the income tax returns, and whose contributions to the inquiry from time to time must always be consulted by those who wish to study the subject thoroughly. Our figures are certainly much lower than his method would have furnished us. He states (see *Economist*, 12th December, 1863)—'Considering, however, the large omissions and under statements of all income tax statistics, and also remembering that the figures before us wholly omit the sub-tax incomes, we have, after taking some trouble, arrived at the conclusion that if we multiply by twenty, or, what is the same thing, capitalize at twenty years' purchase, or at the rate of 5 per cent per annum, the total average annual increase shown in Table A' (a table summarizing the various schedules of the income tax) 'we shall not overstate, but the contrary, the annual savings of the United Kingdom during the five years in review'. Applying the same method now, we find that the increase in all the schedules of the income tax between 1865 and 1875, is from 396 to 571 millions, or 175 millions in the ten years, that is 17½ millions per annum. Capitalizing this at twenty years' purchase, we get a total increase of 3,500 millions in the ten years, or 350 millions per annum, which is certainly a much larger figure than has been arrived at by the method used to-night. There is no doubt that since the period to which the *Economist* referred, viz., 1855–60, a good deal has been done to improve the income tax valuations. Even before 1865, as appears from the report of that year, a good deal has been done to stop the notorious leakages. But making all the new allowances we should make for changed circumstances, the method of 1863 must have brought out considerably higher figures. I am inclined to believe that the estimate to-night errs, if anything, on the side of moderation, and perhaps this confirmation I have brought may convince those who may have been startled at first by the great magnitude of the figures with which we are dealing, that these figures are really not excessive but moderate.

There is yet a different way of estimating the accumulations

of the country, viz., from the Legacy Duty Returns. Mr.
Porter, in his 'Progress of the Nation', makes especial use of
these figures. He prints a long table (pp. 492–3, edition
1851) showing the amount of property which had been
subjected to legacy duty in Great Britain in each year since
the commencement down to 1848. This table I have reprinted and continued in the appendix, both as regards
Great Britain and the United Kingdom, with the exception
of ten years between 1849 and 1857 inclusive, in which it
appears the Inland Revenue Department has not published the
data it has since supplied. With these data Mr. Porter estimated that in 1841 the personal property in the country
might be reckoned at 2,000,000,000l. and in 1845 at
2,200,000,000l.; and comparing these sums with the corresponding amounts of property passing at death in the years
mentioned, viz., 41 millions and 44 millions, it would appear
that he reckoned the personal property in the country, as
from forty-five to fifty times the amount annually subject to
legacy duty. Multiplying by forty-five only the annual
average of two years, 1865–6 and 1875–6, we should arrive
at the following sums as the amount of personal property at
these dates, and the increase in the interval:—

Capital Estimates in 1865 and 1875, deduced from the
Property subject to Legacy Duty

(000's omitted)

		Average Property subject to Duty	Calculated Total Amount of Personal Property
		£	£
1875		104,686	4,710,870
'65		73,216	3,294,720
	Increase	31,470	1,416,150

In other words, in personal property alone there was an
increase of 142 millions per annum, according to this method,
between 1865 and 1875. But this increase would not include

any property subject to succession duty, the increase in which, adopting a similar method of calculation, and allowing for the difference that only the life interest of the succession is subject to duty would be as follows:—

Capital Estimates in 1865 and 1875, deduced from the Property subject to Succession Duty

(000's omitted)

		Calculated Total Amount of Real Property
		£
1875		3,150,720
'65		2,213,550
	Increase	937,170

Adding this last sum to the above figure for personal property, we get an estimated total accumulation between 1865 and 1875 of 235 millions per annum, which corresponds very closely, it will be observed, with the total arrived at by the method used tonight.

Whatever may be thought, therefore, of the estimates which have been made, they are fortified in some degree by the authority of former inquirers. Large as the totals appear at first sight, every one who looks into the subject, is satisfied that very large figures must be dealt with. If necessary, we might derive additional confirmation from a comparison of the increase of railway traffic, increase of the tonnage of shipping entered and cleared, increase of iron and coal production, increase of imports of raw material for manufactures, increase of consumption and revenue, and other data, all showing an enormous progress, which implies, when rightly inquired into, a corresponding increase of property. But the facts, though interesting, might lead us away from the main point, which need not be further illustrated.

IV. Comparative Growth in Former Periods

The question will be asked—How does the increase in recent years compare with the increase in former periods? The reply must be that whether we take the returns of the income tax, or of the legacy duty, or the estimates of property deduced from them, the increase of late years has been much more rapid than at any previous period of the century. The total assessment to the income tax in Great Britain appears to have been about 140 millions at the close of our great wars at the beginning of the century. It is stated to be 130 millions for 1813 in the accompanying table in the appendix, and Mr. Dudley Baxter gives the figures of 146 millions for 1814–15. Few good data unfortunately have been preserved for that period, and there is an additional difficulty in comparing with later times in the differences in the minimum subject to duty. But assuming 140 millions, we find that this compares with a total of 251 millions in 1843, when we have again got income tax data—the increase in the interval of thirty years being 111 millions, or about 80 per cent. In other words, the annual increase in this long period was rather less than 4 millions, and about 2⅔ per cent per annum. Between 1843 and 1853 the increase was from 251 to 262 millions, or 11 millions in ten years, that is little more than 1 million per annum, which is even a lower rate of increase than between 1813 and 1843. In the next decade, which we take for the United Kingdom between 1855 and 1865, Ireland having been subjected to the income tax in 1853, the increase is from 308 to 395 millions, or 87 millions, and about 28 per cent in the ten years. This shows a very different state of things from what had existed in the first half of the century; but great as the increase is, it is still less than what we have been dealing with between 1865 and 1875, in which period, as we have seen, the income assessed to income tax has increased 176 millions, or 44 per cent.

If we look at the returns of the legacy duty we arrive at the same conclusion of a very slow progress in the first half of the century and afterwards a progress at a rapid and accelerating rate. Mr. Porter tells us that in the early years of the century the returns are uncertain, but taking the average of two years at the end of each date since 1820, we get the following comparison:—

(ooo's omitted)

	Property subject to Legacy Duty
	£
1820	30,328
'30	40,443
'40	41,247
'48	44,481
'60	59,701

Thus the increase between 1820 and 1840 was 11 millions, or about 36 per cent, that is, about 550,000l., or rather less than 2 per cent per annum. The increase between 1840 and 1848 was only about 3,200,000l., showing a still slower rate of increase than between 1820 and 1840, corresponding to the indication of the income tax returns between 1843 and 1853. But the increase between 1848 and 1860 is 15,200,000l., or over 1,200,000l., per annum, and at the rate of 34 per cent in the twelve years, or 3 per cent per annum. Since 1860, as we have seen, the increase in the decade we have dealt with in the United Kingdom, has been at the rate of over 43 per cent. Thus there is a great start forward just after 1850, both in the income tax returns and amount of property subject to legacy duty. We have no data for the succession duty in the early part of the century, as it was only imposed in 1853; but since 1859, when we begin to have data, it has progressed with great rapidity, and with greater rapidity in the later than in the earlier years.

It may be interesting to exhibit these facts still more directly for our present purpose, by comparing Mr. Porter's estimates of 'personal property' at different dates in the century with those which can now be made. He gives the following table for Great Britain, at p. 600 of his 'Progress of the Nation'.—

(000,000's omitted)

Years	Personal Property £
1814	1,200
'19	1,300
'24	1,500
'29	1,700
'34	1,800
'41	2,000
'45	2,200

The highest sum reached is thus 2,200 millions, whereas the total for 1875–6, as we have seen, on the same method of valuation, is nearly 5,000 millions, of which nearly 1,500 millions was the increase between 1865 and 1875 alone. In other words, the increase in the last decade exceeded the whole personal property of the country in 1814, and was three-fourths of the amount of that property, even as late as 1841. So great has been the change in the material condition of the country in recent years.

The totals would not be greatly modified by the consideration of the important question in such matters, that of a change in the level of prices at different dates. It is possible— I should almost say probable—that part of the slow increase between 1815 and 1820 and 1840, and even to as late a date as 1850, was due to a gradual appreciation of the standard of value. Part of the great increase up to 1860 may also be ascribed to a rise in the level of prices consequent on the Californian and Australian gold discoveries, which seem to have reached their maximum effect in the first decade. But there can be no such explanation of the improvement since 1865, which has been coincident with events in the money market, significant rather of an appreciation than a depreciation of the standard. There is nothing, therefore, to qualify our sense of the extraordinary accumulation of property in recent years, and which we can only ascribe to the accumulated effects of mechanical and chemical discoveries, so that year by year the industrial machine is more and more productive in proportion to the labourers employed.

V. Comparison with other Countries

It would more than exhaust the limits of a single paper to go into the question of a comparison of our national position, as regards capital, with that of any other country. But such a comparison would be most instructive. In France, for instance, it is known from the estimates of the ministry of Finance, that real property has increased immensely during the present century, while manufacturing industry has also extended. So with Germany and the United States. The latter country, as I have stated, possesses the data of regular valuations at every census, and the gross figures thus arrived at since 1791 are as follows:—

Statement showing the Population and Wealth of the United States by Decades, from 1790 to 1860; Decennial Percentage Increase of Population; Decennial Percentage Increase of National Wealth; and Average Property to each Person.

Year	Population	Decennial Percentage Increase of Wealth	Decennial Percentage Increase of Population	Decennial Percentage Increase of Wealth	Average Property to each Person
		$	Per cent	Per cent	$
1790	3,929,827	750,000,000 (estimated)	—	—	187·00
1800	5,304,937	1,072,000,000 (estimated)	35·02	43·0	202·13
'10	7,239,814	1,500,000,000 (estimated)	36·43	39·0	207·20
'20	9,638,191	1,882,000,000 (estimated)	33·13	25·4	195·00
'30	12,866,020	2,653,000,000 (estimated)	33·49	41·0	206·00
'40	17,069,453	3,764,000,000 (official)	32·67	41·7	220·00
'50	23,191,876	7,135,780,000 (official)	35·87	89·6	307·67
'60	31,500,000	16,159,000,000 (official)	35·59	126·42	510·00
'70	38,558,000	30,069,000,000	22·00	86·13	776·96*

* But allowance ought to be made here for the depreciation of the dollar between 1860 and 1870.

Here again, as with ourselves, the increase has been much smaller between the beginning of the century and 1840, than it has been since, and it is especially noticeable that what increase of property there was in the earlier period, only corresponded to the increase of population. The increase between 1860 and 1870 is at a less rate than in the previous decade, contrary to our experience in this country, but the difference is no doubt mainly due to the civil war in the United States. The contrast would have been more striking but for the depreciation of currency between 1860 and 1870. The total United States' property in 1870, it will be observed, was a good deal less than our own total at the present time, 6,000 millions sterling, against 8,500 millions sterling, while the amount per head, owing to the larger population, must be much smaller. But there would be a great increase in the United States between 1870 and 1875, and in any case the total is a very large one, and is so far confirmatory of the large figures of our own estimates.

VI. Concluding Observations

What is the bearing of the facts brought out on what was stated at the outset as the main object of such inquiry?—that is, the degree of improvement (if any) in the material welfare of the community in consequence of these accumulations of capital, and the addition to the margin of taxation. It is evident, from the mere statement of the percentages of increase, that the improvement in both respects must be great. Since 1855 at least the increase of property must have been 30 per cent in the first decade, and during the second decade the increase must have been 44 per cent, so that the addition to the capital of the community in that time has been immensely greater in proportion than the increase in its numbers. The increase of population has been about 1 per cent per annum, but property has increased 3 to 4 per cent and upwards. Whether the property so increased is productive or unproductive, the resources of the community as a whole must have been greatly enlarged. They have more to enjoy,

even if the means of increasing production have not increased proportionately with other property. But that reproductive capital has increased quite in proportion, if not more
in proportion, is, however, very obvious. The railways,
mines, ironworks and stock-in-trade of trades and professions
are precisely those descriptions of property, with only slight
exceptions, in which there has been the largest proportionate
increase of property. As regards the question of the margin
of taxation, the figures are absolutely astounding. The apparent increase of capital between 1865 and 1875 alone is
2,400 millions sterling—that is, about three times the amount
of the national debt. That is to say, the community has
acquired in ten years three times the amount of its debt. It
could pay the debt three times over, and still be as rich as at
the beginning of the decade. Allowing that to keep things in
equilibrium there ought to be an increase of capital pari passu
with the increase of population, the increase of capital in the
ten years (1865–75) merely to keep the community as rich as
it was, would only have been a little over 600 million. Deducting this from the 2,400 millions of actual increase, we
have still a sum of 1,800 millions, or two and a half times the
national debt, which the nation could afford to pay, and
still be as rich individually as it was ten years ago.

The following figures will, perhaps, bring out the comparison still more clearly:—

	Amount of Property (in Millions)	Amount per Head of Population
	£	£
1875	8,500	260
'65	6,100	204
Increase	2,400= 39½ per cent	56= 27 per cent

Allowing for the increase of population, there is still an
increase of over one-fourth, or 27 per cent, in the capital of
the community in the decade. The nation might lose a
fourth of its property, and still be as rich and prosperous as

it was ten years before. Thus, whether we compare the increase of property per head, or the increase in relation to the national debt, the facts are equally striking.

Incidentally the figures as to income we have been using as the basis of these calculations about property, afford additional evidence as to this increase of the margin of taxation. The capital yielding income by Table A, 1875, is 484,586,000l.; by Table B, 1865, it is 322,045,000l.; showing an increase of 162,541,000l. Deducting 10 per cent for the increase of population, there still remains an excess increase of income from capital beyond the increase of population, amounting to 130 millions sterling. This means that taxation to an immense amount could be imposed, and yet the share taken by the Government of the earnings of the community from capital alone would still leave the community per head as much as it possessed in 1865. If there has been anything like a similar increase in the earnings of the community in wages and salaries, the real margin of taxation must have increased very much more. It is no doubt quite true that the Chancellor of the Exchequer could not deal with the matter in this arithmetical manner. The practical margin of taxation for him to deal with must be very much less. The increase of wealth and wages has brought an increase of the scale of living, which would make a diminution of the profit of the community from capital to the level of ten years ago be greatly resented. A tax just imposed is also by many degrees more burdensome and injurious to industry than one which has long been in existence. But the magnitude of the arithmetical increase of the margin proves that the increase which could be practically dealt with as a resource in time of need must be very large.

If we carry the comparison a little farther back, say for half a century, as some of the figures we have used would suggest, we cannot but be impressed with the marvellous change which has come over the country. We emerged from the great wars at the beginning of the century, with a debt of 900 million sterling, which was practically a burden upon the people of Great Britain, amounting to between a third and a half of their capital. Mr. Porter, as we have seen, estimates the personal property at that time at 1,200 millions sterling, and the real property, the income from Schedule A being under 40 millions, would be little over 1,000 millions more. In other words there was a debt of 900 millions against an estate of say 2,200 millions. Reckoning per head of the population, the debt was about 70l., and the property about 170l. Now the property of the United Kingdom is 8,500 millions, or 251l. per head, and the debt has sunk to about a tenth part of the latter sum, or 25l. per head. According to this reckoning also, the income from capital in 1815, was probably not more than 90 millions sterling, on which the charge of the debt was about one third; now the income from capital is 445 millions, on which the interest charge of the debt, amounting to 21 millions, is only one twenty-second part. Apart from any proportionate increase of the earnings of the people per head, such great changes have passed over the resources and burdens of the people within a period so short that the burden itself is still not infrequently talked of, by a kind of tradition, in the language of the time when it was really crushing. Had we a national debt corresponding to what existed fifty years ago, it would be over 3,000 millions, and not under 800 millions sterling; and the interest charge would be above 100 millions, instead of 21 millions a year.

Before I conclude, I may notice one or two points on which observation may have been expected. One is the distribution of this great increase of wealth. In one respect, as regards the three divisions of the United Kingdom, it has perhaps been unnecessary to do so, while it would be difficult to find sufficient details, owing to the large amounts of income which are earned in one part of the country and which pay income tax in another. The great increase both in amount and per head of population is undoubtedly in England, although the income tax returns show clearly enough that both Ireland and Scotland now progress very rapidly. In another aspect, viz., as to whether capital is being more diffused, or is accumulating in fewer hands, I am afraid the data are not sufficiently good for any sure conclusions. There are certain means for comparing the number of assessments under Schedule D, at different amounts of income, which would appear to show that the number of large incomes is increasing more quickly than the increase of population or the increase of wealth. But the fact of the rich class becoming a little more numerous, would not prove that as a whole the number of people possessed of moderate capital and the average amount they possessed are increasing or diminishing, while the increasing number of company assessments under Schedule D, makes the number of assessments altogether useless for comparison, as we have no information whatever respecting the number of individual shareholders in the different companies, the average amount of each individual interest, and the interests of the holders in Schedules A, B, and C. For these reasons mainly, and also partly for want of time, I have not inquired into this part of the subject; the problem could only be attacked in a most indirect manner.

Another question which has been raised of late, is whether the nation is now spending its capital. The figures tonight may at least be taken to prove, I think, that if the nation has begun to spend its capital, instead of saving capital, the process is a very new one. So far as our researches carry us, the fact we have to deal with is, that the rate of saving has been far greater of late than at any previous period during the present century; that the saving all through has been at an increasing rate. The figures would also show that the only fact alleged in proof that we are living on our capital is insufficient to make out the case. The allegation is that the excess of imports is now so great as to show that we are calling in our capital from abroad. But apart from the incidental evidence which has been before us tonight, as to the great amount of lending in former years, which entitles us to the receipt in each year of an enormous income from foreign countries, so that the excess of imports would need to be much larger than it is to prove any material calling in of capital from abroad;—it must also be apparent that if the nation is calling in some fraction of its foreign investment, it is not therefore stopping its savings or diminishing its capital. The foreign investments, though they were very large in the years before 1875, were by no means the chief part of the national accumulations. Our main savings were at home. Before the nation can be said to be living on its capital, it must be shown that not only is capital being called in from abroad, but that more is so called in than what is being simultaneously invested at home. I have not seen this point considered by any of those who have made the suggestion that the nation is living on its capital.

And this brings me to the next question. on which perhaps some observation may have been expected, viz., whether in point of fact the nation is saving at home in years like the present. In what sort of years are the accumulations, such as those we have been dealing with between 1865 and 1875, the greatest, and in what years are they at a minimum or suspended, or is the process nearly uniform? I am afraid it is impossible to answer this question in anything like a complete manner. The assessments to Schedule A of the income tax have not hitherto been made annually, but at intervals of years. We cannot tell, therefore, from these data what the increase is in a particular year. The assessments of trade profits under Schedule D again may be made on the average of three years' profits, which throws out all possible comparison of annual increases. But we have good reason to believe that in no year is the accumulation absolutely at an end; and that in many directions it is even more active in dull years than it is at other times. We know, for instance, that the capital outlay on railways is incessant; that during the last two or three years of depression, and even now, the nation is saving in railways very nearly as much as the annual income of the capital invested in them. In agriculture again, there is a constant annual reclamation of land in progress, besides an incessant outlay on the older cultivated area. The house-building trades again are as active at the present time, and have been for the last year or two as busy, as for many years previous, showing the absence of any stoppage to accumulation in this direction. We may anticipate from what has happened before, that the enormous increase in mines and ironworks, which was one of the special features of the accumulation between 1865 and 1875, is checked; that the next income tax returns will not improbably exhibit a falling off

on these heads.* But in general the extension of factories and
warehouses, and the increase of machinery, goes on in dull
as well as good times. We all know how Lancashire went on
adding to its cotton spinning and weaving power even
during the cotton famine, and a similar extension of manufacturing power, we may be sure, is going on at the present
time. So far as one can judge, the only direction in addition
to that of mines and ironworks in which saving is now
checked, as compared with the period of which we have
been treating, is in foreign investment. From the nature of
the case, every other species of accumulation is in progress as
before. The truth is, that owing to the division of labour,
there must be a vast disorganization of industry, not a mere
temporary falling off from a former inflation, before accumulation can be wholly checked. A certain portion of the
community is told off, as it were to create the accumulations,
and if the accumulations were not made, we should see in
the building trades, in railway construction, in shipbuilding,
and numerous other directions, a wide-spread stoppage of
works, and masses of unemployed labourers, far exceeding
anything witnessed even in those terrible times of depression
which were frequent before the free trade period, when industry was partially disorganized, and pauperism assumed
most threatening dimensions. In the absence of the effects
which would follow, we must assume that the cause is not
present, that there is no stoppage of accumulation; but that
accumulation, on the contrary, goes on at present in most
directions at an average annual rate, or at a rate greater than
the average.

It is a different question altogether whether there is any
ground for anticipating a permanent change in the extent of
our accumulations at an early date. This is substantially
much the same problem as you will have to consider at your
next meeting; but perhaps we may just glance at it tonight
according to the indications in the facts which have been
before us. What appears to me most striking is the apparent

* The Twentieth Report of the Inland Revenue, which has been issued
since this paper was read at the Statistical Society, exhibits as here anticipated a falling off on these heads.

indestructibility of most of our capital. The drainage and other improvements of land, the roads, railways and canals, the houses, the improvements of towns, the machinery and plant set up in every direction, are all forms of fixed capital, which are there to be used, if the willingness to work and enjoy all this vast estate only exists. Unless a species of paralysis seizes our workmen and capitalists, I do not see what hindrances there are to this vast industrial machine being used, whether to make for ourselves, or to make wherewithal to buy from other countries the surplus they may have to exchange with us. A great deal is said at the present moment which is substantially to the effect that workmen and capitalists are paralysed, but looking at the matter scientifically, and from a point outside as it were, the balance of probability must be held to be that the higgling of the market, as has always happened before, will result in a working compromise, and that industry will be resumed, and go on, after much individual losses, but without, in the aggregate, any loss or destruction of capital. It is said again, that our coal and iron will soon be exhausted, and that our whole position is based upon cheap coal and iron; but, in reply, we may observe that in the above valuation of our capital the value of mines and ironworks has been reckoned at only a few years' purchase; a few years' industry would replace to us the capital value, and all our other capital—our improved soil, our dwelling houses, our machinery, our roads, and much more—would remain. Looking at our capital as a whole, I think it is a strong thing to say that because many years hence we shall not possess as a nation a certain particular form of capital, therefore the other forms of capital will not remain to be used and enjoyed. Against all considerations of this nature, we may perhaps set the continual progress in invention which is being made, and which seems to benefit most the nations with accumulated capital. If the steam engine is improved, so that two pounds of coal can do what three pounds did before, then it is the nation which has most steam machinery, which is clearly the greatest gainer. So with other inventions. It will be the fault of the English people if their progress is not in future even more rapid than it has been in the past.

Further Reading for Part 2

W. Albert, *The Turnpike Road System in England, 1663–1840* (1972).

M. Blaug, 'Productivity of Capital in the Lancashire Cotton Industry during the Nineteenth Century', *Economic History Review*, XIII (1961).

A. K. Cairncross, 'Capital Formation in the Take-Off', in W. W. Roston (ed.), *The Economics of Take-Off into Sustained Growth* (1963).

A. W. Coats, *The Classical Economists and Economic Policy* (1971).

F. Crouzet (ed.), *Capital Formation in the Industrial Revolution* (1972).

Phyllis Deane, 'The Implications of Early National Income Estimates for the Measurement of Long-Term Economic Growth in the United Kingdom', *Economic Development and Cultural Change* (1955); 'The Industrial Revolution and Economic Growth: The Evidence of Early British National Income Estimates', *Economic Development and Cultural Change* (1957); 'Capital Formation in Britain before the Railway Age', *Economic Development and Cultural Change* (1957).

Phyllis Deane and W. A. Cole, *British Economic Growth, 1688–1959* (2nd ed. 1969), VIII.

M. M. Edwards, *The Growth of the British Cotton Trade, 1780–1815* (1967).

Sir R. Giffen, *The Growth of Capital* (1889).

J. R. Harris, 'The Employment of Steam Power in the Eighteenth Century', *History*, LII (1967).

G. R. Hawke and M. C. Read, 'Railway Capital in the United Kingdom in the Nineteenth Century', *Economic History Review*, XXII (1969).

J. P. P. Higgins and S. Pollard (eds.), *Aspects of Capital Investment in Great Britain, 1750–1850* (1971).

A. G. Kenwood, 'Railway Investment in Britain 1825–1875', *Economica*, 32 (1965).

S. Kuznets, 'Capital Formation in Modern Economic Growth', *Third International Conference of Economic History*, Munich, 1965, I (1968).

J. Load, *Capital and Steam Power, 1750–1800* (1966 ed.)

P. Mathias, 'The Social Structure in the Eighteenth Century; A Calculation by Joseph Massie', *Economic History Review*, X (1957).

B. R. Mitchell, 'The Coming of the Railway and United Kingdom Economic Growth', *Journal of Economic History*, XXIV (1964).

M. G. Mulhall, *The Dictionary of Statistics* (1884).

A. E. Musson and E. Robinson, 'The Early Growth of Steam Power', *Economic History Review*, XI (1959).

S. Pollard, 'The Growth and Distribution of Capital in Great Britain c. 1770–1870', *Third International Conference of Economic History*, Munich, 1965, I (1968).

S. Pollard and D. W. Crossley, *The Wealth of Britain, 1085–1966* (1968).

G. R. Porter, *The Progress of the Nation* . . . (1857 ed.).

Royal Statistical Society, *Annals of the Royal Statistical Society, 1834–1394* (1934).

S. Shapiro, *Capital and the Cotton Industry in the Industrial Revolution* (1967).

D. Swann, 'The Pace and Progress of Port Investment in England, 1660–1830', *Yorkshire Bulletin of Economic and Social Research*, XII (1960).